Foundations of
Social Administration

Edited by

Helmuth Heisler

Dean of the Faculty of Social Science
Lanchester Polytechnic, Coventry

First published 1977 by
THE MACMILLAN PRESS LTD
London and Basingstoke
Associated companies in New York Dublin
Melbourne Johannesburg and Delhi

ISBN 0 333 18647 8 (hard cover)
0 333 18648 6 (paper cover)

Typeset by
SANTYPE (COLDTYPE DIVISION)
Salisbury, Wiltshire

Printed and bound in Great Britain by
REDWOOD BURN LIMITED
Trowbridge & Esher

Cc

FOUNDATIONS OF SOCIAL ADMINISTRATION

New books of related interest from Macmillan

The Nature of Social Work
Zofia T. Butrym

The Economics of Social Problems
Julian Le Grand and Ray Robinson

Contents

Knowledge begins with practice, and theoretical knowledge which is acquired through practice must then return to practice.

MAO TSE-TUNG

Preface

Rooted in the anti-rationalism and then the anti-industrialism of the nineteenth century, in the twentieth century the social-welfare outlook has been a major propellant of the growth of public activity in Britain. Expressed as a percentage of gross domestic product this was 10 per cent at the turn of this century, 50 per cent in 1972, and then public expenditure jumped to 60 per cent in 1975. Much of this has been at the expense of a quarter of a century's under-investment in British industry which, if permitted to continue, will lead to zero or minus growth in the gross domestic product. Even so the supply of a certain level of welfare is necessary for economic production. Thus some of this public activity helps the economy. In view of this growth in welfare it is remarkable that, compared to the other social sciences, so little has been spent on social administration. Although it is a recognised subject it has failed to generate appreciable intellectual interest because it has not yet developed into a discipline. This collection of essays is a reflection of a stirring to establish a discipline by paying attention to positivist as well as the long-standing normative considerations of social administration − in truth, the two are inseparable in any social science.

The book can be divided into three parts. The first of these recognises that every subject has its own peculiarities and distinctiveness which influences the reputation and status it is accorded among academic subjects. Hence in this book about foundations it is sensible to begin by consideration of the traits of social administration − primarily the matter of Chapters 1 to 4. The phenomena of social conditions, problems and consequential policies provide the genesis for our subject and so are reviewed from a contemporary standpoint in the second part, which covers Chapters 5 to 7. Certain conditions only are defined as social problems which merit organised help and these chapters consider the more critical conditions and policies intended to cope with them. Three of the several ways in which the handling of adverse social conditions can be studied are identified in the final part of the book which spans Chapters 8 to 12. The traits of social administration permeate the middle and final parts of this book, and both the study of social problems and policies and the specialist study of aspects of the understanding and handling of problems reveal the character of social administration. Approaches such as those described in the final part of the book are human as well as analytical responses to the complexity of problems and measures and are ways in which the social administrator acquires expertise and status.

The character of social administration is revealed by the coexistence of its two versions. The older of these sees it in terms of a technical parasite (Chapter 2) or an academic flea living off other subjects (Chapter 4). This version of social administration confined the subject to multidisciplinary studies of the social services, and therefore established its boundaries as those defined by the convenience of public administration and ostensible social legislation. According to this version social administration as a subject does not have boundaries and matter peculiar to itself.

The evolving version of social administration incorporates some of the traits of that which confines the subject to the study of social services. The salient traits of the evolving version will be capitulated under the labels of frontiers, functions, capitalism, social-science theory and a commitment to an open society. It is appropriate when considering the extent of social administration to think of boundaries when the subject is confined to social services which are clearly demarcated by legal and administrative arrangements as in Britain. But this is a restrictive and inaccurate way of thinking about the extent of the subject universally when, for instance, one is dealing with air traffic and noise abatement because of their effects upon living conditions. This is a 'frontier' of our subject, a marginal area inhabited by different categories of persons and phenomena, rather than a boundary. The concept of 'function' is related to the desirability of using the concept of a frontier. As society changes there is no telling what new social problems will be unveiled, and as the social administrator is interested in their solution it is impossible to forecast all the directions in which his attention will be directed. Many social problems will have the objective consequences of solution by means and agencies not commonly regarded as social services and so the logical concomitant of this functional interest is the no-man's land of the frontier. This may be illustrated by reference to Zambia when it was hatching a development plan during the Second World War. The great social problem of the country was the poverty of the peasantry arising from their agriculture and to improve this was seen to be the key to social development. Public aid was to be supplied specifically for this purpose and in the national accounts this was listed under the heading of 'social services'. All kinds of do-gooders as well as agricultural specialists were involved in this welfare frontier – difficult to contemplate through the blinkers of Britain's social-services boundaries.

Three further aspects of the concept of function require comment. It is argued that social administration could grow as a social science and achieve disciplinary status with a distinctive outlook if it were directed to the allocation of scarce resources to alleviate social problems (Chapter 2). The decision-making involved in this must take account of the beneficial objective consequences for society, that is functions, supposed to result from resource allocations. These are manifest welfare functions that are intended and welcome and latent welfare functions that are unanticipated and also welcome (Chapters 9 and 12). The essence of the contention is that resource allocation is the distinctive purpose of social administration. Tensions created by the persistence of unattended social problems weaken the cohesion of society and this leads to a concept which parallels that of the intended welfare function. This is the possibility that the unintended welfare function of public resource allocation may be better social cohesion (Chapter 1). But the unintended consequences of social administration, called outcomes, are not all desirable. Thus a third concept of latent welfare dysfunction, which arises when more harm than good results from resource allocation (Chapter 8), is required.

The two attitudes to capitalism revealed in this book are typical of social administration. Resources should be redistributed by the state, it is believed, for the benefit of those citizens who, through no fault of their own, become ill, unemployed, destitute and without shelter because they cannot make adequate provision for their own protection due to the vagaries of a capitalist economy. Hence there arises an interest in mediating the unfettered forces of capitalism. More positively there is the opinion that capitalism should be taxed somehow to raise the levels of living for all citizens. Thus a wariness about capitalism characterises many social administrators, some of whom of late, under the influence of the current recession, are revising this attitude. There is a growing understanding that capitalism is not an inexhaustible source of wealth for redistribution after taxation. Capitalism as well as the poor seems to be in need of help and a little more protection than in the past (Chapters 7 and 8). These observations serve to exemplify the functional-frontier nature of the evolving version of social administration.

Social administration has emerged as an empirical study whose outlook has been fashioned by social philosophy more than by social-science theory. There is a large chink in the armoury of social administration as a result, interposed between social philosophy and the assumed understanding of actual conditions. To an extent this incomplete outlook has confined social administration to the boundaries of the social services as defined by law and administrative convenience. Tunnel vision results from this. The restraints on resource

allocation imposed by a political culture or the identification of the
wrong phenomena as facts to which resource allocation should
respond can only be overcome with the aid of explicit social-science
theory (Chapter 1). In connection with the economy and the function
of welfare, the contrary interpretations of how to handle inflation,
exposed by Keynesians and monetarists, testify to the elusiveness of
facts and the necessity of establishing them with the aid of theoretical
perspectives. Hence the exploration of welfare frontiers cannot be
undertaken without reference to a more adequate repertoire of
social-science theory.

A commitment to an open society is an outstanding trait of social
administrators. When their reasoning and pleading are blocked by the
vested interests which do much to influence the ways in which social
problems are dealt with (Chapter 4), their belief in all that belongs to
an open society sustains their effort. To a degree moral values,
particularly the ascendancy or otherwise of one or other of the
important interpretations of justice, contribute to this commitment.
There is some choice between the high valuation of liberty of the
individual and groups, which is the liberal point of view, and the
contrasting high valuation placed on the satisfaction of human needs,
the socialist point of view. The dilemma is that liberties may be
sacrificed if all that concerns society is the achievement of satisfaction
by meeting human needs. A realistic view of justice may involve both
the protection of basic liberties and the achievement of benefits by the
worst off in society (Chapter 3) and to the extent that this is the view
of society also, and it is (Chapter 5), this will temper the importance
attached to satisfying human needs irrespective of the cost to human
liberty. During a Labour administration, seemingly at the beck and call
of the trade-union movement, it is unsurprising that the justice of
meeting human needs, the redistribution of the national income by
recognition of the rights of the least advantaged to be made as well off
as possible, should be the morality which is ascending. But even so this
is constrained by the grip of vested interests, which by seeking to
ensure the continuance of certain advantages for some groups prevent
improvement of the position of others. Are these interests so powerful
as to freeze the social order and prevent progress from within? The
evidence is encouraging. Change can be generated from within because
scope for voluntary action, in defiance of vested interests, is inherent in
our open society. Such voluntary action is often in response to the
investigative procedures and reports of social administrators and to the
extent that this is so they help to provoke the open mind – a
precondition for material progress (Chapter 4).

The connections between the state of society and policies for the
provision of social services, which now employ two million people, is

the focus of Chapters 5 to 7. Social policies are responses to political pressures, which in turn are reactions to social conditions, and in order to appreciate why policies are made and whether they are effective, therefore, three kinds of information are required: knowledge of present conditions, the changes taking place within them and the reasons for these changes. Chapter 5 describes the first two kinds of knowledge about conditions in Britain, including the economic changes which have raised material levels of living, changes in technology which have increased our sensitivity to the predicament of others, organisational changes which have swelled the public service and have added to the power of important groups such as trade unions, and not least the demographic changes which profoundly influence the size of the labour force and economic growth. Knowledge of the economic inequalities brought about by such trends has been of particular interest in the shaping of social policies and forms the subject of Chapter 6, which notes and analyses three categories of economic differences. Here, by the way, it is observed that differences are smaller in income than in wealth. Differences of life styles are reviewed also as are other differences related to work, residence and people's needs.

Social policies by the state are not evolved in response to all trends and conditions. Pressure groups, by identifying only some of these problems, limit those which are subject to policies. The recent increases in social affluence constitute a baseline against which achievement and under-achievement can be assessed and new goals set (Chapter 5). In view of the inclination for social aspirations to rise faster than recordable progress, the appreciable gains which have been recorded should alert us to the possibility of demand for more progress and greater frustration and tension as meagre resources and organisational shortcomings result in measurable under-achievement. Britain's organisational shortcomings, which impede material social progress, arise from its political culture which leads to the laudable search by the state for consensus over so many vital issues. Unfortunately this involves the sharing of power with many groups of people just at the time when, to attain the ever-rising goals of our galloping aspirations, the state should be centralising its power to provide the drive to modernise the country (Chapter 1).

Progress to many entails satisfying the needs of economically disadvantaged groups and the effect of this on economic activity should not be overlooked. This leads to the subject of economic inequalities and the perpetual dispute about the extent to which they should be diminished. Besides the ethical arguments for the reduction of such inequalities (Chapter 3), there is a long-standing concern in Britain that extreme economic inequalities may become the source of deep dispute such as might lead to the overthrow of democracy. On the economic front they may inhibit the co-operation of the advantaged and disadvantaged with adverse effect on industrial productivity. Opinions on matters such as these form some of the background for social policies aimed at the redistribution of wealth by means of income maintenance, health and educational provision. In so far as these policies are directed at preventing economic inequalities, they are hampered by uncertainty about their extent, manifestation and origin (Chapter 6).

Social capital also affects progress. There are many projects which are too costly for an individual producer to provide for himself and yet must be supplied by the state without direct charge to him if economic productivity is to be raised. In this connection, the backwardness of the British economy and the question of how social policies affecting the labour market can help it to recover are of recent interest. While industry opposes such policies as would increase its costs at the expense of its profits, it is as well aware as government that certain social policies catering for health, social security and regional needs often may be of positive assistance to the raising of productivity and profits. Neither individual workers nor industries on their own can afford expensive schemes for industrial training. This and decisions about industrial location to utilise idle pockets of localised resources therefore require the intervention of the state. But exactly what and how much should be done requires consideration of what we know about the impact of social policies (Chapter 7).

The supply, organisation and comparison of social services are the popular approaches to social administration discussed in Chapters 8 to 12. Social administration has tended to ignore the effects on the economy of expenditure on the social services and a lack of conceptual clarity has clouded studies of how best to deploy whatever limited resources are set aside for these services. Thus Chapters 8 and 9 contend that the supply of social services is susceptible to economic analysis and that it is vital that an economic approach should be used to help ensure that the economy retains its productive capacity, which may be starved of funds by the social services, and that the scarce resources available for the social services are used wisely. Without a sound economy public resources are unavailable to satisfy the needs of citizens which are beyond their own means, and as the totality of needs if simply summed far exceeds these resources it is essential that they should be used to the best advantage. Hence a certain rationing of provision by the use of prices and measures of quantities assists the identification of priorities, needs to be met and contributes to the assessment of the implications of social-service expenditure for economic activity.

One may speculate about the future effects of the current recession with its low economic growth and high unemployment and wonder whether this will dampen aspirations and make people more content with their lot. This implies that aspirations and progress, expressed as needs, may vary from situation to situation and that Marx's dictum of 1875, 'to each according to his needs', should be construed as relative to the state of society. The study of need, reflecting this dictum, is the accumulation of statistical data about needs for goods and services wanted by arbitrarily chosen groups of consumers who may be too poor to purchase these goods and services. Often such definitions of needs are accompanied by suggestions that they should be catered for at the expense of other needs for which consumers can pay and which generate industry and trade. Thus the social administrator is called upon to make judgements about two kinds of demand: one is the effective demand of the private consumer, which has a direct effect on economic productivity; and the other is social demand, which refers to the exchange of public funds for resources for the social services. It is contended that a rather more rational resource disposition in the public sector is achieved by means of the economic approach to social demand than is possible by persisting with the high valuation of intangibles which is intrinsic in the needology approach to social administration which has held sway until now (Chapter 8).

Moral and social valuations figure large in the identification of human needs in empirical social studies, whereas economists use need in connection with opportunity cost. In this sense it is the recognition that in a situation of scarcity the welfare benefit of providing a given service with these resources will be the consequential cost of not providing some other defined services. Accordingly the value of a unit of social security may be defined as the unit amount of housing which must be forgone in order to create it. To the economist need and social demand are aspects of the same notion: the power of the public sector to commit resources from society for social services and the decision about what quantities of these resources should be directed to each social service. Behind this view of need is the determination of objectives and the order in which they should be realised if resources will not stretch far enough to achieve all of them. This leads to the commitment of different quantities of resources to each objective and its concomitant services. But the allocation of resources to a particular social-service objective provides no certainty that the objective will be achieved. There is an output implication in every way in which given crude resource inputs may be combined and transformed supposedly with the same service objective. For this reason the study of outputs must accompany the economic study of need in order to plan the optimisation of resource output and the achievement of original need objectives. This leads the social administrator with an economic outlook to search for valid measures of need and output to guide resource allocation and thus improve the efficiency of social-service provision. Tunnel vision is the usual determinant of resource-allocation decisions, it fails to optimise welfare, and cost-benefit analysis should be put in its place (Chapter 9).

The supply of social services and the attainment of their objectives depend on organisations and the men and women who staff them. Although a need may be identified and adequate resources allocated to ameliorate it, the need may not be met because something is wrong with the responsible organisation or staff. Due to this and the increasing concentration of control, continual reorganisation and more compliance of operational units to their governing bodies mark the social services. Effort to increase such control seems to make more comprehensive planning possible. It is hoped that as a result there will be fewer failures in attaining objectives, but this is a chimera because all relevant relationships cannot be encompassed in plans and the organisations to execute them. This implies that gaps or disjunctions in organisations are as usual as under-achievement, which derives from the tendency for organisations to be built to cope with existing rather than emerging needs. The normal response of organisations to disjunctions and shortcomings is to investigate their position against the perspective of what is known already. This certainly helps organisations to react more speedily and surely to minimise difficulties as they present themselves. But there may be a limit to which organisations can be so adapted and they may in time become obsolete due to the magnitude and nature of needs which will arise in the future. To avoid this, and the futile quest for comprehensive planning, organisations should try to construct imaginative futures which take into account needs barely sensed at present. Organisations are better able to determine if instead of mere adaptation they require restructuring once these projected needs are sensed (Chapter 10).

Scarce means in relation to the growing scale of needs in the social services and the tendency for bureaucratic decision-making bodies to seek to increase their power, at the expense of operational units and staff by limiting their discretion, pose increasing problems for those staff of social services who try to cultivate a professional outlook and behaviour. For instance, whereas central bodies in local government with corporate management perspectives are primarily concerned with efficiency, their professional employees are more concerned with questions of effectiveness. Such perspectives are not wholly compatible. There is a school of thought which believes that society is becoming increasingly bureaucratised, which in turn implies that efficiency considerations must increasingly govern the work of operational units and professionals. But there is scope for the professional outlook to survive in influence, indeed the effective discharge of the social-service mission will depend upon this. The improvement of links between bureaucrats and professionals so that the latter can more adequately inject their outlook into corporate decision-making bodies is vital to this, as is the understanding of bureaucrats in these bodies that professional tasks can be performed only in comparative isolation and by the use of discretion by professionally minded operatives. New ways of focusing the opinions of professionals are a countervailing force to the diminution of effectiveness logically inherent in the present operation of local authority corporate management. Some bureaucratic rules are essential if anarchy in professional work is to be avoided, but too many rules may actually prevent the discharge of professional work. Such issues exist within Seebohm social-service departments, and adaptation of the ways in which the professional task and client need should be handled so as to maintain the effectiveness of the social-service mission is necessary (Chapter 11).

The comparative study of social administration is the last approach discussed in this book. Understanding and knowledge of a particular form of social provision in a single country might be deepened when this is compared with similar provision in another country and this may improve the efficiency and effectiveness of further provision. Before commenting on recent comparative studies of the personal social services and social work, consideration is given to the methodology that should guide such studies. A major difficulty is to determine exactly what phenomena are being compared and in this matter constructive definitions help to make intelligible, and at the same time check by exact observation the accuracy and nature of the phenomena subject to comparison. One product of such a preliminary is a functional definition of the personal social services. These are the practical supports needed by those who have become dependent upon others creating substitute homes for the homeless, providing friend substitutes when they are needed, and providing the necessary social element in the treatment of deviants. The kinds of organisations and staff involved in discharging these functions will vary according to the country studied. The achievement of a functional definition such as this is that it facilitates the communication between social administrators working in different countries of information which is of potential value to them (Chapter 12).

By means of its accounts of social problems, policies and progress, it is hoped that this book will contribute to further public understanding of welfare provision and its inadequacies. At the same time it attempts to show that social administration is in its youth and as such its future development depends on improvements in its ways of formulating problems. As an academic subject it has suffered somewhat because there has been too much thinking about how to make an immediate contribution to policies and administration and too little concern about its intellectual tools. This book shows how this is being recognised and the subject reorientated to illuminate more adequately than hitherto how needs are and should be met. Often this leads social administrators beyond the boundaries of the traditional social services into frontiers which will change as society evolves. To cope with this uncertainty about the empirical extent of their subject social administrators are equipping themselves with more adequate theory and methodology.

H. H.

1 Dimensions of Social Administration

Helmuth Heisler

Uncertainty and poverty in the lives of individuals and groups have been major concerns of social administration. As these pathologies of the human condition have been studied by means of different and often unrelated perspectives, a complication of interdisciplinary studies, the result has been that social administration as a subject has appeared to be inchoate. But this under-estimates its strength. By considering its philosophical and historical legacies and constraints, theoretical and empirical issues, academic social administration can be revealed to possess a measure of cohesion.

Wrapped in the cocoon of social policy, too often the administration of social services has been the sole focus of study, no doubt on the grounds that limits to competence must be set to an academic enterprise if the energy at its disposal is to bear fruit.[1] Unhappily, sometimes as a result the search for causal processes has been confined to the social services. Neglect of the prime pressures which shape their character, which are generated outside their system of activity, is a consequence. Another way to express this judgement is to say that 'the quality of our understanding of current problems depends largely on the broadness of our frame of reference'.[2] More orientation towards the interplay of societal pressures which engender policies and social administration, which is one of their objects, is overdue. When this happens, the descriptive character of studies and teaching will give way to analysis, and the ephemeral statistics of the present will make way for the deciphering of trends.

The Commonwealth

> Where are men most useless, would you say?
> When they can't command and can't obey (Goethe).
>
> He that leaveth nothing to chance will do
> few things ill, but he will do very few
> things (Halifax).

The British commonwealth is the context for social policy and administration and dictates its problems, procedures and possibilities. On this account it is the logical starting-point for the study of social administration. From a synoptic consideration, the commonwealth is a product of the interaction of two sets of phenomena, whose present grouping is heuristic. First, there is civil society and the nation, and, second, there is capitalism and the state. Within the single though fractionalised society these phenomena provide separate sources of loyalty, alignment and tension, which, though often acute, do not imperil its perpetuation. Civil society and the nation are integrative forces, as opposed to the disruptive potential of capitalism and the state. Civil society and the nation were formed historically before capitalism and the state, and thus were able to mediate the disruptive potential of these more recent forces as they arose.

In Britain 'the State has been fashioned and moulded by the community, and controlled by it' to a degree greater than in most other countries.[3] The reasons for this may be found in the meaning of the system of representation that has been evolved, the organs of government and the culture of the ruling class. The representatives of the nation have succeeded in maintaining a fair degree of independence. They are not in the pockets of their constituents because they are members of a sovereign body whose considerations can rise above those of locality, religion and class. It is to Edward I that we are indebted for first making possible the notion that parliamentarians might pledge themselves to caring for all citizens and bind them all by their unmandated activities. The last recorded instance of a constituency paying its parliamentary representative was in 1678, and almost one century later the words of Edmund Burke sealed the constitutive rule of the autonomy of parliamentarians when he affirmed that 'Parliament is a *deliberative* assembly of one nation, with one interest, that of the whole'.[4] Nor are they in the pocket of government. Parliament drew together and emerged as the opposition to the monarchy and secular government; the character of parliament has evolved through this process of structural opposition to the government and later the state and has learned how to curb what it considers to be their extreme abuses and so 'our constitution is still, at bottom, based on a continuous parley and conference in Parliament between ... the Government as the directing and energising element, and the representations of the Nation whose assent and acquiescence are essential and are only to be secured by full discussion'.[5]

Organs of control directly answerable to the state failed to be developed on a large and effective scale until living memory. Between the end of the Wars of the Roses and the Napoleonic wars, demilitarisation, revealed through the conscious neglect of the militia, prevailed and left power in the hands of rural landowners. As the balance of population was predominantly rural until 1851, their role as 'molecular' representatives of civil society who co-operated, albeit with occasional reluctance, with the central government was crucial. Through the office of the lay magistrate these landowners discharged such administrative duties as the government allocated them and with which they were in agreement. It was not until 1888 that they were obliged to relinquish their administrative duties in the shires in favour of bureaucratised and full-time local administration — which, however, was not the field service of a Whitehall department but of a local government.

The continuity of the culture of the ruling class is the third reason for the weakness of the state. Two prime structural considerations influenced this culture. First, membership of the ruling class has been open to all those individuals and groups who could establish a claim to be assimilated by it. As a result of this assimilativeness it has not been overthrown, not even in the seventeenth century when factions of this class fell out with one another. Second, the ruling class claimed to represent not only itself but all citizens, the nation, and could on the basis of this broad vision successfully oppose sectional interests which threatened its hegemony. By definition, in the secular sphere it is the class that has dominated parliament and determined its constitution; in the religious sphere it is the class that has upheld the Church of England as the religious manifestation of the nation and has propagated its ecumenicalism in order to open its ranks to all who would join it, most notably Disraeli. Three centuries ago it reached the understanding that it and the nation must be ready to change for the sake of its own conservation. And yet the constitution 'is not as much flexible as elastic, tending to revert to form as the influence which have deflected it in one direction or another have been weakened or superseded'.[6] By developing the cult and practice of empiricism the ruling class ensured that the structure of society has been moulded by its own members in the light of experience, and hence change has been incremental rather than radical, and philosophical divisions within itself and the nation have been minimised and not allowed to become disruptive. Such empiricism 'enables hypotheses to be tested by action and wisdom to be drawn from experience of facts as gold from ore'.[7] This was illuminated by the Permanent Secretary of the Department of Education and Science when he answered criticism of the inactivity of his Department by summing up its character as being 'pragmatic, conservative and evolutionary, not theoretical, futurological and revolutionary'.[8] This is an example of how the bureaucratic cadres of the state, who have been recruited from the ruling class, have tended to mirror its culture and abjure autonomous and leadership roles for their apparatus and preferred to keep in close step with the opinion of the nation, as is incumbent upon those who address themselves as servants of the civil society rather than as officers of state.

The commonwealth as embodied in the nation was sorely strained by the large advance of capitalism which accompanied the industrial and agrarian revolutions of the eighteenth and nineteenth centuries. Almost of necessity these changes were accompanied by the growth of individualism, geographical and social mobility, urbanisation and anomie. These changes created new hazards for individuals and their families, raised the threat of political revolution and altered the relationship of master and servant. Each change materially affected the nature and roles of government and the state.

Dependence on the vagaries of market forces was substituted for the material aid of family networks and settled communities and it proved impossible for substantial numbers of people to cope unaided in the industrial society. Symbolically, a pamphlet available to visitors to the Great Exhibition of British achievement in 1851 made this transparent. It posed the question: 'Who passes from the work to the workman and asks – What of all that glory does he share .... Talk of the development of industry: it is the development of curvature of the spine, concave chests .... Growing civilisation has brought with it some incidental advantages to the people, but it has also brought with it one deadly and universal curse – *uncertainty*.'[9] Many consciences among the ruling class were offended by such conditions; the more long-sighted among them wondered whether if these problems were left unalleviated they would become a source of disaffection and a cancer which might destroy the nation. Buttressing these thoughts was the growing recognition that cholera, illiteracy, malnutrition and other horrors lowered industrial and military productivity as well as the morale of the nation. Modestly, the rulers took the sting out of these problems by a spate of social legislation supervised and inspected by specialised departments of state.

Established order was threatened more seriously between 1770 and 1850 than at any other time since the fourteenth century due to a conjunction of political and economic circumstances. Dissatisfaction by ordinary people with the conduct of national affairs and the denial of their respectability by the respectable, deriving from the struggles of the seventeenth century, were fanned by the manipulations of factions which had places in parliament and competed for office. Example and fuel for discontent were provided by new egalitarian constitutions and revolutions in America (1776) and France (1789). Coincidentally the acceleration of capitalism was accompanied by migration, uprooting of social bonds and the creation of new communities whose social divisions were unlike those of the *status quo ante*. It needed more soldiers than were committed to the Peninsular War to garrison England, overawe and quell populism, and allow time for political solutions to emerge – notably, the Reform Acts of 1832 and 1867 by which the bourgeoisie and the urban working men were given the franchise. Grievances thenceforth were expressed through legitimate channels, and in this way democracy arrived. In the next century the social upheaval of two world wars and further innovations in social legislation heralded the legitimation of collectivism among the right as well as the left in parliament. R. A. Butler claimed for those to the right of the political spectrum that the 'welfare state is as much our creation as it is that of the socialists', who first achieved office as a government in 1923, and a younger Lord Hailsham claimed for the same Tories that 'We are committed to a great experiment – the creation and maintenance of a Social Democratic State.'[10] And so the nation swallowed and contained the British brand of socialism.

Between 1799 (Combination Acts) and 1875 (Conspiracy and Protection of Property Act) there was a turn about in the treatment of the industrial worker by parliament. Savage repression of collaboration for economic and political ends was replaced by unlimited freedom to combine. Working men as a category were granted the exceptional legal privilege of using their civil rights collectively. Economic enfranchisement thus followed in the wake of the political enfranchisement of the urban worker, and by this means a kind of 'secondary industrial citizenship' was created. Prior to Trade Union Acts in 1871, 1875, 1906 and 1965 there were legal decisions in the courts which jeopardised the position of trade unions, and following each adverse decision parliament redressed the balance in favour of the trade unions. By these measures, and trade-union involvement in the work of government, such as in pursuance of the 'Social Contract' (1974) and 'The Attack on Inflation' (1975), national officers of trade unions have been admitted to the ruling class. With their assumption of status they try to reconcile the interest of their members with that of the nation.

But by sharp business practices which the City would not countenance if used among its own kind, an influential number of working people in their economic lives behave precisely like primordial capitalists in a pure market economy. They are determined to maximise their rewards at all costs. Between 1938 and 1975 there has been relatively full employment, which has sustained the value of labour and its bargaining power, and national trade unions have tended to lose control of their members in favour of unofficial leaders at the local level. In this context a tendency for wages to be fixed separately by each plant has grown. Shop stewards and plant managers have been responsible for this trend in place of trade-union officials and employers' associations, who would rather determine industry-wide levels of remuneration. Sudden stoppages and irregular output, wage anomalies within identical industries and the leap-frogging of wages have become normal in many parts of the collective bargaining system, whose freedom from interference has become a constitutive rule among its beneficiaries. It is ironical that a body of legislation to absolve trade unionists engaged in collective bargaining from the litigation to which they might be subject otherwise, a body of legislation that confers protected status on workmen because of their one-time vulnerability from the aggression of employers, should remain in force just at the time when employees have acquired a strength which more than equals that of employers. Sheltering under the privilege of status and protected legal rights, at the plant level many workmen insist also on their right to determine unchecked their own contracts of employment. One-third of the employees in private industries tend to determine their terms of employment at the plant level and give a lead to industries where bargaining is industry-wide. Even at the level of the official system of industrial relations, the ethic of capitalism stalks, and industry and economy may be held at ransom until the demands of the trade unions have been satisfied. Due to their ability to take advantage of what are logically incompatible principles, status protection and the unhindered right to determine their own industrial rewards, the industrial workers have become strong. Industry is strike-prone, wages rise faster than productivity, and the implications of this worries the nation.

Political and capitalist revolutions provided the climate which led to the incorporation of all adults into the polity and raised the question about the limits to individual freedom. Should one be at liberty to exploit to the full one's economic advantages was a grave matter dealt with by parliament. 'Why then may not I run up a house as cheap as I can, and let my rooms as dear as I can? Your lordship does not like a house without drains. Do not take one of mine then. You think my bedrooms filthy. Nobody forces you to sleep in them', thus expostulated Macaulay before he advocated the contrary view before parliament in 1846: 'But higher than pecuniary interests are at stake. It concerns the commonwealth that the great body of the people should not live in a way which would make life wretched and short, which enfeebles the body and pollutes the mind.'[11] To match the interests of an expanding electorate, a body of social and industrial legislation was enacted to limit the inequalities of capitalism. This was notwithstanding the injunction of the protagonist of the rights of man and many others for the state not to attempt that which might be done by other agencies for it 'is no further necessary than to supply the few cases to which society and civilisation are not universally competent'.[12] A state which has grown in capability, since the reforms of the civil service which commenced in 1854, has become the guardian of this legislation.

A critical view of the state manifestly 'strangling the community'[13] has arisen because of the supposed decline of parliament and a misunderstanding of the nature of delegated legislation which has mushroomed since the demise of Queen Victoria. The essential roles of parliament since 1832, to enable a parley to take place so that government can sound public opinion and provide from the ranks of the opposition an alternative government, have remained unchanged. Society curbs the discretion of the state even in the area of delegated legislation, which is not scrutinised easily by parliament. It is a convention that such legislation is enacted only after consultation between the departments of state and organisations reflecting the views of every trade, profession or business that may be affected by it. In reality a wide measure of agreement between the state and society promoting legislation in the areas in which society is not 'universally competent' is achieved in this corporate way by delegated and other legislation.

The essence of the commonwealth is a collection of organisational rules which are manifest partly in a pattern of behaviour. From the absence of certain forms of behaviour which might occur otherwise, however, other organisational rules may be inferred. Reviewing the evolution of the commonwealth, not prescribing for a commonwealth, the organisational rules which have given it shape and which it has generated may be stated in summary propositions, namely (1) the prime object of exchange between two parties is to increase their own wealth; (2) but the parties to such an exchange — consumers and producers, employees and employers — should be of equal power; (3) an unsuccessful party to an exchange, such as life insurance, should not lose all and become a dependent as this is an evil condition; (4) weak and dependent categories of people should not be left to the fate of market forces and should be protected by means of indirect exchanges, channelled through the state, between them and the fit and able; (5) private enterprise is better than public enterprise and co-operation between private and state enterprise is preferable if private enterprise cannot succeed unaided; (6) by public enterprise, however, infrastructure facilities which are of benefit to private enterprise and the individual and which are beyond their means should be provided collectively; (7) the state should try to secure the consent of interests affected by impending legislation before it is determined; (8) social divisions in society are abhorrent and as long as they do not contravene the above rules they should be abolished; and (9) the quality of the commonwealth outweighs any supposed advantages of another state of affairs, such as would increase G.N.P. more certainly, and on this account proposals for evolution should be treated with caution and not proceeded with unless their advantages are certain. Proposition (1) is pro-capitalist; propositions (5) and (7) support the civil society; and propositions (2), (3), (4), (6), (8) and (9) strengthen the nation. Apart from proposition (1), the other rules of the commonwealth require action by the state. But only propositions (4) and (6), protection of the weak and the provision of an infrastructure, require fairly unambiguous action by the state. By dividing these organisational rules into two sets, constitutive and regulative,[14] it is possible to describe the tasks of government and the state. Propositions (5) and (9) are about constitutive rules that have implications for regulative rules. In the commonwealth, government is concerned primarily with regulative rules, and only with the consent of the society and nation are the constitutive rules changed.

Public opinion today expects its government and state not only to conserve the commonwealth but to raise national income, which is a novel expectation. Balancing and unbalancing are the ways by which these contradictory tasks may be achieved. Balance often arises from the triadic structure of societal interaction and the dependence of two parties to an exchange on the sanctions of the state.[15] Everyday examples of such interaction include litigation, social and environmental experiments, and private business projects which involve sanctions by third parties. The 'Social Contract' agreed between the government and the trade unions in 1974 provides a more dramatic example of asymmetrical reciprocity. By means of the 'Social Contract' employees undertook to restrain their demand for higher wages; employers paid less than presumably they might have done; and the government paid the difference between pre-contract and during-contract expectations by pledging itself to control prices and execute the manifesto of the Labour Party. Until now a class struggle has been avoided because political, economic and social ends have not coalesced, and these categories of activity have maintained their identities and distances from one another. But a Prime Minister has observed that this separation may be changing because certain trade-union leaders oppose wage restraint and 'want to prove that Britain can only be run with their consent . . . . Their wage strikes are in fact political strikes.' Within the Labour Party, 'people are going to have to decide whether they are Socialists and Democrats, or Socialists first and Democrats not at all'.[16] When categories of action overlap and coalesce, social tension increases correspondingly. To avoid this, government must become a 'broker' between the categories, insulate them from one another by compelling them to interact indirectly through itself in accordance with its own regulative rules.

An uncertain note must conclude this commentary on the commonwealth and its prospect and overshadow that for social administration. The British people of all ranks have not been molly-coddled by an affluent and comprehensive Welfare State as many of them believe, and indeed the welfare available to them is in many respects inferior to that of their European neighbours. This disparity arises because the first industrial revolution made civil society so strong that it threatens to prevent an overdue second industrial revolution. There is a myth that private enterprise sustained our economy effectively until the mid-twentieth century. Accordingly, as private enterprise has been so successful it needs only a little assistance from government, no more than temporary assistance, for private industry to rejuvenate our obsolete economy. This thought of economic freedom has captivated also many a working man who is now worried about national control of his wages and asks that government should not interfere with free wage bargaining. Faced with resistance from capital and labour a Prime Minister has concluded that 'The issue is ... whether any (social democratic) government, so dedicated to the principle of consent and consensus within our democracy, can lead the nation.'[17]

This poses the first question to be asked about any system of government: not 'whether it represents the will of the people, but whether it is competent to meet their essential needs'.[18] While the flexibility in decision-making in the commonwealth is a priceless asset, it must be said at the same time that the government is 'under-responsive' to its task of promoting economic growth because the unqualified story of the virtues of private enterprise is a mirage which holds us in thralldom. At the same time as the Manchester School of Free Traders bragged about what might be achieved without government intervention in the economy, and claimed that government was a positive hindrance to economic enterprise, from the 1850s onward German and French industrial advance began to outstrip that of Britain. In the case of Germany the reasons for success in her competition with Britain 'were not material but other social and constitutional' factors, and in both France and Germany the polities and states rendered appreciable and indispensable assistance to industrialists.[19] Better economic growth entails the mobilisation of all aspects of society, and comparative studies suggest that this involves paying less attention to democratic procedures and granting the state more capacity for

effective action.[20] Society as well as government is only just beginning
to savour this dilemma, a classic problem of backwardness; on the one
hand there is a tension between the actual state of economic activity
and the existing obstacles to industrial development and, on the other
hand, the 'great promise inherent in such a development'.[21]

Methodological—Theoretical Issues

> Progress is the mother of problems (Chesterton)

> Two elements are needed to form a
> truth — a fact and an abstraction (Gourmont)

While the version of British empiricism which receives most approval is
the belief that theory, though important, depends ultimately for its
validity on observation, another version which is unfortunately sometimes associated with academic social administration asserts the
irrelevance of theory to the construction of knowledge and explanation — which is the concern of methodological—theoretical issues. A
generation ago a snapshot of an undergraduate programme in sociology
might depict a course in sociological theory as its core whereas a similar
purpose would be seen to be served by an earthier and drier course
about social investigation for students of social administration.
Reflecting on his work as the architectural Director of the London
School of Economics, where it could be argued that social administration was born in 1912, Beveridge explained that his 'first aim was
that of treating economics, politics and other social sciences primarily
as sciences based on observation and the analysis of facts, rather than
analysis of concepts'. He proceeded to comment on Sidney and
Beatrice Webb, whose organisational talents had made possible the
L.S.E. and who had negotiated the grant of money to fund in it social
administration, that this was their 'central purpose' and that he 'was
merely following in their footsteps'.[22] By allowing the public to think
that facts were facts the Webbs exposed themselves to the general
censure of their kind by Alfred Marshall, who held that the 'most
reckless and treacherous of all theorists is he who professes to let facts
and figures speak for themselves'.[23] It was little use Beatrice Webb
confessing in private that 'the selection of facts is governed by the
hypothesis of an investigator'.[24] The damage was done. Neglect of the
theoretical requirements of research seemed to be encouraged officially
and brought the credibility of research in this tradition into disrepute.
In all research some data are irrelevant and become non-facts. But if it
is left to intuition and implicit theory to decide which phenomena are
facts, it is hard for the investigator to form conclusions about desirable

policies and action on the basis of scientific evidence. This is most serious because the stuff of social administration is problem-centred research whose findings must appear to be objective if they are to be useful as a pressure for improvement independent of political postures.

Biases in the social sciences cannot be minimised unless paradigms and their components are made explicit, and social planning as a corollary of social investigation cannot become rational without such explication. Only factual conclusions can be derived from facts, which if they are the sole concern of investigation cannot assist the formation of policy. This must result either in the immobilisation of social planning or deception, because a conclusion with policy implications can be deduced from observation only if there are appropriate questions explicit derived from theory included in the questionnaire to be administered to respondents.[25] Accordingly, the basic function of social theory is to prepare the questions which we want to ask of the facts because facts 'arranged in the right way speak for themselves; unarranged, they are as dead as mutton'.[26] Likely as not, an investigator is attracted to his work because of a concern or belief about the shortcomings of society. This may colour a hypothesis with a normative element drawn from general theory. As long as the research design is capable of disproving the normative supposition of a hypothesis through actual observation, this is not out of place. Thus social administration ought to be explicitly concerned with both middle-range theory, by which practical conclusions can be grounded on hard evidence[27] in the best tradition of empiricism, and with general theory.[28] But it is rarely so.

Therefore, if social administration is to remain a credible social science while the other social sciences are becoming more sophisticated, it must become more reflective and cease to despise 'the brooding which has gone on in the armchair'.[29] The scarcity of explicitly theoretical writing and thinking in social policy investigation is the problem of social administration as a nascent discipline. From this standpoint it seems to be held back because the theoretical excitement and stimulation to make the subject develop is absent. Development is a symptom and accompaniment of competing and challenging theories and their absence is a ground for regret; because social administration has suffered from 'over-agreement' among its members,[30] its development has been retarded.

Acknowledgement of a few achievements of deductive theory building must balance these reservations because there has been some awareness that a model or point of view need not be worthless or anathema because it is not completely anchored empirically. For instance, we are acquainted with the possible implications of state planning in democratic industrialised societies;[31] the checks on welfare imposed by the power of self-interest;[32] the meaning of obligation and reciprocity for altruism;[33] and stigma as an effective component and product of welfare.[34] Studies such as these offer 'an analytical pattern against which to hold the experiences of history and appreciate the elements of uniqueness and conformity'. Their value is 'heuristic rather than informative' because they do not tell us what happens but help us to find and understand what happens.[35] As Hugh Gaitskell put it, in a memorial address which touched on the learning and passion of Tawney: 'He was not inventing things, but simply showing them to us — things we had failed to appreciate before, but which we recognised immediately he wrote about them.'[36]

Two studies by T. S. Simey and R. M. Titmuss illustrate the methodology of social administration at its best. Simey was appointed Social Welfare Adviser to the Government of the West Indies in 1941 and recorded the plight of the islands in a book which became admired by social scientists in similar situations. Simey explained that there was an unhappy gulf yawning between government and the governed. To overcome this a solution to the 'more fundamental problems of low productivity had to be found'. This 'in turn implies a solution of the problem of social dynamics which provides the economic machine with its driving power'. He was critical of the expenditure of energy 'on the discovery of mere palliatives for the relief of these symptoms'. One way in which energy was wasted and misapplied was by 'paying disproportionate attention to one specific social problem or another, such as the care of "orphan" children or the technicalities of educational administration'. The problems demanding solution lay much deeper in the social issues of the twentieth century, and so Simey in his capacity as a social administrator felt obliged to review the governmental and economic foundations of the West Indies before considering the possible contributions of social-welfare schemes to nation-building.[37]

The Government of Mauritius in 1957 commissioned Titmuss and two colleagues to advise them 'as to the provisions to be made for social security' in a country plagued by overpopulation and declining output. Like Simey, Titmuss searched for an understanding of problems and their solution in the social fabric, and hence 'our perspective is no doubt broader than that adopted by other students of Mauritius'. So much effort was absorbed by this that there was insufficient time to study the social-welfare department and 'justify practical conclusions'. With confidence, nevertheless, the social administrators reported that 'Our recommendations are designed actively to assist and not retard the processes of economic growth; to spend less rather than more on public assistance; to prevent rather than treat ill-health; to use more efficiently and more fully the scarce and precious social resources and skills of the community.'[38]

Backwardness was the common factor in the islands studied, as it is the present condition of Britain. It is a relative condition[39] which tends to be defined in terms of low productivity, the extent of the political will to raise this, and the social dynamics to drive the economic machine. Simey and Titmuss were in no doubt about priorities and how social administration should proceed in tropical and backward islands. They showed how broad the horizon of social administration must be if it is to cope with the problem of backwardness. But when at home in Britain social administrators retreat into their social-services administration shells, and so far have said little about backwardness; while abroad they can feel uninhibited and apply their understanding of social science more adequately than ever they do at home. In considering the proper nature of social administration and welfare, therefore, these two island reports will prove more illuminating than studies of the British scene.

In the tropics Simey and Titmuss observed inadequacies and failures to the extent that collective purposes and the individual objectives of islanders were less fully realised than they would have been in alternative and workable societies. These technical judgements about the workings and societal pathologies of the tropical islands arose because they were afflicted by the class of social problems known as 'social disorganisation'.[40] Simey and Titmuss wanted to blot out social disorganisation in order to attain welfare. Welfare, without adjectival qualification, is a way to describe ideal societal conditions and may be defined negatively: it exists when there is no social disorganisation. Philosophical and economic approaches to the meaning of welfare have predominated and left its meaning unclear[41] and beyond the comprehension of everyone. By contrast to these approaches, Simey and Titmuss looked at welfare and the obstacles to its achievement in the tropics from the perspectives of the social world. When a significant body of people like the Government of Mauritius reaches an unfavourable definition of an aspect of the human condition, this becomes an experiential definition of non-welfare. It is a definition which by its nature contains the prospect that the world will be made better and welfare attained, because the same exercise of will and power which defines a human situation as non-welfare will hardly rest content until it is alleviated and there is progress towards welfare.

Social policies comprehend the definition of situations as disorganised or non-welfare, the emergence of the will to act, and strategies for progress towards welfare. The latter, according to Simey and Titmuss, might involve directing resources to a secondary class of institutions known variously as 'social service' and 'social welfare'. These institutions are secondary because their fortune depends upon others, located more squarely in the realms of the polity and economy, better placed to influence welfare. Though social services merely deliver many of the goods and services allocated by social policy, they tend to absorb the interest of social administration in the commonwealth, which contrasts with the concentration of Simey and Titmuss in the tropics with problems of policy. Like others engaged with the problem of backwardness they believed that achievement resulted by 'attacking old problems along new lines . . . [hence] the elaboration of welfare machinery can have no appreciable effect on welfare'.[42] The dilemma of social administration in the commonwealth has to do with the supposition that a Welfare State emerged after the Second World War because public policy outlawed unemployment and long-standing industrialisation had created the economic basis to pay of this superstructure. But the current economic crisis has revealed that this belief has been unwarranted. In other words, the great concern of social administration in the commonwealth with the social services is a measure of the imperfect recognition of its backwardness.

Integration

As the state of welfare is a concern of social administrators when they serve as consultants overseas, it is also their business when they are involved in the affairs of their own commonwealth. But neither at home nor abroad do they pretend to be omnicompetent. While they examine the many facets of welfare through the lenses of several disciplines their perception of what is relevant might be coloured by what they believe to be the central interest and competence of their subject. Variously described as solidarity, cohesion and consensus, pattern maintenance, social order, unity, citizenship, this primary area of unifying interest is 'centred in those social institutions that foster integration and discourage alienation' and 'unites our concern with the "ends" (the objectives of social policy) and the "means" (the development and administration of particular public and voluntary organisations)', according to the most influential teacher in recent social administration.[43] Notwithstanding the critical challenge of this perspective, as reflecting the values of the ruling upper and middle classes, who have vested interests in continuity and integration rather than change and conflicts,[44] it requires examination by reason of its dominance, the fact that social administrators who wish to influence social policy here and now can do this only within the values of the commonwealth, and the absence of a radical and alternative perspective which has appeal and persuades many significant social administrators.

    This focus on integration arose from the interconnections between the study of the history of social provision, the influence of leading academics and the nature of the social services. As well as the poor and elementary health and social services, the Elizabethan Poor Law (1597–1601), the Law of Settlement and Removal (1662), and the New Poor Law (1834) involved the unemployed, the supply of labour for industry and the 'sturdy beggars' who might disturb the peace. To the Elizabethans the Peasants' Revolt in Germany 'was their spectre of a Soviet Revolution'[45] and turned thoughts to regulations for the poor; the 'No Popery' Riots of 1780, Jacobins, the outrages of Ludd, Swing and Rebecca led Macaulay in the year before the revolutions of 1848 to defend state education in parliament on the ground that the 'gross ignorance of the common people is a principal cause of danger to our persons and property' and that 'the education of the common people is a most effectual means' of security'.[46] Until the Second World War, when it became politically unrewarding to do so, social provision was interpreted as 'social control'.[47]

Expressed as 'the inevitability of gradualness', Sidney Webb taught the Labour Party how to revolutionise society from within and without undue fuss.[48] R. H. Tawney, director of the Ratan Tata Foundation, which funded the Social Science Department at the London School of Economics for a time until 1919, and analyst of the contradictions of acquisitiveness and equality, clarified for many in the Labour Party how democratic socialism might be approached by institutional changes from within our society.[49] T. H. Marshall, before he handed over the Department of Social Science at the L.S.E., in his analysis of how equality grew in the commonwealth showed that progress was possible with the incremental extension of the rights of citizenship.[50] And then his successor, in diverse ways, showed how individual social institutions worked and could be improved piecemeal.[51] The revolution these men sought was silent, the reforms they promoted were those that minimised upheaval and yet were sure of success. Their methods and outlook were conditioned by the evolutionary, adaptive ecumenicalism of British history rather than that suggested by the functionalist conservative sociology[52] which was dominant for a generation after the Second World War.

Though little influenced by such grand theory, the division of labour in the social sciences has contributed to the shape of social administration. By the time they arrived on the academic scene, social administrators discovered that other social scientists had appropriated for themselves many important perspectives on the human condition. Perhaps in a mood of unconscious rivalry, social administrators, not content to be labelled 'fact-grubbers' and 'practical men', looked for academic space for themselves. While professing to be interdisciplinary, social administrators thrust to develop their own perspective of welfare as the problem of integration. This determines their questions about residual welfare, industrial achievement-performance, and institutional—redistribution models of welfare. By means of this key focus the other social scientists are relegated to the wings until such times as their analytical powers are required to support the drama of integration. For half a century Pigou's *Economics of Welfare* directed social administrators to a search for the specifically social, to the whole range of needs outside the realm of satisfactions which can conveniently be left to the market,[53] crystallised in 'The Social Division of Welfare' which is concerned with the will of society to 'survive as an organic whole'.[54]

Titmuss declared that the goal of social administration was to bring about integration, just as Talcott Parsons performed a similar service for sociology when he declared that the 'problems focussing about the integrative factors of social systems constitute the central core of the concerns of sociological theory'.[55] Following Parsons, integration must be distinguished analytically from the tasks of maintaining cultural patterns, inducing action in accordance with the goals of society, and creating resources which can be used to attain these goals. As all of these activities have aspects which relate to integration social administration is involved in all of them. Society is composed of units which do not necessarily wish either to work together harmoniously or belong to the same society. Maintaining the solidarity of society under these conditions is the problem of societal or system integration, which is more fundamental than social integration.[56] Overseas Titmuss was concerned with societal integration; in Britain, with his concern that alienation should be checked by integration, he seemed more concerned with the latter. Whereas societal integration involves the relationships between units, social integration is about the relationship between individuals; societal integration reflects morphology and the reconciliation of interests whereas social integration has more to do with the moral order; societal integration counterbalances social disorganisation whereas social integration counterbalances another class of social problems known as 'deviance'. Societal integration is the long stop which should act when social integration fails to check deviancy.

Central to the process of integration are rules and the agencies associated with their management which create positive and negative sanctions which are allocated for two purposes. One is to ensure that useful change in response to external pressures, such as the depreciation in the value of currency, occurs, and the other is to prevent societal disintegration. Disorganisation often results from the mismanagement of the allocation of sanctions, especially those that affect the relation between development and solidarity,[57] and it is therefore vital that to 'ensure its welfare, order and happiness society must respond with a continuous process of integration'.[58] Hence social administration is concerned with integration because it is the solution to social disorganisation and the task of attaining welfare.

Welfare and a consensually ordered society are abnormal conditions, and Parsons has been criticised severely for assuming the former in his theoretical work. Though normative functionalism has fallen into disrepute as a result of this defect, this does not mean that all elements of this theory, which might provide social administration with a distinct and convenient identity, need be abandoned. A more realistic theory of functionalism has emerged and a more realistic theory of integration can be deduced from it. The issue is that a satisfactory theory of the working of society must take account of disorder and conflict as endemic and not an aberration, even when a unit tries to secede from its society and welfare is lowered towards zero, and must appreciate the resilience of society under stress and indeed the positive virtues of discomfort to a society.[59] Fortunately, a theory of social disorganisation based on the concepts of the tense and disorderly society is now available.[60]

One interesting way in which integration can be approached and understood is by considering the tensions of social change as in part constituted by human rights which have to be fought for and protected. We are familiar already with the cultural displacement created in Britain by two world wars[61] which has revolved around the study of what has happened to citizenship rights. Less well known are the studies of the interaction of citizenship and nation-building.[62] Either single-country or comparative studies can be undertaken by a focus on citizenship, and the latter prospect is attractive at a time when the methodology of comparative studies in social administration is unclear.

Social planning

It follows that as integration becomes the speciality of social administration the integrative features of social policy and planning fall under its purview. As integration is a driving force in society – with tasks arising from discrepancies in expectations, roles and positions in every sphere – this means also that through social policy and planning social administration must be concerned with the state of culture, the economy and the polity. Thus social planning includes alteration to social structure and national and local attitudes as well as social services.[63] Though this brief cannot be broader, social administration, if it is to grow in effectiveness, will do well to curb any ambition to raise welfare overnight, avoid the advocacy of central and holistic planning, which becomes more and more attractive to those who are impatient with the slowness of progress, the bleakness of a deepening recession, and who feel powerless to save society from within. For the three practical reasons which will be described it is suggested that a totally different way of proceeding is not obviously superior to the present mode, which given a little patience is capable of considerable improvement.

First, any innovation must, like a transplant, have a high degree of compatability with the host system; though in itself important it must be a small part of the whole if it is not to be rejected on account of its alien nature.[64] The greater part of what a society has is an inheritance to be enjoyed which people will try to keep — even if this attitude is a symptom of false consciousness. Composite revolutions take several decades before their claims to success can be taken seriously because of this tenacity and culture lag. Apart from the support of influential groups.there must be widespread recognition of the need for an innovation if it is to take root and so 'seamanship consists in using the resources of a traditional manner of behaviour in order to make a friend of every inimical occasion'.[65]

Second, the contention that the power of government should be increased is not an argument for systematic and composite planning. Because the output of goods and services falls short of demand, and private enterprise unaided cannot satisfy our needs, government activity to raise productivity has grown. It seems to be agreed that short-term approaches to economic problems do not resolve them and that the French and Japanese governments are to be admired for steering their resiliant economies for a fair while without squashing private enterprise. More social-overhead capital, the absence of which is supposed to inhibit economic activity, is required in the form of education for literacy, training for occupational skills, social security and housing to facilitate the mobility of labour, energy, and perhaps the unprofitable 'lame ducks' of industry. At the same time the Treasury must hold down public expenditure — which as a proportion of G.N.P. has risen from 30 per cent in 1938 to 50 per cent in 1970 — by an unprecedented overview of the whole range of government spending, which, in addition to an audit of the past and present, must peep into the future. Both piecemeal and systematic planning have need of such a rational framework of interconnected information; but the ingredients of this framework, the location of decision-makers, and the kinds of decisions made tend to diverge. With some notable exceptions, such as energy and air transport, money rather than quantities is used as a measuring rod because it is the more sensitive measure of worth capable of reflecting quickly changing economic circumstances. A plurality of producers and buyers can therefore be substituted for many of the decisions that must be made by a handful of centrally located planners when systematic planning is attempted, and though planning in this manner in a free society lacks the potentials of single-minded systematic planning, its gross miscalculations of output and consumption can be avoided.

Third, the answers to the question whether welfare is attainable will provide clues as to the kind of policies and planning that should be undertaken. Utopians and Marxists see the whole of society as being corrupt and disorganised. It is incapable, therefore, of being reformed, and the only solution to disorganisation is to completely change society and thus a blueprint for a new society is required. A disjunction between the old and new arrangements is required, and as the old society has failed there is no place for any of its processes in the new. By one leap, a systematic reconstruction, welfare will be attained, and because the blueprint for this is comprehensive it is not envisaged that there will be disorganisation once the reconstruction according to this design has been completed. By contrast, there is a view that social change is continuous and that there is no end to conflict of institutions, social mobility and anomie. Every reform and change has its unanticipated consequence which might contribute to further disorganisation. Welfare is therefore unattainable though we orientate ourselves to it because we are human, rational beings and believe we can influence our destiny and so improve our lot. Piecemeal policies and planning have the virtue of being flexible and responsible to changing realities and are best suited to coping with the problematic nature of social change; in other words, 'we can learn only from our mistakes' and we must be cautious and prepared for 'unavoidable surprises'[66] as is impossible through systematic planning.

There is a point of view that attention to planning in a democratic industrial society is fruitless either because in reality it does not exist, or that it neglects the overriding imperatives of the moment which exclude attention to the aims of planning, however deserving they may be. Such thoughts arise from the belief that the only true planning is systematic and that only a structural perspective of policy and planning is valid. Whether there can be planning in a commonwealth is a matter of definition, and in view of the preceding discussion this need not detain us, but as the second line of criticism of concern with planning in a society such as Britain has a partial validity it requires comment. This structural explanation of social action is illustrated by two approaches to the study of nineteenth-century social policy: a group of contemporary historians provide a 'Tory interpretation' of this phenomena, and a social scientist of a contrary disposition arrives at a similar conclusion. Both sets of conclusions tally in finding a lack of premeditation and planning in social policy which is a product of 'the historical process' or of 'blind forces';[67] 'the objective "demands" of certain situations . . . are seen as virtually imposing particular courses of action'.[68] From these conclusions it may be inferred that their authors assume that only pressures external to people are relevant for the making of social policy or the determination of any other social action, and that ties between people within the same situation are the most relevant factors which fashion social policy. People are therefore chameleons who proceed through life by assuming an appropriate hue for each and every situation, and planning, which is a process extending over a series of situations, is impossible.

This would appear to invalidate the underlying premise of the editor of the *British Parliamentary Papers* who, reflecting on his learning in a substantial study of methodological importance, tries to show that there has been a process of conscious social planning during the past century or so.[69] He reveals how the making of policies and plans are to be understood through an understanding of the fourfold pressures on decision-makers: the obstacles to their constructive thinking; the handicap of inadequate information; the inadequacies of their social theory; and administrative institutions. People — decision-makers — and situations interact, and that social planning is a product of this is an inference to be drawn from his study. While it cannot be denied that the dynamics of human situations tend to induce alternative behaviour in a person over time, his behaviour is influenced also by some consistency in his character. An explanation of latent character is the essential complement to a structural mode of explanation.[70] Were this otherwise there would be no scope for generational styles, class and paradigmatic experiences, for example, to modify structural interaction and affect the outcome of policy and planning. Planning programmes need not appear as manifestos, constitutions and legislation if through a process of child and adult enculturation they are imprinted on the social consciousness of the participants in political processes. Hence the synchronic analysis of structures must be joined with the diachronic study of latent character in order to approach an understanding of the making of social policy and planning; or, put in another way, in order to achieve an understanding of social planning there must be a blending of sociological determinism, with its situational and institutional analysis, and a theory of voluntaryism which makes an allowance for rationality and leadership.

Methodological–Empirical Issues

> A dog starved at his master's gate
> Predicts the ruin of the State (Blake).

> Truth is a clumsy scullery maid who
> breaks the dishes as she washes them up (Kraus).

Social administration is the body of intelligence which contributes to the making of policies and the distribution of sanctions to eradicate social disorganisation. It is well aware that intelligence may fail to anticipate all the spin-offs generated by social policy and administration[71] and that destabilisation is the outcome of the anxiety and pressure which arises, among the low and the high, when ignorance on every point is dispelled and intelligence shared equally.[72] Slim though expanding resources prevent the anticipation of many side effects of policy and the collection and communication of complete intelligence. Voluntary effort in the study of poverty was the first mainspring of social intelligence. During modern wars the usefulness of intelligence became manifest and it has grown in prestige among those organisations that are determined to increase their own effectiveness in society. Now public authorities, whose scale of operations have expanded vastly since the Second World War, are engendering an imminent revolution in social intelligence in their roles of sponsors of this activity and as critical objects worthy of investigation.

Academic and organisational intelligence, though they have grown in response to the same stimuli, because they are the products of different settings generate different goals and products. Both forms of social intelligence exhibit the increase of measures by man to shape his destiny by the exercise of social science rather than the application of philosophy. Immediately after the Second World War, many important matters were still disposed by recourse to fundamental principles, but by the 1970s, according to the editor of the *Reviews of United Kingdom Statistical Sources*, there has been a radical change in the attitude to the use of data: 'on almost every issue now at least the *desideratum* of factually based conclusions is broadly accepted'.[73] We are surrounded by problems which urgently require solution, and so this change has occurred before it can be founded on the perfection of a fully fledged social science; hence many factually based conclusions are not as safe as they might be had social science not been so embryonic. This does not mean, however, that the facts which influence policy are without value because 'an *implicit* unstated theoretical system had emerged . . . equipped with explanatory, i.e. integration powers'. It came about by trial and error through the adaptation of survey methods to social problems, and so, 'unbeknown to the researchers, a standardised repertoire of major explanatory variables was gradually established, such as age, sex, occupation, level of education, ethnic origin, etc.'[74] These explanatory variables have overspilled from survey methods into many major arrangements for the collection of information which now enter into social accounting.[75] The systematic and regular preparation of social accounts by public agencies, their publication notably in *Social Trends*, provide much of the base-line information for factually derived conclusions. Another form of organisational intelligence is *ad hoc* and requires the investigation of specific issues for which it is believed urgent remedies may prove necessary. But this form of intelligence is less useful than the systematically derived social accounts because the information gathered, as well as the pressures which cause the search for such specific intelligence, becomes quickly out of date.

Alongside social accounting, the most important intelligence resource should be the public administrators, whose actions it is hoped might be guided by knowledge as much as expediency. After all they are appointed in part by virtue of their education and training. Ideally, they bring two qualities to their work. One is the cultivation of the habit of agnosticism exercised in relation to the results of researches undertaken by others and which require evaluation — even if this process leads to a cheerless conclusion such as that 'the precise investigation into questions of social pathology has been to undermine the credibility of virtually all the current myths'.[76] While they must conduct their business with the advantage of working theories, or else become immobilised, they should not allow themselves to be deluded into the belief either that they are proven or are without need of refinement. Moreover, the lack of certainty 'about the why and wherefore of any given social event' is not a necessary constraint upon sensible policy-making because 'we may yet be in a position to indicate which of a limited range of decisions is most likely to produce desired results'.[77] In contrast to the complexity of unravelling causation the range of possible policy alternatives is 'so closely limited'. Thus agnosticism and a willingness to experiment offer something to good administration. To these should be added the skill of elementary statistical criticism exercised by administrators, few of whom have research officers on tap. Unfortunately the casualness of much undergraduate social-science education in developing this facility rarely produces more than hit-and-miss and tubular criticism.[78] It may take a long while before intelligence influences the behaviour of an organisation. Given agnosticism, empiricism and statistical skills, the saddest fact in the whole drama of organisational intelligence is that it is notorious 'that ideas often ramble over long and roundabout courses from their origins' to influential persons[79] because they compete with deeply rooted interests and values and unclear expectations.[80] The competition is especially uneven when these forces of inertia are symbolised by simple and misleading slogans, such as that propagated by Mrs Thatcher in the summer of 1975, to the effect that the Welfare State has reduced inequality to such an extent that it is the latent cause of Britain's shoddy economic performance.

Implicit in academic intelligence is the notion that its 'proper calling' is to illuminate opinions[81] in order to uncover the public interest. Though ways to examine the public interest exist there is no public-interest theory 'that offers much promise either as a guide to public officials who are supposed to make decisions in the public interest, or to research scholars who might wish to investigate the extent to which governmental decisions are empirically made in the public interest .... The concept itself is significant primarily as a datum of politics.'[82] Nevertheless, the quest for the truth which might guide public action continues, often leading to uncomfortable conclusions for public administrators. In stark contrast to the agnosticism of organisational intelligence, which nevertheless seeks to strengthen its employers' power, academic intelligence is 'conducted in a radically iconoclastic mood ... almost always directed against authority [and] There is often an outcome that those in authority have acted wrongly, out of incompetence, blindness or disregard for the common good. The result is an outlook that radically distrusts the intended order of society.'[83] In the absence of a useful theory of the public interest and useful results, is academic intelligence a worthless activity? The answer is 'no'. The immediate relevance of research findings is not necessarily the justification of this activity because 'although useful results are likely to be important, what is important need not be evidently useful'.[84] Though many research findings do not make a direct impact on public affairs, through their accumulation they become diffusely mediated and expressed in ideology and general habits of thought, and in these ways may improve the character of social action.[85]

What Bertrand Russell described as the paradox of exact science, that it is dominated by the idea of approximation, tends to be overlooked by much social intelligence which strives to become exact. Social intelligence has less reason to be exact than natural science because it must by its nature handle poor-quality data. The three reasons for this are well-known: the affairs of human society at a particular point in history are more complicated than those of nature; because our subject-matter is living and free men, direct experiment under the most carefully controlled conditions is impossible; and, not least, the constants of a society change from epoch to epoch, which is to say that as well as the position in time of a society changing its own constitution is inconstant.[86] Hence there is a difference of exactness between hard data, like the number of rooms in a house, which are discernable to our physical senses, and soft data, such as broken homes, which are not. The difficulty of social intelligence is compounded because it is the soft data which tend to be the more valuable.[87] Soft data scrutinised too meticulously 'easily lead to sterile debates where the plain fact that quite a lot of contemporary sociology *works* is lost' in effort to become too exact.[88] Nevertheless, it must be admitted that because of the inadequacy of its data, social intelligence 'must always speak with an uncertain voice'.[89]

Inequality is emerging as the central empirical concern in academic intelligence. There has been considerable advance since inequality was viewed solely in terms of wealth and income. It is widely acknowledged that the pricing mechanism by itself is an unsatisfactory index of inequality, and thus, to illustrate, in the Third World 'few people are so well housed as the prisoners in jail, but the only people who appreciate the comforts of prison life are the warders'.[90] Moreover, in given circumstances the economic causes of inequality are 'partially dependent on non economic circumstances'.[91] Academic intelligence about inequality has been most illuminating when it has dealt with people's sense of justice, disorder, economic needs and the availability of resources in a single context[92] — because of the limited pertinence of empirical findings about one context or another.

Another way of looking at social intelligence is to distinguish its usages: clinical and engineering. Whereas organisational and some academic intelligence are employed for clinical reasons, much academic intelligence is utilised for engineering purposes; whereas the former accepts the clients' formulations of problems as the most efficient way of solving them, the latter may regard such formulation as no more than the symptoms of underlying difficulties which themselves merit consideration and action.[93] Hence the Welfare State, to illustrate, may be seen from a clinical approach as reacting only in response to the undesirable emergence of problems and seeking solutions within the framework of master institutions that lie beneath and cause the problems. Though the distinction between these usages is stark for heuristic purposes, in practice the distinction may become blurred because the historical evidence is that by the cumulative tinkering with the social problems that present themselves, men of affairs and vision may improve the form of society from within. But, whichever approach is adopted by the social administrator, he is distinguished among social scientists because his most fertile insights derive often from practical experience of the business of this world and he joins with Clarendon in believing that the 'Wise Man that should reform and establish Governments ... must compound his life both out of Action and Contemplation; and they must as it were succeed each other.'[94]

2 Social Administration as Social Science

John Carrier and Ian Kendall

'Social administration as a subject is not a messy conglomeration of the technical *ad-hoc*.'[1] This comment was made by Titmuss in an essay on the subject of social administration. A significant part of our aim in this essay is to examine this claim. We are concerned with the status of social administration and its relationship to the social sciences generally and to sociology in particular. We would like to begin our examination of these issues by referring to definitions of social administration, including our own. This may be construed as a rather predictable way to begin an evaluation of the subject. Certainly the well-known textbooks typically include such definitions in their introductory chapters.[2] Is it an exercise that needs to be repeated yet again? We would argue that it does — even if only to make clear what we are referring to when we write about social administration. However, definitions of subject-matter take on greater significance in this context than that of simply avoiding misconceptions of what is being written about. It is our contention that definitions of the subject reveal two main traditions in writing about social administration which have different implications for its place amongst the social sciences. We will call the first tradition 'social administration as a technical parasite'; the rationale for the terminology will become clear in due course.

Social Administration as a 'Technical Parasite'

This tradition tends to emphasise three things about social administration. They are as follows:

    (*a*) social administration is *not* a discipline but a multi-disciplinary field of study[3] – it is therefore possible to view the subject as being largely parasitic in relation to the 'real' social sciences;[4]

(b) social administration's field of study is essentially statutory welfare provision;[5] and

(c) statutory welfare provision is distinguished by its aim of meeting individual needs – there is thus a distinction drawn between 'personal' social services and public services that benefit the 'community at large' in an indiscriminate way.[6]

What observations can be made about this 'technical-parasite' tradition? First, let us look at the notion of social administration as a multi-disciplinary field of study rather than as a discipline in its own right. If adhered to, this idea has important implications for the status of social administration, for it must be seen as relying largely, if not entirely, on the theoretical developments of the 'real' social sciences for its own development. As a multi-disciplinary field it will involve the utilisation and application of the concepts of sociology, political science, economics, and so on – it will be an importer and user of ideas rather than a producer of them. As one sociologist has observed, social administration 'draws its ideas from [sociology] . . . and contributes facts and techniques to it'.[7] Social administration is thus cast not only in a 'parasitic' role but is also presented as being primarily concerned with factual and technical issues.[8] As a subject for academic study social administration becomes only as good as its sociological inputs (or whatever it draws from economics, political science, psychology, and so on). In terms of its relationship with sociology the issue becomes one of how best to utilise the resources of sociology in the study of welfare. However, we are inclined to reject this view of social administration as a purely multi-disciplinary field of study based on the other social sciences. Other considerations apart, and which follow, the notion may be said to be faintly ridiculous in the context of the social sciences where demarcation lines between the various disciplines are so vague. In fact many social-science disciplines could be said to be in constant danger of conceptual annihilation by the expansion of those disciplines most closely related to them. Thus, whilst it may be possible to make social administration disappear into the sociology of welfare, the economics of welfare, the politics of welfare (and so on), it may be equally feasible to make sociology disappear into social history, social psychology, social anthropology, economics and political science.[9] It might of course be said that the argument is more substantial than one about boundaries between disciplines. That unlike other 'genuine' disciplines social administration 'appears to have failed to generate any substantial body of theory of its own'.[10] This is a criticism which we wish to return to and examine below. For the moment we would simply wish to reiterate that an identification of social administration as simply a multi-disciplinary field of study tends to confirm on it the status that Titmuss denied it — a collection of the technical *ad hoc* given some academic status by the importation of ideas and concepts from the 'real' social-science disciplines such as sociology.

If we proceed to look at the second and third points emphasised by the 'technical-parasite' tradition we will find that they lend support to the view of social administration that we have just presented. This is largely because they delineate the subject-matter of social administration in a very narrow way and to a large extent in terms of contemporary administrative arrangements. This reinforces the notion of social administration as a rather specialised subject concerned with technical details about the administration of specific government agencies. In such circumstances it would be surprising if the subject were not largely descriptive and derivative. However, our second tradition of defining social administration — which we will call 'social administration as social science' — provides us with a valuable critique of these second and third aspects of the 'technical-parasite' definitions. In so doing it opens up quite a different view of social administration as a subject, its position amongst the social sciences and its relationship to a discipline like sociology.

Social Administration as Social Science

It is at this stage in the discussion that we would like to introduce our definition of social administration and its subject-matter. We would define social administration as the study of the welfare activities of societies. We would define welfare activities by saying that their distinctive feature is that their manifest purpose is to influence differential 'command over resources' according to some criteria of need. Apart from the particular configuration of words used in the last two sentences, we do not take this definition to be particularly unique. It is in fact based on definitions produced by other writers[11] who have contrasted welfare activities with those of private markets. Thus welfare provision and private markets are presented as alternative agencies for distributing resources in society. This tradition of defining social administration gives it not only a broader subject-matter but one that is much less obviously tied in with how certain societies have functioned at certain points in time. This broader perspective has been justified by criticisms made of the narrow view of social administration implied by the 'technical-parasite' definitions. The most well-known one — which was made twenty years ago — is that by Titmuss in his essay on 'The Social Division of Welfare'. He made it clear that to fully understand the role of welfare in modern industrial societies we will almost certainly have to look beyond the traditional textbook limits of

statutory social-services and voluntary provision and examine statutory
fiscal and occupational welfare provision.[12] Titmuss also commented
on the difficulty of separating 'individual needs' from those of the
community as a whole – a distinction which is the rationale for
distinguishing 'personal social services' from 'community public
services' with only the former coming within the purview of social
administration. Pinker has subsequently argued that this distinction is
both 'illogical and misleading'.[13] He points out that we utilise the
'impersonal' public services as individuals to meet our own individual
needs.[14] Similarly, it is possible to see many of the 'personal' social
services as having a benefit for the wider community – clearly the
treatment of an individual's infectious disease meets both his personal
needs and those of the wider community.[15] These criticisms of the
narrow 'technical-parasite'-type of definitions make us see the subject-
matter of social administration as the broad-ranging one of welfare as a
distributive device. One is then forced to become aware of the fact that
the private-market/welfare distinction has a significance for more than
the resources typically examined by the textbooks (medical care,
education, income maintenance, housing and social-work services). The
'technical-parasite' tradition tends to limit social administration to
study that which is officially defined as 'a social service', despite the
problems involved in setting such limits.[16] The result is to avoid the
type of discussion that Pinker engages in with reference to 'public
transport as welfare',[17] and thus the subject becomes not only
concerned with technical details, but technical details in officially
prescribed areas – those that are officially defined as social services. By
contrast, a concern with welfare activities in general will embrace fiscal
and occupational welfare as well as voluntary and traditional social-
welfare provision. It will also be concerned not simply with medical
care, social-work services, income maintenance, housing and education
but with transport, legal services, food, recreational facilities and in fact
all resources where the issue of welfare distribution or private-market
distribution can be seen as significant.[18]

Social administration can thus be seen to have included two
divergent traditions which are represented by differences in how the
subject is defined. One tradition we have called the 'technical-parasite'
because it defines the subject-matter of social administration very
narrowly, so that the subject has as major interests technical issues
concerning very specific institutional arrangements for welfare and
relies on the established social sciences to provide ideas, theories,
concepts, and so on to analyse these issues – the subject is essentially
parasitic on the social sciences, making little or no contribution itself to
their advancement. We have contrasted this with a tradition which we
have called 'social administration as social science', which, by defining

the subject-matter much more broadly, indicates that the nature of social administration may well be a discipline that parallels political science and economics in its concern for a particular but significant area of social action. This view of social administration as a separate discipline implies the existence of a distinctive social-administration perspective that would be equivalent to the sociological perspective. To what extent is this a reasonable view to adhere to given the criticism which has been voiced concerning the failure of social administration to develop its own body of theory? One area in which we can explore this view is in the relationship between social administration and sociology, for, as has been noted, the former 'is often identified with' the latter,[19] and we have already referred to observations concerning the uses made by social administration of the ideas of sociology. To what extent should social administration be identified with sociology? To what extent should it utilise the sociological perspective rather than develop its own? An examination of these questions may enable us to arrive at an answer to the question of whether the tradition of 'social administration as social science' has real validity or whether, despite our own definition of the subject, it remains a parasitic conglomeration of the technical *ad hoc*.

Let us examine why social administration should be identified with sociology. However broad or narrow the subject-matter of social administration may be, one would certainly anticipate sociologists having studied the area. This anticipation is based on the typically all-embracing definitions of sociology made by sociologists, that it is concerned with 'all human activities'[20] and 'the whole complex system of social institutions and social groups which constitute society'.[21] Certainly, whether social administration's concern is all welfare activities or simply statutory social-welfare services, both clearly come within the ambit of sociology. Moreover, if one does take social administration to be a multi-disciplinary field of study then instead of the possibility of a close association between it and sociology one is faced with the certainty of its dependence on sociology. However, an examination of the actual relationship between sociology and social administration suggests that the former's claim to ubiquity starts to look somewhat thin. In fact there seems to be a case for saying that there is a long-standing sociological tradition of ignoring welfare as an area of study. Pinker has concluded that the 'founding fathers' of sociology (Marx, Durkheim, Weber and Spencer) had a tendency to be 'not greatly interested ... [in] remedies for social problems'; he also makes the general observation that 'sociologists have been oddly diffident about the subject matter of social administration'.[22] Certainly, a search through standard sociology textbooks reveals a general paucity of references to welfare.[23]

A similar examination of the textbooks of social administration casts some doubt on the observation we quoted above, that social administration draws its ideas from sociology.[24] On the contrary, we would suggest that there is more evidence to support a previous observation of our own that 'the resources of sociology do not appear to have been extensively or systematically utilised in the study of . . . social administration',[25] for the social-administration textbooks contain few explicit references to sociological theories.[26] Thus the theoretically feasible close association between sociology and social administration is not matched by the reality of the situation. For what are probably a variety of reasons[27] sociologists have ignored the subject-matter of social administration and students of social administration have made relatively limited use of the resources of sociology. This separation of sociology and social administration may be viewed as an unfortunate situation – and a closer association advocated.[28] However, whilst not wishing to appear as advocates of academic isolationism, we would express doubts about the advisability of embarking on an exercise that sought to 'remedy' the situation we have described above by an attempt to make social administration more sociological.

There are two reasons for our reservations about the development of a more sociological social administration. The first concerns the nature of what have been – and to a significant extent still remain – the dominant sociological perspectives, which are essentially 'positivistic' in their approach. We have in another context sought to demonstrate the extent to which a 'positivist' approach has been implicity utilised in explanations of the development of British social policy and indicated the ways in which we consider this approach to be inadequate and misleading.[29] Thus the first element in our doubts about a more sociological social administration concerns the nature and value of the sociology that is utilised. Regardless of what many sociologists may claim, it does not automatically follow that the traditional social-administration texts have lost a great deal by their failure to incorporate an explicitly sociological framework into their analyses of welfare. It is at this point that we re-introduce briefly the criticism that social administration has failed to develop any 'substantial body of theory of its own'.[30] There are two observations one could make about this: the first is that the subject of social administration has at present a relatively short history compared with other social sciences and therefore this criticism could not be said to constitute a major indictment of the subject at this point in time; second, it might also be pointed out that a discipline such as sociology has developed a 'substantial body of theory' in terms of the amount of sociological theorising that has taken place, but the value of much of this theorising may be open to question.[31] A more sociological social administration may be a more theoretical social administration but it may not be a 'better' social administration.

Our second reason for doubting the value of making social administration more sociological concerns the nature of the former rather than the latter. We would lend support to the view that social administration 'is not . . . [a] discipline of the traditional sort',[32] that its distinctive features are worthy of retention and may be threatened by any attempt to turn the subject into some kind of sociology. In particular the concern of social administration with 'exposing the value choices and value conflicts which are inherent in any social policy development'[33] rests on the assumption that the resolution of such choices and conflicts will not depend on 'the impersonal forces beloved by sociologists'.[34] Yet such 'impersonal forces' are the essence of the 'positivist' approach to understanding society, and this approach is the essence of much sociology. There is thus a very real sense in which much sociology denies the significance of the social-administration perspective by denying the reality and significance of the choices about welfare policy that face members of societies. However, this denial of value choices reflects not only the 'positivist' perspective, with its emphasis on impersonal social forces determining what happens in society, but also the implicit faith that many social scientists have in reason being used to resolve such choices and conflicts.[35] This faith springs from a deeply held methodological principle concerning the separation of fact and value. Examples can be found in the writings of the most eminent social scientists, whose intellectual rigour in setting out the distinction often does not allow for the layman's inability or unconcern with such academic nicety. This is not to say that such a distinction is not important; it is, but to state the difference is not to resolve it.[36]

Thus our two reasons in fact come together at the end. A more sociological social administration is not to be automatically desired in our opinion. This is not only because we have reservations about the value of the 'positivist' sociological perspective as a means of understanding societies and their welfare activities, but also because this perspective is antithetical to the distinctive perspective and concerns of social administration. In fact, for social administration to become more sociological would be to confirm its status as a 'technical parasite'. We would argue for social administration having and retaining the status of 'social science'. It can be seen as having as subject-matter a particular but none the less significant aspect of society which the other social sciences have tended to ignore.[37] The subject should develop by attempting to understand its subject-matter on its own terms rather than on the assumption that the ideas of the other social sciences, developed to suit their own purposes, can somehow be imported into social administration to produce something that is more theoretical and therefore perhaps more acceptable within the academic community. The concern of social administration with 'dilemmas of choice and change' and possible resolutions to such dilemmas gives it a distinctive approach worthy of preservation. We might also suggest that social administration's 'atheoretical' development to date is itself no bad tradition. It can be construed as partly a result of its 'empirical tradition'[38] but perhaps also of an implicit commitment to avoiding the forcing of data into preconceived existing theoretical constructs. There is much to be said for generating theories from what we know about welfare activities rather than attempting to impose on what we know an assortment of imported theories from the other social sciences. There are, we think, justifications for seeing 'social administration as a social science' — the most fundamental one is that there lies the way, in our opinion, to a better understanding of the welfare activities of societies.

3 Responsibility and Justice

Thomas McPherson

Introduction

It may be useful to indicate in summary form the main themes of this chapter. I begin by noting that although the closeness of the relationship between social justice and economic justice is not likely to be questioned, there is less agreement on what exactly the relationship is. There are important differences between any one of the three following views and the other two: (*a*) that the achievement of economic justice is simply one means among several to the achievement of social justice; (*b*) that the achievement of economic justice is overwhelmingly the most important condition of the achievement of social justice; (*c*) that the achievement of economic justice actually is the achievement of social justice – that is, that social justice has no content over and above economic justice. I mention these here simply as examples of views that might be held; I do not discuss them in what follows. At any rate, it is obvious that the association of social justice with economic justice is one that no theoretical discussion of social justice can ignore.

I next comment on the distinction between distributive and commutative interpretations of justice; the distinction reflects political differences. Indeed, even if we disregard commutative justice and concentrate on distributive justice – as being in any case the approach that tends to be taken for granted in discussion of social justice and social welfare – there are political or ideological differences within this more limited field, for example over the status of utilitarianism.

Although utilitarianism has been sometimes regarded as the moral-political theory justifying, or at least inspiring (at any rate, accompanying) the Welfare State, it has not been universally so regarded. From a theoretical point of view it is important to remember that utilitarianism has been subjected to serious criticisms. Some of these criticisms are new, or at least appear to be so; others are revivals of older, standard objections. I attempt an assessment of some of these.

But before that I discuss the difficulty which the existence of political differences puts in the way of providing objective criteria for distributive justice.

I pass finally to the question: whose is the responsibility for social justice? Responsibility for justice exists on several levels — in particular, responsibility for declaring (and it may even be for creating) men's needs and deserts, and responsibility for meeting them.

Social Justice and Economic Justice

'Social' justice seems to be a vaguer notion than either 'legal' or 'economic' justice, which suggests that there are advantages in the way of greater clarity and precision in its being attached to one or other of these two notions. Let us consider how a linking with economic justice may be supposed to give precision or backbone to the notion of social justice. There is both a theoretical and a practical answer to this question.

Take first the theoretical. In the modern period the science of economics grew up following the development of the modern nation-state, of liberalism and of a competitive market economy. Its seniority ensured it a dominant position over the other social sciences as these in time began to develop. Being first on the scene, it functioned as a stimulus for, and provided a shape to, social thinking in other fields: the most obvious example is in the work of Marx. Furthermore, economics had the great virtue of being a quantitative study. 'Economic' justice suggests a precise and measurable kind of justice (money can be counted) which anyone interested in social justice or social welfare might in any case be pleased to have offered to him as a model, even if the economists had not historically got there first; the idea of a just society as one in which justice is a matter of the distribution of units of wealth and income is an attractively neat and simple one.

The practical answer is obvious. The demand for social justice takes the form of a demand for economic justice for the reason that the most pressing of men's needs are material. When a man is starving he needs food first; the sustaining of a person's physical or material life is a necessary condition for possible improvement in the non-material quality of that life.

Economic considerations, in Western industrial societies, have tended to be dominant. Nevertheless, of course, in these same societies, other considerations have also often seemed important. Indeed we sometimes make a point of drawing a contrast between economic and social demands — for example, in discussions about the environment.

We may note two significant differences between social justice and economic justice; no doubt there are others. First, economic justice basically is a matter of the proper distribution of wealth and income, whereas social justice (this is admittedly a somewhat dogmatic assertion) involves the recognition of other goods also — for example, the respect of others, self-respect, liberty — which are not always dependent on wealth or income. Second, even if economic *equality* could be achieved (the relevance of this lies in the close relation between the concepts of 'equality' and 'justice') it would not follow that social equality had been achieved. Social inequalities dependent upon ancestry, or physical attributes, or occupation, for instance, could remain; there is no good reason to suppose that such differences between people would totally cease to be socially important if redistribution of wealth, and so on, were to greatly reduce economic inequalities.

Supposing, then, that economic justice and social justice are not identical, we may pass to a different question, namely whether either, or both, can be described as an end in itself or only as a means to some further end. The achievement of what a given person would regard as the proper distribution of wealth or income is unlikely to be for him self-justifying. A proper distribution of wealth, like wealth itself, seems to be a means to an end. It is true that it can come to be regarded as an end in itself; but this is surely a perversion. On the other hand, it would seem, social justice can be more plausibly represented as an end in itself. If a particular society is agreed by two persons to be one in which there is social justice, will there be further questions about what this social justice is *for*? However, one must be careful here. The means/end distinction is sometimes hard to maintain. The obvious candidate for the overriding end to which both economic justice and social justice might be claimed to be means, by someone who wanted to classify them both thus, is 'happiness'. But the concept of 'happiness' is notoriously a vague one. As J. S. Mill said, 'the ingredients of happiness are very various'.[1] Mill's belief was that what might have begun as a means to happiness could become in time sought for its own sake and an ingredient of happiness rather than a means to it. He instanced money, power, fame — but also virtue. We could add economic justice and social justice to the list. Such a doctrine as Mill's virtually does away with the means/end distinction in this context; but also, by incorporating too much into it, it largely empties 'happiness' of precise content. Yet who can doubt either that happiness does indeed have many and various ingredients, or even that 'happiness' is still the most plausible answer to the question: 'If economic justice and/or social justice are means to an end, what is the end to which they are means?'? In short, there are difficulties involved in making precise what might at first sight seem a difference between economic justice and social justice, namely, that one definitely is, and the other definitely is not, a means to some end beyond itself. The apparent difference may indeed be ideological – or, to put it more mildly, it may reflect the different political assumptions of different societies or of groups within a single society. There is no agreed answer to the question whether one of these is more obviously than the other no more than a means to an end. A value judgement is involved here about the relative importance of economic and other considerations. However, it is certainly the case that to suppose that economic justice is an end in itself would strike many as unattractively materialistic. The basic necessity of economic justice can more acceptably be admitted if it is seen as literally no more than basic – a basis for some other, more 'spiritual' condition. It may be that 'social justice' has a stronger moral connotation than 'economic justice'. Certainly, for what it is worth, if we look to nothing beyond the two terms 'economic justice' and 'social justice' themselves, it seems more natural to suppose that social justice might be the end to which economic justice is a means than that economic justice might be the end to which social justice is the means.

Political Differences

Anyone attempting an account of social justice faces the problem of identifying 'objective' features of social justice – in the sense of features that would be agreed on by adherents of different political or ideological persuasions. I am not thinking of differences between assumptions held in widely different political systems, but rather of differences of 'philosophy' within a liberal democracy.

W. B. Gallie has brought out effectively the contrast between what he calls, in an essay of that title, 'Liberal Morality and Socialist Morality', two ways of thinking which he presents as intertwined in the attitudes of people in our liberal-democratic society. One of the differences between these 'moralities' as he presents them is in their conceptions of justice. 'For Liberal Morality . . . justice consists primarily in those arrangements whereby the meritorious individual, wherever his work or services are publicly available, shall receive back his (commutative) due.'[2]

For Socialist Morality justice is essentially a distributive, not a commutative conception. Nor is it based on any of the *actual* claims men make, or have made, on one another in respect of fair rewards and returns; for all such claims are subject to the taint of non-moral self-interests and pressures, whether from individuals or groups. Justice, like all other strictly moral notions, is derived from an ideal — conceived as realizable in the future and already in some measure affecting men's aspirations — an ideal state of affairs in which moral claims would act as motives entirely without the taint of self-interest.[3]

Gallie is reluctant to press too strongly his own distinction, or the suggestion of a real conflict between the two moralities; but the distinction is a useful and illuminating one. There indeed are these two strands, or something like them, in 'our' thinking about justice;[4] and people's views about what would constitute social justice differ according to the extent to which they emphasise one of these tendencies rather than the other. Gallie's choice of the terms 'Liberal' and 'Socialist' brings out the political or ideological connections of these views of justice — a point further underlined by the fact that in his discussion justice is only one of three concepts in terms of which he expounds the distinction between 'Liberal Morality' and 'Socialist Morality' — for he interrelates the views of the two moralities on justice with their views on liberty and on good government.

Although people of all political colours may nowadays be heard to speak in favour of the Welfare State, adherence to a 'liberal' view of justice nevertheless constitutes a theoretical obstacle, just as adherence to a 'socialist' view of justice constitutes a theoretical encouragement, to whole-hearted involvement in the working or extension of the Welfare State. This way of putting the matter assumes that ideas determine policy, which is no doubt a rather simple point of view; but it does not really matter for our purposes what comes first or what depends on what. There is a general association here which is of relevance to the understanding of the concept of 'social justice'. The important point is that neither a socialist nor a liberal view of justice as such is singly 'right' or singly 'wrong' (though there might be moral objections to particular workings-out of either view); and as long as both views are held by individuals in the same society with different emphases, agreement on what social justice 'really' is will be difficult to find. Views about social justice are, among other things, political views. The very expression 'social justice' has been associated much more with one political position than with others. The very idea that the achievement of social justice is a prime task of government is taken for granted in one political view where it is only grafted on to another. That a central responsibility of the social philosopher is the examination, or the recommendation, of criteria for distributive justice seems a natural assumption. But the philosopher must from time to time remind himself of his duties, first to see things whole, and second not to be content to see things through particular spectacles but also to examine the spectacles through which he sees things. In the present context one fundamental question that presents itself to him is the following: how far in arriving at an account of social justice must 'liberal' criteria be combined with criteria of distributive justice? Social justice (again to be dogmatic) involves the recognition of people's *rights*, and these include more than rights to a particular sort of share in some quantifiable stuff that is capable of being distributed in one way rather than another.

Criteria of Distributive Justice

Nevertheless, social justice is most commonly thought of as distributive justice. Let us therefore now take up the question of criteria of distributive justice. The simplest and most natural way to consider this is in terms of distribution of income – though we need to remember that rules for the distribution of income will not of themselves guarantee even distributive social justice, let alone social justice in a wider sense; for there are things that money cannot, or cannot always, buy, and for which there may need to be rules of distribution (for example wives or husbands).

The most convenient point at which to begin is, as in so many cases, with the existing pattern of things, whatever that may be. Our own present situation is the result of historical processes, which have included deliberate efforts to bring about a nearer approximation to social justice. Of course, historical processes which have in practice tended to lead to increased social justice also include some which are only partly, or even not at all, the effect of deliberate human engineering.

Let us assume (however unreasonably, but we must start somewhere) that in any period the existing distribution of income is broadly just, and that any proposal for altering it needs to be argued for. This will put the onus on the person who wants to change things. If the arguments of the advocate of change are powerful enough, those who are doing well out of the *status quo* may then be put in the position of having to defend their advantages by argument; but argument generally comes more appropriately from the minority that actively wants social change. It is perhaps hardly necessary to say that argument is not the only, nor is it the most effective, weapon in the hands of those who want social change. The argumentative inertia of those who accept the *status quo* we may take as reflecting a belief that the *status quo* is on the whole just. The criteria of distributive justice which are discoverable in the *status quo* tend equally to be taken for granted. If we leave aside cases — which may in fact be quite numerous — where tacitly agreed criteria are simply not applied, it would seem that the would-be reformer has to offer either new criteria or new interpretations (or applications) of existing criteria. But in practice he can hardly offer totally new criteria; there can be no fruitful argument about social justice between people who hold quite different criteria of social justice. So it is the latter way that he must take. The would-be reformer and the upholder of the *status quo* will share broadly the same criteria of distributive justice. It is the task of the reformer to point out that the existing criteria are not being applied consistently or are being interpreted wrongly.

Let us look at criteria of desert, for the present taking these for convenience in isolation from criteria of need. Where there are no differences in desert, justice requires that people be treated equally — the same rate for the same job, and comparable rates for comparable jobs. But what is a relevant difference in desert? And if several criteria of desert seem relevant, what weighting is to be allowed to each? An intending minister of the Church of Scotland may be required to take at least as long in training for his work as a medical student of the University of Edinburgh is required to take for his; but it is unlikely that a Scottish parish minister would argue that he ought to receive as high an income as his local general practitioner, and even more unlikely that the general practitioner would argue that *he* ought to be paid no more than the minister. If any differences between them are relevant to the justification, on grounds of desert, of the differences in their income, they presumably lie elsewhere than in the length of training. Do they lie in vocation? But both professions are apt to talk in terms of vocation. Do they lie in amounts or types of responsibility for others? No doubt at one time men valued their souls higher than their bodies, and perhaps the direction of the difference of income we are considering indicates that they no longer do. Yet the cure of souls can be as responsible as the cure of bodies and minds. Is the difference to be justified by reference to the higher social status of the general practitioner? But supposing the doctor's social status to be indeed higher, which might well not be the case in a Scottish rural community, this itself is as much an effect as a cause of his higher income. Do they lie in the difference of sex? This is probably not relevant here. The doctor in any case is the only one of the two who is likely to be a woman, and attacks on income discrimination are usually directed against higher incomes for *men*. Perhaps there are other criteria than those I have mentioned that are more relevant than those that I have. But this example — a deliberately uncontroversial one — illustrates both the kind of criteria that come to mind in cases of income difference and the general point that the responsibility to find arguments rests on the person who wants to change the *status quo*. In a case like this, where the persons concerned are themselves likely to be contented with their position, at any rate as relative to each other, the assumption that the situation as it is is broadly just presumably seems to them a reasonable one. (The example I have given is presented in a very over-simplified way; for an important and wide-ranging discussion of attitudes to social inequality see W. G. Runciman's *Relative Deprivation and Social Justice*.)[5]

We need to distinguish between the acknowledgement of the relevance of particular criteria of desert to certain cases, and insistence that they should actually determine social policy. Quite apart from the fact that criteria of need as well as criteria of desert may be relevant and may lead in another direction, and apart also from the inertia already referred to, there is the criterion of the market. Some occupations, in the view of everybody other than the majority of their own members, may be rewarded financially far beyond what 'objectively' seems to be their deserts, but in judging that they get more than they 'deserve' we are not necessarily committed to saying that anything should be done about it. There are two reasons for this. One is that, as we have noted, deliberate action is only one of the causal factors involved in establishing relative incomes. It is realistic to accept that *action* to bring about a distribution of income more in accordance with desert may sometimes be ill-advised, if even possible. It may sometimes be better to wait for change to happen rather than try to bring it about. There may be bad consequential effects on other groups (some of these effects unforeseen or unforeseeable) of deliberate action to bring about change. The injustice may be only temporary – a market advantage dependent on passing public taste – and an attempt to change things might not take effect until after the public taste has in any case altered.

It may be thought unfair on criteria of desert that a successful pop singer should earn more than a nurse – by the criterion of length and arduousness of training, perhaps, or that of responsibility for others. But this does not mean that we must propose special action to change this particular circumstance. The world is full of 'unfairness', and sometimes, for the considerations mentioned, we ought not to seek to do anything about it.

This leads on to the second reason why we often ought not to attempt to alter things in accordance with our convictions about desert – in particular, perhaps, why we ought not to seek to get a reduction in incomes that we may consider too high (not that this is ever a very practical thing to do). The argument we are about to note applies less sharply to cases of attempting to raise incomes that we consider undeservedly low; nevertheless, it does apply here also, for the rather obvious reason that rates of income are relative, and to raise *A*'s has the effect of depressing B's or C's or D's, and these may then in their turn come to be seen as being undeservedly low. The argument is of the 'patriotism is not enough' variety. Now, although it is neither a necessary nor a sufficient condition for a society to be just that its members should *think* that their social arrangements are broadly just, it does seem to be a necessary condition for a society to be contented — one lacking in envy, and so on — that its members should think their social arrangements broadly just. The judgement then needs to be made how justice and contentment are to be rated as against each other. I do not myself think that I should rate highly membership in a society which might seem to me as an outsider to exhibit social justice (equity, fairness) but whose members were themselves markedly discontented with their lot — if they detected many inequities that, in the absence of what I might regard as much more serious inequities, assumed *for them* large proportions. In the interests of social contentment, people sometimes ought not to be made aware of the inequities of a situation about which little can be done, or about which, because of its temporary character, little needs to be done. (This is not to deny the need for action in the case of inequities apparently more permanent or more easily changeable by government or other action.) Too much reflection on desert — which includes demerit as well as merit — can be an obstacle to a good atmosphere in any society. The argument can perhaps be made stronger. One of the elements of justice is respect for one's fellow men. The practically just man is considerate of people's feelings. He will be sensitive to the ways in which too remorseless a pursuit of some rather remote ideal of justice can damage the foundation of mutual trust and respect on which any practically just society has to rest.

We may now turn to criteria of need. Although criteria of need can for purposes of discussion be considered apart from criteria of desert, when it comes to matters of policy or of practical decision they will sometimes be inter-involved. It will be a political — and in some cases also a moral — question whether an undoubted need should be met in the absence of desert. For example, two politicians may differ over whether unemployment, which they are able to agree creates needs (for work, and more basically for the continued provision of food, clothing and shelter, or for an income to ensure their continued provision), should be met by state action of various kinds. Here the distinction between voluntary and involuntary unemployment may appear important to one of the politicians but not to the other. It may seem to one that the condition can in some cases be remedied by the actions of the unemployed themselves, or that it is good for the character or — a utilitarian argument to which we shall be returning — that a just society is one in which there is justice over all, but not one where justice is guaranteed for every individual — where, indeed, justice over all can sometimes only be achieved, it may be, by denying justice to some individuals. It is no doubt possible to say that it is men's needs and men's needs alone that should be taken into account; but in practice criteria of need are not always used on their own. One reason why this might anyway have been expected is that men's needs are various, and some are specific to certain occupations or classes of persons. A scholar or writer needs quiet, a diabetic needs insulin; or they need the income, etc. to acquire them. It is therefore often necessary to weigh needs against needs in deciding priorities between individuals. And in making such decisions it sometimes seems natural to appeal to criteria of desert. (Not always; for we may class some needs as more basic than others quite irrespective of desert.) This is not to imply that criteria of desert have some sort of logical priority over criteria of need, for we sometimes make the appeal in the opposite direction. The point is merely that we do not always operate with one of these types of criterion in isolation from the other. For example, in conditions of real scarcity it may not be possible to meet equal needs equally, and here criteria of desert might be appealed to as a way of differentiating between people. Such an appeal would of course be resisted by many; my point is that this kind of appeal would not be inappropriate, not necessarily that it could be justified in every case.

Utilitarianism and Rawlsian Liberalism

It is impossible to discuss social justice without mention of the Welfare State, and impossible to mention the Welfare State without referring to utilitarianism. It is noticeable that movements towards social justice have often been closely linked with the very philosophy whose treatment of justice has commonly been claimed by its critics to be its weakest part. (Not only its critics. Mill himself admitted that 'the only real difficulty in the utilitarian system of morals'[6] arose from its handling of justice.) The plausibility of those attacks on utilitarianism which amount to saying that it cannot account adequately for justice have certainly not prevented utilitarianism from being a powerful movement for social reform and an inspiration to greater social justice. But this is not as paradoxical as it may appear. The utilitarian view of justice sees it as chiefly distributive and as chiefly concerned with need. Liberal attacks on utilitarianism, whether in the last century (as by T. H. Green) or in the present century (as by John Rawls), essentially seek to meet these emphases with their own emphasis on basic rights and liberties.

In many passages in his book *A Theory of Justice* John Rawls develops objections to both average utilitarianism and total ('classical') utilitarianism. Some of his arguments may be read as objections, from a liberal point of view, to a theory which sees social justice as a matter of the maximisation of social and economic advantage. Rawls himself says of some of his objections to utilitarianism (those that he refers to as 'the strong arguments from liberty') that they do not hold against a mixed doctrine, that is one which combines elements of utilitarianism and liberalism.[7] Many utilitarians, from Mill onwards, have in fact held mixed doctrines.

I shall confine myself to Rawls's objections to 'classical' utilitarianism, the doctrine that society should maximise total utility. Rawls's objection to this is that it does not take individuals seriously enough. It is a long-standing objection to utilitarianism that the utilitarian would be prepared to sacrifice individuals in the interests of an increase in the *total* happiness of a society. But, although it is permissible for an individual to sacrifice advantages in some periods or departments of his life in order to get advantages in some others, it is not permissible for society as a whole to sacrifice the interests of some of its members in order to gain satisfaction for others. Utilitarianism 'does not take seriously the distinction between persons'.[8] It supposes that what would be the rational principle of choice for one person is also the rational principle of choice for a society. The utilitarian, says Rawls, mistakes impersonality for impartiality. It is right to seek impartiality, but quite wrong to suppose that this requires ignoring differences between individuals; on the contrary, it means taking individuals seriously. (On the matter of the possible sacrifice of some for the general good, consider the advocacy by some politicians of deflationary measures which it is admitted will lead to increased unemployment but which are said to be necessary for 'the country'. It may be that they *are* necessary; and such examples are clearly relevant to the assessment of this criticism of utilitarianism.)

Rawls's other main objection to classical utilitarianism is that it sacrifices right to good — that is, it sacrifices basic liberties to the achievement of satisfaction. According to Rawls, the utilitarian has no independent criterion for right: whatever gives satisfaction is right. So if by curtailing someone's liberty you could increase the total happiness it would be in order to do so. According to Rawls's own theory of justice, on the other hand, the principle of equal liberty is independent of, and prior to, the principle about maximising social and economic advantage; so you must not restrict someone's liberty in the interests of total satisfaction.

The great virtue of Rawls's own view of justice, as his criticisms of utilitarianism help to bring out, lies in the way in which he sees a just society as, at the least, one in which social and economic advantages are distributed in such a way as to benefit the worst-off, but also, and in his view more importantly, one in which 'basic liberties' are put first. It is thus a richer view of social justice than would be that of a pure classical utilitarianism. It is, however, a defect of Rawls's theory, in my opinion, that it assumes a view of human nature according to which men are fundamentally interested in their own welfare. The motivation behind men's wanting to arrange things so that the least-advantaged are as well off as possible, and so that all men's basic liberties are respected, is assumed by Rawls to be that men cannot be sure that they themselves will not turn out to be among the least-advantaged. Utilitarianism is more altruistic, more 'idealistic', than Rawls's theory. The issue comes down to whether a theory of justice ought to be constructed on principles which people, *given their moral failings*, would agree to be fair, or on principles which suppose that just men *ought* to rise above their limitations and aim at something more than a rather grudging 'fairness'. I am not saying either that utilitarian writers themselves would necessarily agree that their view is intended to present ideals rather than to be realistic, or that Rawls himself would see the contrast between his own view and utilitarianism in such terms. The point is rather that utilitarianism *can* be presented as offering a kind of 'idealistic' contrast to Rawlsian realism; and that if justice is a *moral* notion then there is point in saying that it might be expected of a theory of justice that it lay down a standard that rises above what can in practice be expected from not very altruistic human beings.

Declaring, Creating and Meeting Needs

In conclusion, a number of rather obvious points require to be made. However commonplace they may seem, they are both important enough to deserve reiteration and basic enough not to be killed by it.

On the most general level, responsibility for *declaring* the needs of men probably rests with philosophers or philosopher-surrogates. When it comes down to detail, however, empirical investigation is called for to uncover precisely what are the needs of individuals or groups. Voluntary agencies, government agencies, university and other-supported researchers carry out the more detailed task; and unless this more detailed task is done we do not know what *precisely* the needs of individuals or groups, as opposed to the needs of 'men', are. In declaring that something is either a general human need or a specific need of certain groups, the philosopher or the social researcher (or, indeed, the social worker) may be assuming a particular view about what people *ought* to have, or even, perhaps, helping to create such a view. Certainly people can come to have, or be made to have, needs they did not have before.

But it is not philosophers with their theories, or social researchers, who are apt to come first to mind when we think of the *creation* of needs. It is more likely to be the manufacturers and advertisers of unnecessary products, which people are encouraged to want to the extent that in time they become unhappy if they do not have them, so that they might have to be said eventually to need them. If our criterion is immediate human happiness, then people – other things being equal – ought to have these things. In the longer run, they might be happier if they could be got not to want them: though to achieve that would now require radical changes in our society. In this sense to assign responsibility for creating needs is probably a preliminary to condemning those who are said to be responsible (as in the case of medically induced dependence on drugs). But, of course, it is not inherent in the notion of creating needs that the creation of new needs is to be deplored. Religious or moral teaching can create in a person needs he did not have before – for example, the need to please God or to labour in the service of others – whose creation we might not in the least regret. (I should perhaps say that the relation between 'needs' and 'wants' calls for examination that cannot be given to it here.)

Whose responsibility is it to *meet* men's needs? That depends on what needs we have in mind, but take the case of the basic human need for food and clothing. There is a question whether the state can more effectively meet such a need than can private agencies, but that question does not much concern social philosophers. The question that does concern them is whether the state rather than private agencies *ought* to undertake this responsibility. To attempt to answer this would lead us back to the 'political' differences we have found presenting themselves several times already.

4 Value Choices in Social Administration

Howard Jones

There was a time when it was hoped that the application of the scientific method to social issues would produce solutions as objective and conclusive as those of the natural sciences. In spite of the operation of an 'uncertainty principle', even in physics at the sub-atomic level[1] we have become used to making predictions in physical science with a high level of certainty. To take a rudimentary example, chemists would be disconcerted, to say the least, if the burning of hydrogen in oxygen did not eventuate in the production of water. Consequently, many people confidently looked forward to the time when we should gain the kind of control over our social environment and our human problems which science has given us over our physical world.

We should have known better. Not only are the problems of social explanation infinitely more complex, but intractable human nature constantly reacts both to research itself (the famous 'Hawthorne effect'),[2] and to any conclusions reached, so as to change the nature of the problem itself. Thus the development of objective statistical tables for predicting the outcome of borstal training with delinquents[3] goaded borstal staffs into attempts to 'break the tables' by improving their performance − as well as bringing about changes in the borstal system itself.

But the finally insuperable difficulty confronting a natural-science approach is the impossibility of eliminating 'non-scientific' value elements from the social situations under investigation. Economics, of all the social sciences, made the largest claims in this connection. As

Professor Lionel Robbins put it: 'Economics is neutral as between ends. Economics cannot pronounce on the validity of ultimate judgements of value.'[4] There would seem to be some justification in such a viewpoint in that economics has an objective measuring rod for 'value in exchange', in the shape of a money price. As a result the analysis of economic problems has taken place in the past almost entirely in terms of money values, any factors such as sentiment or beliefs, not measurable in cash, being treated as a sort of friction, preventing the free operation of 'economic forces'. The plain facts are that the so-called frictions are genuine preferences, or values, of a similar kind to those to which a monetary value has been attached, but that they are not normally saleable in the market, so that their 'market value' is difficult to assess. A good example is that of the pollution of the environment. How do you set a price on our feelings about the quality of our environment? Other factors, like, for example, the wider costs of the closing of railway lines (the costs of road-building, policing, road accidents, and so on), are often not easily discerned, and, even now when their reality is acknowledged, are very difficult to calculate. There is also the fact that different evaluations may be made by different people; some may value the convenience of the motor-car as compared with the train more than others.[5]

As a result the economics of price and of the firm place all the emphasis on monetary values, and of profitability determined by such values, thus attaining a degree of objectivity, but at the expense of over-simplifying the situation — and of under-estimating the real costs of many commodities. The community, willy-nilly (and often unwittingly) is left to bear costs which (however difficult to estimate) should be borne by the producers or consumers of the commodity in question. This is more than a theoretical question, though it has important implications for theoretical economics. For this allegedly non-normative concept of wealth has been decisive in controlling many decisions made by government and private business, for example railway closures, the location of industry where sites were cheapest to buy or to operate, without enough regard for the effect on people or the environment, the use of plastic containers because they were cheap, largely ignoring the almost indestructible excrement which this leaves for the community to clear up.

Similarly, psychology or psychiatry, as ways of dealing with our personal and social ills, have a prestige at present which may appear exaggerated, when one realises how, in the quest for 'scientific rigour', they too have left out of account important subjective value judgements which exercise a powerful influence on human motivations and behaviour. Thus the central concepts of 'adaptation' and 'normality'[6] may prove to reflect merely that image of man which we in our kind of society and in our historical situation happen to find most congenial. There is no suggestion, of course, that our view of normality is thus in some way accidental or trivial; it may be deeply rooted in our kind of industrial society, furnishing it with the kinds of people who can best serve and enjoy it. But, by the same token, other kinds of culture may need other kinds of person. Our idea of normality may not be exportable. Even within our own culture, however, such monistic concepts as normality are suspect. In a pluralistic society such as ours, many different modes of adaptation are possible and would seem legitimate. For instance, some of the behaviour reported as characteristic of the lower working class in this country, and highly valued by them,[7] bears a remarkable resemblance to some forms of behaviour stigmatised by psychiatrists as 'inadequate'.[8]

Even sociology, the youngest of these disciplines, under the persuasive influence of Max Weber's ideas about a *wertfrei* social science,[9] has flirted with the same kind of scientism. Weber was at least willing to admit that one's choice of problems for study must reflect one's value system, in the sense of one's scale of priorities, even though he went on to argue that, after that first step, an entirely neutral approach was possible, and indeed essential. But it does appear that he attached too little significance to that fatal first bias. When one thus chooses a problem for study, one is also choosing a concept which reflects one's initial orientation as faithfully as does the choice of the problem itself.

A good example of this is research on crime. Why is this considered worthwhile? Presumably because crime is a social problem, a bad thing. Thus crime as a 'bad thing' is part of the concept with which one embarks on one's research, and it is to other 'bad things' that one is therefore led in looking for its causes – things like low intelligence, psychological maladjustment, broken homes, poverty. Some selection among the multitude of conceivable causes (ranging from possessing blue eyes to being born under the sign of Cancer) has to be effected, and is bound to follow the lead given by one's concept of the problem under investigation. In countering this we do not necessarily have to go as far as Durkheim[10] and argue that crime (up to a certain level) is good – one feels that Durkheim could never have had his home broken into or his daughter assaulted. Nevertheless, we might ask ourselves if crime might not sometimes be positively associated with factors which we usually see as 'good things' and not only with the bad. For instance, many researches have been carried out to explore the relationship between poverty and crime, such a relationship having usually been taken for granted. Yet our post-war record crime rates have been associated with a degree of affluence unequalled in our history. And the increase in criminality has often been greatest among the older teenagers, who have most improved their relative economic position in the years since the war. Only with the emergence of newer concepts of crime have factors of this kind begun to receive attention.

The parallel between this traditional approach to crime and the use made of the concept of normality by psychology is clear. The more recent 'labelling perspective' in sociology differs in seeing criminals as not distinct from other people in their personal make-up and social circumstances, their status as criminals having been imposed on them by a process of social selection and labelling at the hands of those with social power. Nevertheless, labelling theorists do not entirely escape the charge of reflecting a particular set of values. While they do replace the word 'crime' by the word 'deviance', deviance must always be from some set of norms — not markedly less biased a concept than that of crime. And from the initial discovery of a 'bad thing', in the form of labelling by the authorities, they often travel along a road of social criticism, a radical commitment which may be only the mirror image of the establishment commitment for which they attack conventional criminologists. More recent sympathisers with the labelling and deviance perspectives have recognised the nature of the problem, and some, particularly those with a Marxist background,[11] not only accept the inevitability of some sort of commitment, but embrace it eagerly.

Social administration draws on all these (and other) social sciences, and so is affected by all these doubts about their 'ethical neutrality'. It would be unjust and also imperceptive to see it therefore as a kind of parasite: an academic flea living solely off the substance of its sister disciplines. For unlike them it is not concerned primarily with the elaboration of a theoretical structure, but with the elucidation of a social problem. To do this it must become broader and more hospitable than social sciences are usually willing to contemplate being: willing to follow the argument wherever it leads — even into its neighbour's garden. In the course of all this inter-disciplinary activity, genuinely generic concepts and theories emerge, indigenous to social administration.

But a 'problem' focus finally gives the *coup de grâce* to any hope of eliminating subjective value elements. Social administration starts out with an explicitly critical attitude towards some social situations which it defines as a social problem. Such might be criminal behaviour, the unsatisfied needs of our more elderly fellow-citizens, or the privations inflicted on people by poverty or slum-life. Although a habitual way of thinking about these as social problems makes us take their status as such for granted, this status is not self-evidently true. They are to be seen as problems only in the light of a set of values which may not be shared by everybody.

To take a single example: most people will agree that poverty is undesirable, but the amount of relief to be afforded remains a live social and political issue. Some would be concerned about the possible demoralising effect of over-dependence on the state and the injustice and fatuity of penalising the successful and hard-working to provide such aid. As Sir Keith Joseph puts it:

> Who would train as a doctor if he thought that after all that effort plus the long and unsocial hours and the meagre initial earnings he would end up with the same earnings as a hospital orderly? Who would endure the rigours and dangers of life on an oil rig for a postman's pay? Woe betide any society where the common or official view of differentials is narrower than that held by the most talented and vigorous strata of the population.[12]

Opponents of this view are more impressed by the deprivations suffered by the poor, and would argue for more generosity. A few even, seeing poverty as essentially 'relative deprivation',[13] and thus defining inequality as a social problem in itself, would go so far as to expand the aid provided for the poor by the Welfare State as a step towards greater equality of incomes in society at large — much as we have seen, to Sir Keith Joseph's alarm. Among the latter group, Coates and Silburn[14] confront Joseph's 'market' philosophy frontally:

> The truth is that welfare and market principles are incompatible .... In the case of Britain, welfare legislation has failed to humanise the economic and social system because it has been a strategy of people who have avoided a confrontation with the market on at least two crucial issues. The first of these concerns the distribution of income. Welfare-oriented measures have never been intended to produce an initial distribution of income sensitive to individual and family need .... Then as we have already documented, the success of welfare intervention in securing a post-income redistribution through progressive taxation, subsidies and social benefits has been, at best, marginal.

If one teases out the various issues implicated in this controversy, the impossibility of settling it on a purely objective basis becomes clear. Suppose one could determine which kinds of individuals, in which circumstances, and subject to what amounts of state aid, were likely as a result to be made over-dependent or to lose their motivation to do difficult or unpleasant jobs. It would obviously be a complex equation, subject to many exceptions, though it might be conceivable with the aid of a computer-based mathematical model. Suppose social science could give us that much of a lead. It would still leave the question of whether the suffering caused in restricting aid to the poor would be justified whatever the gains to the community in terms of personal self-dependence; or, alternatively, whether the relief of suffering achieved by additional welfare expenditure justified the burden placed on the 'achievers' in our society.

And it leaves out of account the possibility that 'root and branch' socialist reform of the economic system, eliminating its market focus, might produce a quite different social ethic premissed on interdependence rather than independence, and setting in train a whole new pattern of other-centred motivations in place of the self-centred ones on which Sir Keith lays so much stress. There is even less chance of determining the actual effects of such a socialist revolution than those of welfare support in a market economy; for quite apart from similar fantastic technical difficulties, such research is faced by the fact that a revolution of this kind has not yet been implemented in any country with the cultural traditions and attitudes of Western Europe. As Coates and Silburn point out, all our welfare measures take the persistence of a market economy for granted, and are shaped accordingly. But if it were possible, we would still not solve our basic problem. Even if either a market economy, with welfare services which are restrained in the Joseph manner, or alternatively a new socialist system, proves the more productive in the material sense, it would still not answer the question of which we *ought* to prefer. To answer that question we have to decide what model of man or of society we ought to aim at – a moral question, or more modestly a question of taste. This cannot be decided solely by the practical outcomes of alternative programmes.

It is nevertheless true that moral thinkers and the man in the street alike sometimes attempt to distinguish too sharply between 'what will pay' and 'what is right'. As we shall see, in making one's moral choices, pragmatic consequences cannot be left entirely out of account; and in what follows it is suggested that there may be an even more basic connection between the two – that our moral arguments may be unconcious rationalisations for our own vested interests.

One has only to say that something is a 'moral question' in order to give it a new and grander status; all at once it becomes important. People resign their jobs, face social ostracism or even suffer martyrdom for their moral beliefs. Any attempt to cut morality down to size is bound to meet with violent opposition. However, what has just been said suggests a need for a close examination of how we come to acquire our moral beliefs, even if this does destroy a few myths; and we have then to consider carefully how we can then justify them.

If one considers the division of opinion on the social-welfare issues with which social administration is concerned, some clue can be gained as to the answer to the first of these questions. Views do seem to be divided systematically, so that the 'haves' tend to opt for the less generous, and the 'have-nots' for the more generous provision. There are of course many exceptions, such as millionaire socialists, middle-class Welfare State politicians, and working-class Tories, and their emergence calls for explanation; but, broadly speaking, the moral standpoint seems to rest on sectional interest. Thus it is the welfare-orientated Labour Party which is supported by the working class, deprived minority groups and others near the base of the social pyramid; and it is the rich and privileged, and industry and commerce, who offer their backing to the Conservative Party, with its philosophy of individualism, and the limitation of taxation and state expenditure. Thus whether mutual interdependence is seen as a personality-destroying serfdom, or as eliciting the better, more neighbourly side of human nature, may be related to which of these views leads to policies which are broadly in line with the interest of the group you belong to. Arguments about the rights and wrongs of particular policies then begin to look like an attempt to provide moral justification for a view rooted in self-interest. In the light of this, the old expediency versus morals debate referred to above takes a new form.

There is of course no suggestion that this use of moral arguments as a justification for self-centred claims is a deliberate and conscious act. People do seem to believe that the views that they are putting forward are genuine and morally justifiable — even if they have more difficulty in conceding the same integrity to their opponents. Nevertheless, if, in the terminology of R. K. Merton,[15] you take a look at 'objective social consequences' rather than subjectively experienced 'motivations', it is difficult to escape the conclusion being drawn here.

There is nothing very new about this view. Since Marx, sociologists of knowledge have related the beliefs of groups to their position in society. Thus Karl Mannheim, perhaps the most distinguished of them, speaks of a perspective derived from class position.[16] But the illumination provided by the sociology of knowledge goes far beyond this, to argue in a more general way that the prevailing belief system of a society is shaped by the relations of production in that society. Each economic system generates and inculcates in people a philosophy which justifies it. Even Max Weber tempered his support for the independent influence of ideas to the extent of recognising the fundamental and ultimately inescapable process of economic causation.[17] Not surprisingly, the dominant ideology shaped in this way turns out to be that of the ruling class, which has the greatest stake in the survival of the system. One can now begin to understand why, in a capitalist society, welfare provision has to be so formulated as not to challenge the market mechanisms which are so important for capitalism.

Although we are primarily concerned here with the effects of social forces on social values, they can have their influence on other mental products, even on natural science. Unlike social values, science does have an empirical reference, so there is a factual basis which social forces, however powerful, can hardly set aside. Nevertheless, the direction of research is strongly influenced by social demand and the ease of obtaining research funding; and there are plenty of examples of the suppression of discoveries (especially in the applied sciences) when they are seen as threatening to powerful economic or political interests. An important difference to note is that in totalitarian regimes they are suppressed by fiat, while in democracies (in conformity with their market ethos) they are either starved of social approval and finance, or bought up and suppressed.

What are the implications for social reform of what has been said above? There is a common belief that social reforms take place as a result of rational and moral progress. People understand social problems more than they did, and also come to care more about what happens to their less-fortunate fellows, and as a result reforms take place. However, if we accept that dominant social values are a byproduct of the economic conditions of the time, social reforms too must arise out of these conditions. At first sight this may appear a very conservative viewpoint, implying as it does that there will be no chance of bringing about changes which challenge the *status quo*. In such circumstances why bother to try? More must be said about this argument shortly.

This approach to social policy has not received anything like as much attention from social-administration researchers as it deserves; the evidence for the social determination of social-reform ideas is at present piecemeal, and therefore not as convincing as it might be. An exception from the kindred field of penal reform is the work of Rusche and Kirchheimer,[18] They argue that penal methods at any particular time are determined by conditions in the labour market. Punitive reactions ensue when labour is plentiful, and more constructive methods involving the productive use of convict labour when labour is harder to come by and therefore expensive. Thus the interest in prison labour from the sixteenth and the middle of the seventeenth century (represented in this country by the development of 'houses of correction') was connected with the need for labour in the booming mercantile era. The development of powered machinery in the eighteenth century meant the decline of the houses of correction; instead prisoners were transported to meet the labour needs of the colonies. As the supply of free labour in our overseas possessions became more adequate, the transportation system, in its turn, waned. But there was still a labour surplus at home, hence the solitary or 'separate' confinement of prisoners, making workshops impossible and facilitating the use of the unproductive treadmill and crank as forms of prison work. Finally came modern constructive methods of training and rehabilitation, to fit the individual for an industry which was hungry for skilled labour. This analysis corresponds closely to the historical facts, and indeed, for confirmation, trade-union and industrial opposition to prison industries in recent years has been greatest at times of unemployment and economic recession.

A number of pessimistic conclusions may seem to follow from all this. One is the 'relativist' conclusion. Value positions, it is said, being value positions, cannot be *justified* by whether their consequences are desired or not. Because of this, and because they can legitimately differ according to the social position of those who hold to them, there would appear to be no basis for choosing between them. And if all are equally valid, how do we make choices between social policies reflecting different value positions? It does look as though only scepticism about values is possible; and yet we cannot abandon the value element entirely in this way. Otherwise, decisions made on the basis of naked self-interest would go unchallenged, victory always going to those with power. Keeping the debate going at least means that action taken does have to be justified by arguments about the 'rights' and 'wrongs' of the matter. Even *rationalisations* of a moral character have their purpose, because they can be refuted, and people do in any case have to live up to them. What is being suggested here is that even if, human nature and the human situation being what they are, we never find any final answers to our moral questionings, the search for such answers may itself be worthwhile. 'To travel hopefully', says R. L. Stevenson in *El Dorado*, 'is a better thing than to arrive, and the true success is to labour.' Maybe we also are searching for a non-existent *El Dorado*, but like Stevenson's searchers we also can learn a good deal on the way.

It is also important to examine more critically the view that a moral judgement about a social policy ought not to be influenced by its consequences. Taken to its logical conclusion this would make such judgements so purely intuitive that you could not cavil about an individual's value judgements, no matter how limited his experience, or distorted his mental processes, might be. On such a basis the judgements of a young child or a deluded paranoic would have to be treated as entirely valid. Even Kant, in basing the 'categorical imperative' on what would happen if a moral decision became universally applicable as 'a general natural law', fell back ultimately on a kind of empirical justification.[19]

And of course if one were indifferent to the suffering caused or the relief afforded by this, that or the other approach to welfare, one would be displaying a cruelty, or at least a lack of compassion, which everybody nowadays, whatever his value perspectives might be, would consider morally wrong. If only one could follow this particular clue to its logical conclusion and adopt a utilitarian point of view! Many problems would be solved for us if we could, with Jeremy Bentham, adopt 'the greatest good of the greatest number' as our guide.[20]

However, quite apart from the impossibility of interpreting these words (who is to say what constitutes 'good'? Bentham's 'hedonistic calculus' leads us right back to self-interest), the rights of minorities ought not to be treated so lightly.

So neat encapsulated resolutions of our moral dilemmas are unlikely to be found. We have to live with uncertainty in this as in so many other aspects of our lives. But this does not mean that we are doomed to relativism. Even if we never find the ultimate answer, we are entitled to go on searching for it.

The other sombre possibility, as an outcome of what has been said above, is fatalism. If dominant values are merely a byproduct of the socio-economic conditions of the time, is there any point in engaging in any dialogue about them at all? *Che sará sará.* We may just as well wait for it to happen. Such fatalism would only be appropriate to those Marxists who take an extreme position on historical determinism. For those who believe that man can alter the course of his destiny by intelligent and determined action, it becomes important to 'know the enemy'. One can then plan a campaign for social reform in the full knowledge of the nature and strength of the resistance when it arises. Only if you do understand these forces can you hope to circumvent or neutralise them.

But there is another virtue in this kind of understanding, and this applies not only to social policy-makers, but also to administrators and social workers, who, on the whole, have to operate within a given context of social-welfare provision. In the 1950s and 1960s, the heyday of psychoanalytic case work, it was contended that good case workers needed to know as much about their own psychological make-up as about that of their clients. Otherwise, their own insecurities and blind spots would adversely affect their work. Thus a social worker with marital problems might find it difficult to be objective in dealing with the marital problems of others; or somebody who was personally insecure, and therefore fearful of rejection, might unwittingly try to ingratiate himself with a client when a firmer approach might be required. The clientele of social agencies are often people in miserable life situations — situations which would arouse sympathy in the minds of most people. Under the pressure of personal feelings of this kind, young and inexperienced social workers are often so anxious to comfort their clients (and relieve their own feelings in the process) that they sometimes forget, it is said, that people have to learn to solve their own problems; and that the painful experience of being anxious or guilty about their present situation may be the only powerful internal motivation impelling them to do something about it. So to relieve a client's feelings may not always be helpful to him. But once the social worker knows that this apparently compassionate behaviour is really motivated by a wish to palliate unpleasant feelings in himself, he either gives it up as self-centred and damaging to his client, or continues with it knowing that he is reacting to his own needs rather than to those of the people whose problems he is supposed to be tackling. This is the therapeutic role of 'insight' as Freudians see it operating.

But it is not only our psychological predispositions that we often fail to take into account. We often take our social beliefs for granted in the same way. A case in point is the belief that poverty is always due to laziness, incompetence or some other personal failing of the individual. This had undisputed currency throughout most of the nineteenth century. The 'less-eligibility' principles of the nineteenth century poor law were formulated as a way of coercing such unsatisfactory citizens into more effort; nor are such ideas dead, even now, in certain sections of the population. One has only to scan the research on class differences in values[21] to realise that those which the policy-makers, administrators and social workers adopt, not only as personal ideals, but as self-evidently true, may be very different from those of their mainly working-class customers. But such values also impose a limitation on the range of possibilities which one considers in the course of formulating or operating a social policy. A social worker or social-welfare administrator with a 'taken for granted' belief that people often 'deserve' the good or bad things that happen to them is going to approach people in need in a very narrow way. This kind of tunnel-vision may be even more serious in its consequences when it is manifested by a policy-maker whose decisions affect large numbers of people.

But suppose these powerful persons could be helped to see that their attitudes were open to challenge, that indeed they were largely shaped by social and economic conditions and in particular by a perspective derived from their class position. It is at least arguable that they would then be more willing to entertain alternative viewpoints than they had been before acquiring these new insights.

Social administration is a discipline orientated towards social action in the real world, towards 'doing something' about real social problems, or it is nothing. A similar reality aspect is inescapable also for its social-science kinfolk. But in being involved in a culture-laden 'real society', one takes on the coloration of one's surroundings, and becomes value-orientated too. We do not therefore become impotent; the very fact that what we do always involves a value element imposes on us an obligation to try to adopt a critical posture towards our own values. And that calls not only for an explicit recognition of the effect which they thus have on the lives of so many others, but also a determined attempt to understand their origin in our own and our society's history. For only thus can we expect to be able to take control of them.

5 Government, Data and Social Change*

Muriel Nissel

Introduction

This century has seen steadily increasing involvement by government in social policy and, since the Second World War, the emergence of the Welfare State. Expenditure of money and manpower on the social services has risen rapidly. By 1974, Social Security, Health and Personal Social Services, Education and Housing made up about half of total public expenditure in the United Kingdom. The social services, which are very labour intensive, also take up a high proportion of the country's manpower, particularly highly qualified manpower. At the time of the 1971 Census of Population they absorbed some two million people.

It is not surprising that against the background of this outpouring of resources on the social services, social statistics have proliferated. Good administration needs reliable statistics for monitoring day-to-day operations of the social services both at national and local level. Those running the system must know how resources are deployed — how staff, buildings and equipment are used and how much is spent.

* This chapter is based in part on a talk given by the author at a joint conference of the Market Research Society and the American Marketing Association at Oxford in June 1974. The author was in the Central Statistical Office until April 1976 and the chapter is reproduced with the kind permission of Her Majesty's Stationery Office.

Without this information it is not possible to run an efficient organisation.

However, superimposed on the growing pressure for better statistics for administrative purposes, there has been a further influence. There is now a much keener interest in the impact of policies, both economic and social, on the individuals they are intended to serve. No longer is it simply assumed that, providing output grows, social conditions will get better. People and governments are increasingly asking questions about the value of the benefits these policies provide: whether they are in fact doing what was intended and are improving 'the quality of life'. This involves being explicit about the aims of policies and specifying them in such ways as can be quantified. Policies, by definition, are intended to bring about a certain course of action, but before a judgement can be made about their effectiveness at least three types of information are required: first, it is necessary to know what the present situation is, second, what changes are taking place in it, and, finally, why these things are happening. Without the third, which is one of the weakest parts of our information system in the social field, there is no satisfactory means of developing explanatory or predictive models to evaluate policies or to establish priorities between them. It is here that the statistician needs the help of the social scientist in developing hypotheses which can be systematically tested.

The main part of this chapter, which in the immediately following paragraphs briefly reviews some of the major changes in society during the last generation, is concerned with statistical evidence which enables us to identify these changes. It thus deals with those two aspects of the information system which describe the present state of society and the changes taking place in it. It is only incidentally concerned with trying to explain why they are taking place. The final section takes a brief look at some of the ways government has reacted with legislative and administrative changes.

Social Change

Many of the changes which have taken place since the war have been economic, technological and organisational rather than explicitly social but they have had a profound impact on society, and no paper concerned with social changes would be complete without reference to them. In the economic field, the main influences on society have been the rising material standard of living and, more recently, stagnation, rapid inflation and unemployment. In the twenty years from 1953, before the onset of the recent depression, personal disposable income per head in the United Kingdom measured at constant prices went up by 75 per cent. Thus despite present high levels of unemployment and uncertainty over future economic prospects, the standard of living over the past generation has almost doubled. This has brought with it big changes in attitudes and expectations. Once their basic material needs have been met, people put more emphasis on better provision of services, such as education and health, and give greater attention to the satisfaction that can be derived from, for example, employment, leisure and the environment. In the technological field, one of the main impacts has been the rapid spread of communications, particularly the car, air travel and television. This has enormously enhanced awareness of how other people live and brought with it an uneasy concern about the lot of those who are materially below an acceptable standard of living. At the same time it has broadened our reference groups so that 'keeping up with the Joneses' has taken on a new and wider meaning. In the organisational field the dominant influences have been the expansion of the public sector and the growing size and concentration of authority in power groups, particularly in industry and the trade unions. At the end of the 1950s 17 per cent of all employees in industry were in private firms employing 20,000 or more workers; some ten years later this had risen to 27 per cent. Similarly, whereas at the end of the 1950s less than 70 per cent of trade-union members were in unions containing 100,000 or more members, by the 1970s this had risen to nearly 80 per cent. In the face of these massive organisations, the individual, better educated and better informed than ever before, has experienced a sense of frustration, which in its turn has forced the present generation to seek new ways of asserting the importance of the individual and of his right to privacy. It has led to questioning of authority and, amongst some, cynicism at the ineffectiveness of traditional forms of government in the face of these power groups. Sometimes the reaction has been to 'opt out' and to revolt against a too-materialistic society. Other consequences have been various forms of community action and the formation of pressure groups representing the consumer and particular sectional interests. At the parliamentary level, Scottish and Welsh Nationalists vie with the main political parties for representation in the House of Commons, and the government has put forward proposals for devolving certain powers to Scottish and Welsh Assemblies.

In many ways, though it is a more tolerant age, it is in other respects more violent than anything we have known this century. It is also a time when society is changing rapidly. Because we move around more, we spend less time in one town getting to know people and places; our friends and acquaintances are more widely scattered and our relations with them perhaps more superficial. We change jobs and even occupations more frequently, and technology makes our skills more quickly out of date. The family, though perhaps more home-centred, is less tightly knit and has less day-to-day contact with its kin. Children mature younger and are more independent and mothers more frequently work outside the home. One of the most profound changes in the present century has been the changing status of women. Nowhere has this been more evident than in the employment field, where women, though still disadvantaged, are now more accepted than at any time in our history.

People's spending habits have changed. They eat more 'convenience foods', and foreign travel and the presence of many different cultural groups within the country have made them more adventurous in the types of foods they choose. Affluence has increased spending on goods for the home and for leisure activities. More leisure time in total is spent using – or justifying expenditure on – these goods and, with costs of servicing rising relatively more than prices in general, in repairing and looking after them. Not only have the rising relative costs of services led to a boom in 'do-it-yourself' activities but, because it is often cheaper to buy new goods than repair old ones, it has changed attitudes and fostered what has become pejoratively known as the 'chuck-away' society. With increased prosperity time has become more precious. It is moreover debatable whether the much talked of increase in leisure time has in fact happened, at least in terms of the life span up to age 65. Many more women take up paid work, and children and young people are subject to greater educational pressures. However, growing prosperity has altered the form which leisure activities take. In particular, over 50 per cent of households in the United Kingdom now have use of a car, so bringing the countryside and other recreational facilities more easily within the reach of many more people. Cars – and lorries – in their turn have given rise to congestion in our cities and to noise and air pollution. This has caused growing concern to a society, which, as it becomes more affluent, is increasingly sensitive to environmental problems.

Data

What evidence is there to substantiate these statements? How far do statistics, such as those published, for example, in the Central Statistical Office's *Social Trends*, help to measure these changes? The answer is inconclusive. Though statistics may help in the process, many of the statements about social change in the foregoing paragraphs are the result of a process of knitting together an assortment of varied threads of information. In this piecemeal manner opinions are formed and judgements made. The middle section of this chapter examines some of the more detailed statistical evidence available for identifying social change. Before doing this, however, it outlines in the next few paragraphs some of the demographic changes which set the background to our society.

Demographic changes

The population of the United Kingdom has increased from 38 million at the turn of the century to 56 million today (1976) and is currently projected to rise to nearly 60 million by the beginning of the twenty-first century. Its age structure has changed substantially. In 1900 a quarter were under the age of 11 and a quarter over 40; today a quarter are under 16 and nearly a quarter over 55. Thus there are now relatively fewer children and many more old people, particularly women.

The sex balance has also changed; in the age group 16–45, when most people marry, there were, in 1901, 108 women to every 100 men, whereas today there are 103 men to every 100 women. More people marry and they marry younger. Whereas in the early 1900s only 17 per cent of men and 27 per cent of women in the 20–4 age group were married, today the figures are 36 per cent and 59 per cent. Families are smaller and they are completed within a shorter time span. This, together with longer life expectancy, has led to a noticeable lengthening of both the last stage of marriage, when the couple are alone, and also the stage when one is widowed. More couples now divorce; figures for England and Wales show that only 1 per cent of those marrying in 1921 had divorced fifteen years later compared with 7 per cent of those marrying in 1956. Although more families tend to lose a parent through divorce, lower mortality rates mean that fewer now suffer the premature death of a parent.

These demographic changes, which result from multiple social and economic causes, in turn have a profound impact on other social trends. A few examples illustrate the point. The changing age structure of the population has a direct effect on the size of the labour force and hence on economic growth. Earlier marriage and increased longevity, combined with economic prosperity, have all contributed to a rise in the number of small households, and this in turn has put pressure on the housing market. Thus, whereas in the twenty years from 1951 to 1971 the number of households in Britain increased by nearly 26 per cent, the number of people in private households went up by only about 13 per cent. Because families are smaller, and child-bearing is concentrated into a shorter time span, women spend less of their time rearing children, and this, together with a variety of other factors such as better education and better equipped houses, has led many more of them to take up full- or part-time employment. These changes, in their turn, have their own impact on fertility patterns.

This interrelationship between demographic, social, economic and technological change is complex, and, because we know so little about its workings, it would seem that governments intervene at their peril. However, having sounded the warning, and before going on to consider some of the ways government has tried to intervene, let us look in rather more detail at some of the facts about social trends in particular fields.

Employment

First, let us consider the employment field. The principal factors, apart from demographic ones, affecting the size of the labour force in recent years have been, on the one hand, increases in the proportion remaining in full-time education beyond the minimum school-leaving age (which was raised to 16 in the educational year 1972—3) and of those retiring on pension and, on the other hand, the growing number and proportion of married women in employment, often on a part-time basis.

These changes can be illustrated by what are described as 'activity rates', showing, for any particular group of the population, the proportion in the working population. The first two factors, more education and earlier retirement, are reflected in the declining rates for men and unmarried women. For married women, on the other hand, increasing participation in the labour force has more than outweighed other factors working in the opposite direction. Looked at over a longer period and particularly over different generations, some of these changes have been very striking. Thus whereas only one-quarter of the 50—54-year-old married women born at the turn of the century were working in 1951, twenty years later in 1971 over half the married women of that age group were working. (On this see Table 5.1.)

A second significant change in employment, which has had important social repercussions, has been the structural decline in the primary industries, agriculture and mining, and the growth in the service industries, which now account for over half of all employees in employment. Half the employees in the service industries are women, many of them part time, and the shift has thus gone hand in hand with the growing participation of women in the labour force.

Another important change in the employment field has been the improvement in working conditions. In particular there has been, in the last few years, a rapid growth in paid holidays. By 1974, 98 per cent of full-time male manual workers in the United Kingdom covered by

TABLE 5.1   *Working population (Britain)*

	Census	
Working population (millions)	*1961*	*1971*
Males	16·2	15·9
Females	7·8	9·1
of whom married	3·9	5·8
others	3·9	3·4
Total	24·0	25·0
Activity rates (percentages of total population aged 15 and over)		
Males	86	81
Females	37	43
of whom married	30	42
others	52	44

National Agreements and Statutory Wages Orders had minimum entitlement to paid holidays of three weeks or more; in 1966 the figure was only 4 per cent. Employers have also been increasingly concerned with covering their employees for sickness absence and for occupational pensions; at the time the last Survey of Occupational Pensions was conducted by the Government Actuary in 1971, about half of all full-time employees in the United Kingdom were covered by occupational pension and sick-pay schemes. More recently – under the 1975 *Employment Protection Act* – employees' rights against unfair dismissal have been greatly extended and they have been granted guaranteed payments during short-time working.

Though a number of surveys, such as the *General Household Survey* and the special surveys on subjective indicators carried out by the Social Science Research Council Survey Unit, now seek to quantify job satisfaction and attitudes towards specific aspects of working life, this work is still in its developmental stage and it is as yet too early to quote statistics to demonstrate these changing trends and values. It would none the less be fair to conclude that there has been increasing concern with job satisfaction and human relations generally and with the particular need to break down class attitudes within the work place.

The changing attitude to job satisfaction and working conditions has been developing at a time when labour relations, as evidenced by strikes, have been deteriorating. Stoppages at work resulting from industrial disputes, mostly about wage claims, led to an average annual loss of over 12½ million working days in the United Kingdom from 1970 to 1975 compared with an average 3½ million during the 1960s;

much of this increase was due to a few major stoppages and the disruption which they caused, such as the three-day week at the beginning of 1974.

Income and expenditure

In recent years, particularly since about 1970, there has been a number of significant changes in relative earnings. During the 1960s, the average earnings of manual workers and of non-manual workers, both men and women, doubled, but the relationship between them did not alter very much nor was there much change in the shape of the distributions around the averages. More recently, however, the position of the lower paid has tended to improve; earnings of manual workers have increased faster than those of non-manual workers; women's earnings — partly in anticipation of the full implementation of the *Equal Pay Act* at the end of 1975 — have risen faster than men's and younger people's earnings faster than older people's.

For those who depend on social-security benefits the various flat-rate benefits more or less kept pace with average earnings during the 1960s, and since the end of 1971 there has been built into national insurance retirement pensions an automatic annual review to protect their purchasing position. Moreover, many retirement pensioners now receive graduated pensions and many workers are entitled to earnings-related supplements when off sick or unemployed. Policies to help the lower paid have also been reflected in the Family Income Supplement, whereby the income of the head of the family in full-time employment is supplemented when it is below a certain prescribed amount.

Within the rising trend of incomes generally, certain shifts in distribution have been taking place. The share of income taken by the top 10 per cent of tax units (either individuals or married couples) decreased over the period 1949 to 1972–3 from one-third to about a quarter: after tax it shrank from 27 per cent to 23½ per cent. Most of the change was concentrated in the top 1 per cent of incomes. The share of the bottom half of the distribution remained unchanged at about a quarter of total incomes both before and after tax. The groups immediately below the top 10 per cent slightly increased their share of total incomes, one of the factors probably being the increasing number of tax units with both husband and wife earning. (On this see Table 5.2.)

Little of the extra income of the past decade has been spent on food; although consumption of food has risen in real terms it now accounts for a much smaller share of total consumers' expenditure than it did ten years ago. There have also been relative falls in expenditure

TABLE 5.2

*Percentage increase in average gross weekly earnings of full-time employees, Britain (April 1970–April 1975)**

Men (21 and over)	
Manual	108
Non-manual	91
Women (18 and over)	
Manual	140
Non-manual	122
Youths and boys (under 21)	136
Girls (under 18)	296

* Excluding those whose pay was affected by absence.

on tobacco and clothing and footwear. The big increases have been on motor vehicles, alcoholic drink, entertainment and recreation, and housing. Expenditure on motor vehicles reflects in particular the increase in the last decade in the proportion of households with cars. Although the relative rise in expenditure on housing reflects a higher level of real consumption, it has also been substantially affected by the sharp increase in costs. (On this see Table 5.3.)

The previous paragraphs have been principally concerned with the economic well-being of individuals and households. The sections which follow look more closely at those aspects of social concern, such as health, education, housing and the physical environment, justice and law, etc. which might be said to enhance the quality of life.

Health

The physical health of the nation has traditionally been measured by mortality rates. In 1973 expectation of life at birth was 69 years for men and 75 years for women. This was some twenty-one and twenty-three years, respectively, greater than at the beginning of the century but, since it has been mainly due to lower mortality at infancy and in early childhood, by the age of 5 life expectancy had improved by only ten and thirteen years respectively. In recent years the decline in mortality rates has slowed (for middle-aged men life expectancy has even tended to fall slightly) and the figures have become less sensitive as health indicators. Moreover, they tell us little about the quality of life during the life span; for this we need statistics which measure and weigh the varying degrees of intensity and duration of illness, including mental illness. At present there is very little statistical material which

TABLE 5.3
Consumers' expenditure: shares of total (United Kingdom)

Consumers' expenditure at current prices	1965 (per cent)	1975* (per cent)
Food	22·1	19·4
Alcoholic drink	6·6	7·8
Tobacco	6·2	4·4
Housing	11·4	13·8
Fuel and light	4·8	4·6
Clothing and footwear	9·2	8·3
Household goods	7·8	7·3
Entertainment and recreational goods and services	3·8	4·1
Motor vehicles	7·2	9·6
Other expenditure	20·9	20·7
TOTAL — percentage	100·0	100·0
TOTAL — £ million	22,864	62,695
Consumers' expenditure at 1970 prices		
TOTAL — £ million	28,760	35,434

* Provisional.

can be directly used for this purpose but data from a variety of sources can be pieced together to give some kind of morbidity picture.

One of the more dramatic trends in recent years has been the fall in the incidence of infectious diseases such as tuberculosis, diphtheria, poliomyelitis, scarlet fever, measles and whooping cough. However, influenza and bronchitis remain serious, and between them (but excluding acute bronchitis) they accounted for 35 million working days of certified sickness incapacity amongst men in Great Britain in the year mid-1973 to mid-1974.

Amongst men aged 45–54 there has been a heavy and increasing incidence of heart disease, and cancer also still takes a severe toll. The incidence of cancer, particularly lung cancer, amongst women in this age group continues to increase.

When we come to consider trends in mental health, current statistics help very little because they record only the use of particular services, such as hospitals, rather than the incidence of mental illness. Various research studies have tried to establish prevalence rates but they run up against severe definitional problems. One substantial survey conducted in 1966 could do no more than conclude that 'the evidence points to the prevalence in all communities surveyed of a large sub-group of emotionally sick, or emotionally disturbed, patients amounting to between one fifth and one tenth of the total population'.[1]

Education

Education is also both difficult to define and, once defined, difficult to measure. We do know, however, that people are both exposed to the educational process for a longer part of their lives and that they obtain more formal qualifications than they used to. Whereas 90 per cent of children born in 1922 had left school by the time they were 16, thirty years later — before the raising of the school leaving age — only 50 per cent had done so. Over half of all males in Great Britain aged 25—34 in 1971, that is those born between 1937 and 1946, have some formal qualification compared with only one-third of those born between 1917 and 1926. One in ten of men aged 25—34 in 1966 were 'highly qualified' (that is with qualifications above G.C.E. 'A' level or its equivalent) compared with one in fifteen of those aged 45—54.

The type of institution in which children and young people receive their education has changed. Many more are now in comprehensive schools, many more in large schools, fewer in large classes and fewer in single-sex schools. In 1975 about 70 per cent of all pupils in secondary schools in England and Wales were in comprehensive schools; maintained secondary schools of 600 pupils or over doubled in number between 1964 and 1974 and by 1974 over three-quarters of secondary-school pupils were in schools of this size. Although universities in Britain in 1973—4 had nearly twice the number of students they had ten years earlier, most of those going on to some form of higher education have gone predominantly to further-education institutions other than universities.

Housing and the environment

Against what kind of environmental background have these health and education changes taken place? Housing conditions are on the average markedly better than they were a generation, or even a decade, ago. Many more people, particularly the younger generation, own their own homes. The number of households and dwellings has increased proportionately much more than the population, a particular feature being the growth in one- or two-person households. Although this has been partly due to demographic changes, such as earlier marriage and the much greater number of old people in the population, much of it is a reflection of greater economic prosperity, which has enabled young people to move out of the family at an earlier age and old people to maintain an independent existence for a longer time. The 1971 Census revealed that in Great Britain only 2½ per cent of households of two or more persons were sharing dwellings compared with 4½ per cent in 1961 and that 2 per cent of households were living at a density of over 1½ persons per room compared with 4 per cent in 1961. Not only has the degree of overcrowding lessened but the quality of the housing stock has improved. For example, in 1971, 88 per cent of all dwellings had sole use of a bath compared with 73 per cent in 1961; moreover, in 1974, 41 per cent had some form of central heating as against 7 per cent in 1964.

Why then do we hear so much about housing problems? The reason of course is that averages may conceal more than they reveal. There are wide variations between different parts of the country, and even in regions where needs appear to be adequately met there may be local shortages. In London there is a general shortage of housing and a serious shortage in particular areas. Moreover, particular types of housing do not necessarily best meet the needs of their occupants. Evidence from the *Census of Population*, from housing surveys and from the *General Household Survey* shows that households with children tend to be overcrowded but, as they also tend to live in newer houses, the quality of their accommodation is, on balance, above average. It is mainly the old, particularly those 70 and over, who lack central heating, have no bath or are without a W.C. inside the house. Not only are old people who own their own houses more likely to live in older property but the many who rely heavily on privately rented unfurnished accommodation are also often in dwellings of poor quality.

The growth in housing and urbanisation in post-war years has gone hand in hand with much greater use of the private car and much less reliance on public transport. During the decade from 1964 to 1974 the number of private cars and vans in Britain went up by about two-thirds from 8¼ million to over 13½ million. During the same period the number of railway passenger stations in Britain decreased from 3800 to less than 2700 and the number of bus passenger-miles fell from 40,000 million to 34,000 million.

Although part of the price of increased road and air traffic has been air and noise pollution, the disappearance of the steam-engine from the railways as well as smoke-control legislation have brought about a marked diminution in the general level of smoke emission. This is particularly noticeable in the absence of fog and the increased sunshine which now benefits places like Sheffield and London. In the winter months, the average hours of sunshine recorded at the London Weather

Centre have nearly doubled from an average of about one hour per day in 1949 to about 1¾ hours in 1975. As a result of legislation preventing water pollution, rivers are cleaner, and fish now pass through the Pool of London, whereas a few years ago they did not.

To those households in Britain who have regular use of it, the car, with all its disadvantages of congestion and pollution, has brought freedom and independence. The countryside in particular has become accessible not only for leisure activities but also as a place to live in. Many more people have their homes there and travel long distances to work. Over the period 1921–66 the economically active population in rural districts of England went up by nearly 50 per cent to 4 million and the percentage travelling into urban areas rose from 14 to 37 per cent.

The car, together with rising incomes and more paid annual holidays for those in employment, has also changed leisure and holiday patterns. Many more people can now afford to journey to places where they can ride, sail or fish. In 1975 holidays of four or more nights spent away from home by residents of Britain totalled over 48 million compared with 35 million ten years earlier; 40 million were within Britain and 8 million abroad. The car has also led to different types of holidays with relatively more caravanning and camping (25 per cent of all main holidays in Britain in 1975 compared with 17 per cent in 1965).

In the field of communications more generally, the telephone and television have had a profound impact on the social environment, particularly on leisure patterns. In 1974 50 per cent of all households in the United Kingdom had a telephone (compared with 22 per cent in 1964) and as many as 94 per cent had television sets (compared with 80 per cent in 1964 and roughly 25 per cent in 1954). In 1975 people over the age of 5 spent, on average, twenty hours per week in the winter (February) and 14 hours per week in the summer (August) watching television.

Safety

It is not possible from available statistics to evaluate the extent to which the physical environment has become more or less congenial. Although much attention is now being given to 'subjective' indicators derived from attitude surveys, it is conceptually difficult to determine what type of series would produce valid results, particularly for studying trends, and the work is still in its experimental stages.

Statistics, however, can give some, though inadequate, guidance on whether the environment is safer or more dangerous to live in. Despite the increased number of motor vehicles, the number of persons killed and seriously injured in Britain has declined in the last decade; some

6900 people were killed in 1974 and 82,000 seriously injured compared with 7800 and 95,500 in 1964. The work place has tended to become safer. Whereas in the early 1970s (1970 to 1974), industrial accidents killed an average of just over 800 people a year in the United Kingdom, in the 1950s the toll was 1500 and at the beginning of the century it was over 4000.

Crime, on the other hand, as reflected in the number of crimes and indictable offences in England and Wales recorded as being known to the police, has been increasing. The number recorded almost doubled to nearly 2 million in the ten years leading up to 1974 and, although differences in recording practices make comparisons between individual years difficult, the general upward trend is clear. Although 95 per cent of these crimes are offences against property, those which might be considered as violent crimes against the person, excluding sexual offences, rose at an even faster rate from 23,500 in 1964 to nearly 64,000 in 1974. This is symptomatic of an increasing tendency to use violence and other illegal means as an instrument of protest, particularly in pursuit of the politics of a community or minority interest.

Drugs

During the post-war period, drug dependence in the form of tobacco smoking and alcoholism has remained a serious problem. The proportion of smokers in the population in the early 1970s was not very much less than in the 1950s: about two-thirds of males aged 16 and over were smokers in 1972 and of those about half smoked twenty or more cigarettes a day. The proportion of females smoking has remained about 40 per cent. These high rates have been maintained despite the known association of smoking with lung cancer, which caused 33,000 deaths in the United Kingdom in 1974. The number of hospital admissions each year for alcoholism has shown a steady increase, almost doubling in the period from the early 1960s to the early 1970s. Deaths from diseases associated with heavy drinking have also increased. For example, the number of deaths in the United Kingdom from cirrhosis of the liver went up by about 50 per cent in the twenty years from 1954 to 1974. The post-war period has also seen the rise in drug-taking in other forms and this has been particularly marked since the end of the 1950s. It is difficult to produce hard facts to measure the phenomenon but the number of narcotic addicts in the United Kingdom known to the Home Office rose from 454 in 1959 to 753 in 1964 and, between 1969 and 1974, after notification of addicts of dangerous drugs to the Home Office had become compulsory, the numbers registered rose by about a third to nearly 2000. There has, however, been a decline in addiction to dangerous drugs amongst those under 20; the number of addicts of this age registered in 1974 was sixty-four compared with 224 in 1969.

Government Reaction

In the face of those trends, how have governments reacted? And to what extent has government itself perhaps been in some degree responsible for the trends? What have been the main legislative and administrative changes over the past decade?

In general, it might fairly be said that governments in this country do not react directly to changing values and social trends. They only react if some group which they wish to protect appears to be threatened. If hem lines go up and hair lengths come down, if people drink more coffee and less tea, watch television rather than go to the cinema, buy more cars, have more holidays abroad, marry earlier and divorce more often, the government of the day is not interested unless the repercussions are such as to have a substantial effect on those with whom it is politically concerned. Change creates tension; even if on balance its results are thought to be good, it nearly always harms somebody, and it is the degree of harm which determines whether there should be intervention to mitigate its impact. Thus if changing fashions lead to unemployment in the clothing or hairdressing industries, if changing eating habits and more holidays abroad have an adverse impact on our balance of payments or on that of a particular country with whom we have trade agreements, if more cars destroy the environment, if people have more children and this puts pressure on limited housing and education resources and if higher divorce rates lead to more single-parent families living in poverty, then governments may be moved to intervene.

Different governments of course react differently depending on the particular political party in power. After the Conservative defeat in 1964 a Labour Government was in power up to June 1970, followed by a Conservative Government up to February 1974 and thereafter a Labour Government once again. Running through much of the legislation, however, there has been a common thread, though the emphasis has been different. Moreover, it is interesting and significant that the active back-bencher in both parties has often taken the lead in instigating social reforms, the Abortion Law reforms being an outstanding example. Another trend blurring the edges of national party policies in the social field has been the greater power of local authorities and the growing pressuré for constitutional reform leading to further devolution of power from Westminister.

In the social field the changes can be grouped around three main concerns: the first is a keener awareness of the rights of the individual; the second, closely connected with the first, an attempt to mitigate the impact of inequality on the less fortunate members of society; and the third a growing concern with the physical environment.

The individual

The most important piece of legislation in recent years affecting the rights of the individual has been the *Equal Pay Act* of 1970, which contained measures to make sex discrimination illegal by the end of 1975 in the terms and conditions of employment. This was followed, in December 1975, by the setting up of the Equal Opportunities Commission designed to enforce the *Sex Discrimination Act* and to promote equal opportunities between the sexes. Other important legislation directly affecting women has been the *Abortion Act* of 1967 and the *Guardianship Act* of 1973, providing equal rights for both parents for guardianship of children. The *Divorce Reform Act* of 1969 recognised irretrievable breakdown of marriages as grounds for divorce in England and Wales. It applied to men and women equally, and was thus a significant piece of legislation reflecting recognition that women were no longer subordinate partners in a marriage. Attitudes towards the role of women in society are changing rapidly and there is a keen awareness of the extent to which women have been treated as second-class citizens. There is, however, uncertainty about how this can best be remedied and, consequently, a confused and fumbling approach to social-security and tax legislation and legislation on other issues which deeply affect the economic position and respective roles of men and women. For the married woman in particular, social-security and tax policy and some aspects of the law generally still reflect traditional attitudes regarding her as a dependent of her husband and an intruder into a man's world.

There has been a whole range of legislation affecting children and young persons. In particular, in 1969 the age of majority and of the right to vote was lowered to 18, thus reflecting a variety of factors, such as the lower age of maturity, the higher level of education and the greater economic independence of young people which have led to their earlier acceptance as adults. In September 1972 the statutory minimum school-leaving age was raised to 16. Another group of Acts and administrative changes has reflected a more humane attitude towards children. Thus the *Children and Young Persons Act* in 1969 abolished the prosecution of children under 14 and redefined the role of the juvenile courts. Other Acts have made provision for educating mentally handicapped children in normal schools and transferred responsibility for child services in England and Wales, including the treatment of young offenders, from the Home Office to the Department of Health and Social Security. Indeed the very setting up of both the D.H.S.S. at the end of 1968, which brought together at national level the administration of many of the social services, and the requirement put upon local authorities in Scotland in 1968 and in England and Wales in 1970 to integrate their social services, was a big administrative step towards treating the people who use these services more as individuals rather than as units in separate institutional frameworks.

Legislation affecting handicapped people has similarly reflected the change towards more humane and individual treatment. It has ranged from placing a duty on local authorities to find out how many chronically sick and disabled persons live in their areas, and to make provision for them (the *Chronically Sick and Disabled Persons Act* of 1970), to the provision in December 1971 of 'attendance allowances' for severely handicapped persons needing constant attention. Plans published at the end of 1971 outlined a long-term programme for replacing the many old-style large mental hospitals with new psychiatric units in general hospitals as well as extending out-patient treatment.

Though the various Acts restricting the free entry of Commonwealth immigrants might seem to run counter to this trend of greater attention to the individual, the *Race Relations Act* of 1968, which set up the Community Relations Commission and strengthened the Race Relations Board, sought to guarantee that those who come into the country are not discriminated against in work or in the provision of goods and services. These two organisations are being replaced by the Race Relations Commission, which will be able to undertake investigations into alleged discrimination.

In the employment field, in addition to these special Acts concerned with race discrimination and the *Equal Pay Act* relating to women, the *Redundancy Payments Act* of 1965 gave the employee some compensation for loss of job through no fault of his own and the *Employment Protection Act* of 1975 has extended the employee's rights against unfair dismissal.

In the field of law, a better-educated and more articulate population has become more vocal about its rights and more critical of a legal system which seems to cater for the needs of firms and organisations and of the wealthy rather than the individual of modest means. The *Legal Advice and Assistance Act* of 1972 has gone some way to extend legal aid by making wider provision of legal services and, in October 1973, provision was made for dealing with small claims in a less formal manner within the county court system. Local authorities now have discretionary authority to set up or provide financial assistance to citizens' advice bureaux, one of their many functions being to offer limited legal advice.

Incidents, such as the thalidomide tragedy, have called into question many assumptions about the rights of individuals, and whether the complex laws which have grown up and led to differing rates of compensation for different individuals in different circumstances can be justified in present-day society. These changing attitudes to compensation led in 1972 to the appointment of a Royal Commission under Lord Pearson to look into the whole question of civil liability and compensation for personal injury.

A significant new institution for protecting the individual against administrative injustice has been the appointment of the Parliamentary Commissioner for Administration (the 'Ombudsman') in 1967, the appointment of a similar commissioner for the health services in 1973 and of two Commissions for Local Administration – one for England and one for Wales – in 1974. In the field of consumer protection the government has also begun to react, not only with legislation such as the *Trade Description Act* in 1968 prohibiting false or misleading indication relating to the sale of goods, but more recently with the appointment by the Labour Government in 1974 of a Cabinet Minister heading a government department specifically responsible for prices and consumer protection.

Equality

Government reaction to changing attitudes about inequality is coloured by the political complexion of the government of the day. However, running through Conservative and Labour policy, there has been concern to reduce inequality, at least at the bottom end of the scale; the extent of intervention has been more a question of degree than approach and the policies have been carried out with varying degrees of success. Tax policy and public expenditure on benefits in cash and kind are the chief means of redistributing income and, although demographic changes have affected the income distribution, so making it difficult to assess the effect of other factors, the net effect of taxes and benefits in recent years has probably become rather more progressive. There has grown up a network of means-tested benefits designed to help the under privileged, such as Supplementary Benefit, Family Income Supplement, rent and rate rebates and free school meals. The various *Housing and Rent Acts* and the operation of the rent tribunals for furnished lettings and rent registration for unfurnished accommodation have sought to prevent exploitation and harassment of tenants by controlling rent increases and giving security of tenure. The government has also given selective help to deprived groups by means of funds disbursed to Educational Priority Areas and to particular projects in areas of special social need through the Urban Programme. In a more general way the comprehensive-schools policy, associated with the Labour Government, the raising of the school-leaving age, and the provision of more nursery schools, have all been attempts to attack the problem of inequality either at its early stages in the life cycle or, for example, through the Open University, by giving a second chance to the educationally under-privileged at a later stage.

The environment

A more affluent society generally has become more sensitive to its physical environment, resulting in 1969 in the setting up of a Royal Commission on Environmental Pollution. A number of Acts in recent years have been concerned with pollution, the most significant perhaps being the *Clean Air Act* of 1968, which, by means of smoke-control orders, has markedly reduced smoke pollution of the air. Control of noise is more difficult but in 1968 limits for vehicle-noise levels were laid down. Measures to conserve, and prevent pollution of, water were features of the 1973 *Water Act*. Other Acts have dealt with derelict land, general improvement of blighted residential areas, disposal of poisonous waste and use of insecticides. At a more positive level the Countryside Commission was set up in 1968, and other legislation, such as that providing for countryside parks, picnic sites and caravan sites, are pointers towards the type of legislation which government has been prompted to carry out by the growing demand for more planned use of the environment for leisure and recreational activities.

The statistician

This very selective review of recent legislative and administrative changes shows some of the ways government has reacted to changing trends and social values. How far, however, can it be said that statistics, such as those quoted in the earlier part of the paper, have been useful to government in helping it to identify and act upon these changes? To a statistician the answer is perhaps disappointingly negative. For the most part one is tempted to say that broad decisions about policies are based neither on statistics nor perhaps on any systematic information but more on the subjective hunches of politicians who have for their antennae the Press, television and radio, pressure groups, constituency parties, and so on. What statisticians can do is to isolate some of the main factors which lead to social change, to project and to forecast, and thus warn that certain things may happen. Moreover, once a problem has been identified and defined they can help to quantify it and to set it in its perspective so that priorities can be assessed. When policies are being formulated statisticians can endeavour to estimate the numbers and types of people who will be affected and, where expenditure is involved, what resources will be required. A government can then begin to assess both what the cost of its policies is likely to be and to put a value on the benefits which particular groups of people may receive. This is the basis for building an information system for setting priorities on a systematic and explicit basis so that government can, it is hoped, react to changing trends and social values in a more rational way.

6 Inequality

Peter Kaim-Caudle

Introduction

This chapter is concerned with differences in economic welfare and not, except incidentally, with the related but distinct issues of differences in power, status and security; nor is it concerned with inequality of opportunity. Such inequality is one of the causes of differences in economic welfare and its reduction may be a desirable policy objective but it is erroneous to consider such a reduction as either a first step towards, or as an alternative to, a diminution of economic differences — equality of opportunity is no more and no less than a situation in which everybody has an equal chance of attaining or suffering states of economic welfare which may differ widely.

The desire 'to have one's cake and eat it' is one of the most common human traits. Ambivalence about inequality is almost as common. Most people desire to be equal to others in the sense of not being 'the odd man out' and simultaneously desire to be unequal to others in the sense of being superior in strength, industry, looks, intelligence or a host of other characteristics.

It is also widely but mistakenly thought that equality is synonymous with equity but few will dispute that it may be as unfair to treat people alike (equally) who are different as it is to treat people differently who are alike. Judgement about fairness in any particular situation has to depend on an assessment of the relevant likenesses and differences that ought to be taken into consideration.

Another popular view is that social justice has three facets: equality before the law; political equality; and economic equality. This attitude takes no cognisance of the fact that the state of legal and political equality in one country does not directly affect the level of social justice prevailing in other countries. The position as regards economic equality is quite different. A redistribution of income between households within a developed country aimed at reducing inequality may appear to the people of underdeveloped (poor) countries as beneficial and relevant as a redistribution of income between the whites in South Africa would appear to the blacks; or as a redistribution of income between middle-class professional families in Britain would appear to agricultural workers.

There are strong ethical arguments for a reduction in economic inequality and a consequent need for redistribution of income, but it is difficult to deny that the arguments for redistribution are as valid when applied to the people of the world as they are to the people of one country. Some income redistribution within a country, not necessarily motivated by ethical arguments, may however be more feasible and practical than any redistribution on a global scale.

The case for a reduction of economic inequality has also been advocated on other than ethical grounds. R. H. Tawney, at the end of the 1930s, considered it as a condition for the survival of political democracy:

That democracy and extreme economic inequality form, when combined, an unstable compound, is no novel doctrine. It was a commonplace of political science four centuries before our era. Nevertheless, though a venerable truism, it remains an important one, which is periodically forgotten, and periodically, therefore, requires to be rediscovered.[1]

R. M. Titmuss suggested that a reduction of economic inequality might be a precondition of economic growth.[2] Looking back to the early 1950s he wrote in 1964: 'the more privileged . . . had hardly begun to see that more equality in income and wealth, education, and the enjoyment of the decencies of social living might conceivably be a democratic precondition of faster economic growth'.

Economic equality is more complex than other types of equality and is in its nature multi-dimensional. It certainly cannot be brought about by a Magna Charta, a Bill of Rights or a number of Reform Acts.

In that score of countries which are most developed and which are governed by parliamentary institutions, equality before the law and equality of entitlement to participate in the political process are considered basic to a democratic way of life. While in reality these characteristics prevail only partially, their desirability is fairly undisputed. The position as regards economic equality is quite different.

Only very few people favour absolute economic equality. The ideological dispute is about the extent, if any, to which gross economic inequalities should be modified.

Inequalities of Income and Wealth

Inequalities in the distribution of income and wealth have always been, and still are, ubiquitous, but tolerance of varying degrees of inequality has differed, and continues to differ, between places and over time. These two inequalities are of particular social importance because they result in a variety of economic inequalities as well as some non-economic ones, status for example.

The endeavour to measure the distribution of income and wealth is beset by innumerable conceptual and statistical problems. These are accentuated by lack of data and reasonable doubts about the accuracy of the data. Both income and wealth are ambiguous terms. Income is traditionally defined as deriving from three sources: earned income from employment and self-employment; investment income from the ownership of assets; and transfer incomes from public bodies. It thus excludes capital transfers and realised and unrealised capital gains as sources of income. An alternative definition of income is the aggregate of personal consumption and net capital accumulation, that is the expenditure which could be incurred without increasing or diminishing the value of assets owned. This definition includes capital transfers as well as realised and unrealised capital gains. An income computation on this basis requires an annual valuation of all personal capital assets.

The traditional definition of wealth is the ownership of assets which can be sold. However, some rights like those to state pensions or to free health care are valuable assets but cannot be sold. One of the major issues in measuring the distribution of wealth is to determine which, if any, non-marketable assets should be included.

The whole process of measuring the distribution of income has been aptly described as 'a term of art – the sharing of arbitrarily defined "income" among arbitrarily defined "income units" over an arbitrarily defined "income period".'[3] The process of measuring the distribution of wealth has very similar characteristics. The whole subject has been fully discussed in the Report No. 1 of the Royal Commission on the Distribution of Income and Wealth[4] and in several books and articles.[5]

There is thus no need to cover this ground again. Let it suffice to emphasise two matters. First, no measure of inequality can summarise all the relevant characteristics of an income or wealth distribution in one single index. The changes in the degree of inequality, and even the direction of the changes, may depend on the particular index which is used to measure them. Has inequality increased or diminished if the share of personal incomes accruing to the top quintile of income receivers has declined from 40 per cent to 30 per cent and that accruing to the bottom quintile has simultaneously declined from 10 per cent to 5 per cent? In this case there has been a diminution of inequality according to an index of the differences in income shares (as a percentage of all incomes) of the top and the bottom quintile — a fall from 30 per cent to 25 per cent. However, an index of the ratio of income shares of the top to the bottom quintile shows an increase in inequality — a rise from 4·0 to 6·0. Both indexes measure important and interesting changes in the distribution of income but in this example the first index emphasises the large decline (proportionate to all incomes) in the share of the top quintile of income receivers while the second index emphasises the large decline (proportionate to its previous share) of the bottom quintile.

Various statistical indexes summarising the whole distribution and not only the extremes give equally contrary results. The Gini coefficient of inequality may be the same for two distributions of income in which quite different proportions of total income accrue to the top and the bottom quintiles of income receivers.

The second matter which deserves emphasis is the tendency for earnings to show a marked 'regression towards the mean'. The remuneration of high earners in any one year tends on average to be lower, relative to the mean of all earnings, in the following year, while that of low earners tends on average to be higher. This generalisation is based on two large official sample surveys which refer to two different periods and which use different sources of data.[6] It appears to be equally valid for the annual earnings of all employees as for the weekly earnings of men and women manual workers and of men and women non-manual workers.

The regression toward the mean does not necessarily alter the dispersion of earnings as the positions vacated by some of the high earners whose relative remuneration has declined, and by low earners whose relative remuneration has increased, are taken up by earners who previously were nearer the middle. The regression cannot be explained, even for manual workers whose remuneration was not affected by absence from work, by the age factor: young men with low earnings receiving high increases and old men with high earnings losing ground. It operates quite markedly even in the middle years of working life; nor is it due to variations in overtime earnings between one year and another. The regression for earnings excluding overtime is quite substantial, though for earnings including overtime it is even greater.

The matched sample studies excluding the effect of recruitment to, and retirement from, the labour force also show that the lowest tenth of earners are a changing group. Less than half of those who are in the lowest tenth in a given survey week in a given year are likely to be also in the lowest tenth in the two following years. There is no completely satisfactory explanation of the factors which result in earnings regressing towards the mean. The fact that in Britain every year 24 million employees change their jobs at least 10 million times, and that many of them change the industries and occupations in which they work, explains why changes in earnings of individuals are frequently much greater than the average changes in particular industries and occupations. The available data show quite clearly and conclusively that large changes in the relative earnings of large proportions of all earners have not resulted in any changes in the distribution of earnings.

The distribution of personal incomes in Britain is certainly quite uneven.[7] The Royal Commission, on the best evidence available, concluded that in 1972–3 the top 10 per cent and the bottom 50 per cent each had about one-quarter of all personal incomes while the other half went to that 40 per cent of recipients whose incomes were between the median and the top decile. In the past the distribution had been still more uneven. Between 1938 and 1949 the share of the top 10 per cent of income recipients declined quite sharply. This decline continued between 1949 and 1972–3 and increased the share of the next 40 per cent of income recipients while that of the bottom half remained at about a quarter throughout this period (see Table 6.1).

The distribution of earned incomes is somewhat less widely dispersed than that of all personal incomes, as is shown in Table 6.2.

The distribution of earnings seems to have remained remarkably stable over long periods of time. For adult male manual workers it has remained virtually unaltered for the last ninety years in spite of all the changes in the composition of the labour force, in the structure of

TABLE 6.1

*Percentage shares of total personal incomes before tax received by certain quantile groups**

United Kingdom	Income tax units		
	1949	1959	1972–3
Top 5 per cent	23·8	19·9	17·2
6–10 per cent	9·4	9·5	9·2
11–50 per cent	43·1	47·5	49·1
51–100 per cent	23·7	23·1	24·0

* The term 'quantiles' is a general description which covers the median, quartiles, quintiles and percentiles.

SOURCE: Royal Commission on the Distribution of Income and Wealth, *Report No. 1* (1975) table G5.

TABLE 6.2
Quantiles, as percentage of median of personal incomes before tax,
1972–3*

| | Personal income | Earnings | |
	Tax units	Males	Females
Highest decile	214	161	167
Upper quartile	157	126	129
Lower quartile	56	80	80

SOURCE * See table 6.1. 1. Royal Commission, *Report No. 1*, table G6. 2. Royal
Commission, *Report No. 1*, table 21.

industry, in the relative rates of pay, and in the purchasing power of
earnings which have taken place during this period.[8]

In the eight years between 1964 and 1972 retail prices in Britain
increased by 53 per cent. During these years the distribution of earnings
for men over the age of 18 as recorded by the D.H.S.S. in connection
with the Graduated Pension Scheme shows little change but there
appears to have been a slight tendency for the dispersion of earnings to
widen.[9] It is as yet too early to assess the effect of the more rapid
inflation of the mid-1970s and the attempt to enforce income policies
on the distribution of earnings.

The effect of taxes and social-insurance contributions on income
reduces the degree of inequality of incomes. However, in spite of the
very high marginal rates of tax on higher incomes in Britain, the extent
of the redistribution in 1972–3 was modest. The share of the top
quintile after tax was reduced from 42·7 per cent to 39·4 per cent and
that of the bottom quintile increased from 5·8 per cent to 6·8 per
cent.[10] The progressive impact of taxes on income in that year appears
to have been completely offset by the regressive impact of taxes on
goods and services.

The distribution of personal wealth is substantially more uneven
than that of personal incomes, but the trend towards greater equality in
the twentieth century has been more marked. The best evidence
indicates that the top quintile of the total population above 18 years
owned four-fifths of all personal wealth excluding state pension rights.
Even if these rights are included, the share of the top quintile was still
three-fifths of all personal wealth.

Inequality of Life Styles

The distribution of personal incomes and wealth should be considered
as an important but by no means the only indicator of economic

inequality between families. There are alternatives which are less bedevilled by conceptual and statistical problems and by errors and omissions. These other indicators are less comprehensive and not always quantitative but they are quite possibly more accurate and more persuasive.

Economic inequalities can be grouped into three categories of differences: first, personal incomes and wealth; second, a host of factors, some of which are discussed in the next section; and third, life styles, which are discussed in this section. These three categories are partly interdependent; they illustrate different aspects of inequality.

One of the byproducts of increased material prosperity and of increased application of technical knowledge in Western Europe and North America has been a greater similarity in the life styles of different social and income groups.

The validity of this statement can easily be illustrated but it cannot be proved. Increased prosperity has brought it about that today most families have a bathroom and an increasing proportion of upper-income-group families have two or more, while before 1945 many families had no bathroom. The number of bathrooms can be recorded but the greater equality in life styles between a one- and a two-bathroom family than between a family that has a bathroom and another that has not cannot be quantified but is true all the same. The assertion that the difference between no bathroom and one is greater than that between one and two bathrooms accords with common sense and is based on a knowledge of social conditions and attitudes.

The large increase in private motor-cars, especially since the early 1950s, has had a similar effect. About half of all families in Britain and more than four-fifths of all families in North America now own a car, while, in the recent past, car ownership was confined to the fairly well-off, who nowadays often own two or more cars. Here again the difference in life style between a one- and a two-car family or between one who has an old small car and one who has a large new one is much less than the difference between the one-car and the no-car family.

Before the war, most housewives in Britain washed their clothes, sheets and curtains in a tub using a scrubbing board while upper-income-group women either had a woman come in to do the washing or sent it to the laundry. Today the great majority of women either have an electric washing machine or take their washing to a launderette. There can be no doubt that these changes also represent a lessening of inequality.

Personal clothing is another aspect of life where one can observe a move away from inequality. Increased standards of living, new fibres and improved manufacturing techniques have created a society where a woman's coat, dress and accessories do not reveal her or her husband's income to anything like the same extent as they did forty years ago. In the streets of Durham City one can today not easily distinguish between the mine manager's and the pitman's wife; in the past this distinction was obvious.

Dress, however, has not only changed due to increased prosperity and new techniques but also on account of changes in attitude especially amongst the young. In the 1940s and 1950s, university and college students wanted to be seen to be students and thus wore scarves and blazers. Today the ubiquitous jeans are quite as much uni-class as they are uni-sex.

In Britain, to go abroad for the summer holidays and to have a telephone used to be characteristics of an upper-income-group style of life; they are so no longer. The Population Census of 1931 recorded one and a half million private domestic servants, the 1951 Census recorded half a million. Since that date, this classification has been discontinued but it seems probable that there has been a further marked decline during the last twenty-five years. The reduction in the number of domestic servants has diminished the standard of living of the upper-income groups, while in all the other examples given differences have narrowed by the middle-income groups improving their standard of living.

This cursory discussion of changes in life styles shows quite clearly that the differences between the upper-income groups (the top 10 or 20 per cent) and the middle-income groups (the next 50 or 60 per cent) have narrowed substantially in several important respects. There is, however, no indication of a narrowing of differences between these and the lower-income groups. On the contrary, there is reason to think that the very factors which have narrowed the differences between the upper- and the middle-income groups have widened the gap between them and the lower-income groups. Today, not to have a bathroom, a car, a washing machine or an annual holiday may be an indication of relative deprivation while before the war it was the normal experience of wide sections of the population.

There is little evidence of increased prosperity and technical advances having accentuated inequalities of life styles in new and important respects. Second homes, boats, yachts and light aeroplanes are some of the new indicators of high-income status but they are marginal when compared with bathrooms, motor-cars, washing machines and annual holidays. Table 6.3 contains some illustrations of the rapid changes which have taken place over comparatively short periods.

Inequalities Caused by Other Differences

Differences in personal incomes, in wealth, in family composition and in age are four major causes of inequality in economic and social

TABLE 6.3
Estimated percentage of household possessions

		Telephone	Washing machine	Refrigerator	Car
United Kingdom	1964	22	53	34	37
	1974	50	69	82	56
United States	1952	62*	76	80	65
	1971	94			83
	1973		98†	99†	

* Refers to 1950.
† Percentages based on total number of homes wired for electricity.
SOURCES: United Kingdom — 1974 Department of Employment, *Family Expenditure Survey, 1974* (London: H.M.S.O., 1975). 1964 Ministry of Labour, *Family Expenditure Survey, 1964* (London: H.M.S.O., 1965). United States — 1952 U.S. Bureau of the Census, *Statistical Abstract of the United States, 1953*, 74th edn (Washington D.C.). 1973 U.S. Bureau of the Census, *Statistical Abstract of the United States*, 94th edn (Washington D.C.).

welfare. However, even families which are identical in these respects may be subject to numerous differences which lead to inequalities. These other differences are of three types: work-related; residence-related; and needs-related. They are summarised in the schedule (Table 6.4), which is meant to be suggestive rather than exhaustive.

Some of these differences can be quantified and expressed as income equivalents. This can easily be done for the five items classified as 'occupational welfare'. Between the man who enjoys generous provisions in all five respects and the man who does not receive any of

TABLE 6.4
Factors contributing to inequalities in welfare which may be experienced by families who are identical in four respects

1. Income — £3000 p.a.
2. Wealth — £6000
3. Family composition — father, mother, son and daughter
4. Ages — 33, 30, 7 and 5

A.   Work-related

I *Occupational welfare*
   1. Superannuation provisions
   2. Survivors' benefits
   3. Sick-pay entitlement
   4. Subsidised meals
   5. Subsidised leisure activities

Continued on next page

TABLE 6.4 (*cont.*)

A.	*Work-related* (*cont.*)	II *Terms of employment* 1. Length of paid holidays 2. Benefits in kind, for example, house, phone, car, meals 3. Purchase of goods at less than retail price 4. Loans on favourable terms 5. Prospects of promotion 6. Security of tenure, length of notice
		III *Nature of employment* 1. Hours worked 2. Shift and weekend work 3. Accident and health risks 4. Level of congeniality 5. Level of prestige 6. Risk of redundancy
		IV *Journey to work* 1. Duration 2. Method and ease 3. Cost
		V *Wife working* 1. Full-time ⎫ same differences 2. Part-time ⎭ as in I, II, III and IV
B.	*Residence-related*	VI *Economic* 1. Regional and local retail prices 2. Access to shopping facilities 3. Price of houses, level of rents, local rates
		VII *Neighbourhood* 1. Access to recreational facilities 2. Quality of schools and health care
		VIII *Specific* 1. Proximity to near relatives 2. Social identification with neighbourhood
C.	*Needs-related*	IX *Disability* 1. Member of family disabled 2. Caring for aged self-supporting parent

these provisions there may be a variation of 20 per cent or more in the real benefit they receive. The six items shown under 'terms of employment' can normally also be quantified but benefits in kind present occasionally some difficulty as the benefits may be associated with disadvantages, for example tied cottages, entertaining awkward customers, accessibility by phone. The six differences under 'nature of employment' cannot easily be expressed as income equivalents but they may result in crucial differences in economic and social welfare.

For all these seventeen items the general tendency is that undesirable conditions are linked with low incomes, but for most of them differences between low-income recipients may also be quite substantial, for example postmen and municipal workers usually enjoy more favourable occupational welfare and terms of employment than persons with similar incomes in private industries. To a lesser rather than a greater extent people can determine where they live in relation to their place of work. The duration, method and ease of the journey to work have for many people important welfare implications. A man may quite rationally decide to take a job at £2800 near his home in preference to one at £3000 which requires an hour's journey each way in a crowded bus or tube. To the loss of time and the discomfort of the journey must be added the cost of travelling long distances. High marginal rates of income tax further discourage long and expensive journeys to work.

An income of £60 per week earned jointly by a married couple is in some significant respects, which are not easily quantified, less beneficial than the same income earned by the husband alone. For the same reasons a couple earning that amount with the wife working only part time are better off than a couple both of whom work full time. The differences enumerated under I, II, III and IV do of course apply as much to the working wife as to her husband.

The region or the locality within a region where families reside may have a substantial effect on their economic and social welfare. Variations in purchasing power of incomes between places caused by differences in retail prices, local rates, level of rents and price of houses may bring about marked inequalities. Distance from, or inaccessibility of, shopping facilities may have a similar effect.

Differences related to the neighbourhood of residence include access to leisure facilities — parks, baths, playing fields, cinemas — as well as differences in the quality of schools, colleges, hospitals and health centres. Local inequalities in all these respects are quite great and have a considerable effect on the quality of life enjoyed by families.

Certain differences related to the place of residence are specific to a particular family and not to the neighbourhood. A family close to near relatives may consider themselves better off, for example baby-sitting, child-minding, help in emergencies, social contact, than one who is a long distance from their nearest kin. Some families experience problems in settling down in an unfamiliar environment and they too may quite rationally feel that they are more favourably placed at home on a lower wage than earning more but having to live amongst strangers.

A ninth major cause of inequality in welfare is the differences in needs, other than those of family size and age, to which reference has already been made. A family in any circumstances is likely to be worse off if one of them is seriously disabled. This is most likely to result in a reduction of earning capacity, but in addition any disabled person requiring constant care or a housewife unable to look after her family imposes burdens (however willingly borne) on the other members of the family which create inequalities between them and other more fortunately situated families. Much the same type of inequality comes about when a family cares for an aged parent even if that parent is economically self-supporting. The difference in life style between two families may be much greater if they have the same income but one cares for a disabled member than if their incomes differ by some 20 or 30 per cent.

Inequality and Communal Services

In all developed countries a substantial proportion of the national income, often more than a fifth, is spent on three social services: income maintenance, health and education. All three have greatly expanded in this century and all have contributed to a reduction of inequality and a redistribution of resources.

The extent, nature and direction of the redistribution of incomes which takes place when public agencies make payments to persons whose income has ceased due to retirement, invalidity or the death of the wage earner, or whose income is temporarily interrupted due to unemployment or sickness, depends on many complex factors. Some of the consequences of such income-support schemes are unintended and unexpected. Redistribution is the combined effect of the method of financing payments and of the schemes of awarding them. In considering the impact of the financing of payments it must always be borne in mind that those who are called upon to make payments may be able to transfer the real burden to others.

Employers who have to pay social-insurance contributions may in certain market conditions be able to pass them on to the purchasers of the goods and services they sell or be able to pass them back to their employees by paying lower wages than they would have paid had they not been compelled to pay social-insurance contributions. In certain conditions it may also be possible for employees who have to pay social-insurance contributions to pass them on in whole or in part to their employers by demanding higher remuneration. The extent to which a shifting of contributions and taxes is possible depends on the state of supply and demand in the markets for specific goods and services and for specific types of labour. It therefore varies between industries and over time.

The payment of unemployment benefit may be the result of a variety of motives, including: charity, compensation for loss of income due to no fault of those who suffer it, the wish to minimise militancy, the discouragement of resistance to technical progress or the maintenance of consumers' expenditure in periods of recession. However, all such payments do have the incidental effect of redistributing income not merely between the unemployed and those at work but also between regions, occupations, industries, men and women, age groups and over a person's life span. These incidental redistributions are the side-effects of paying benefits and levying the contribution and taxes which finance them at uniform national rates quite irrespective of the risks experienced by particular groups. This 'false standardisation' is of course one of the major characteristics which distinguish social-welfare payments from commercial insurance with its risk-related premiums.

Unemployment benefits thus result in areas of high unemployment (Newfoundland in Canada or Scotland in Britain) being subsidised by areas of low unemployment (Alberta or South-east England). Similarly, occupations and industries where the risk of unemployment is low (teaching or banking) subsidise those where it is high (labouring or construction). As in most countries unemployment is more prevalent among men than women, the latter tending to subsidise the former. Income will be transferred from those in the middle years to the old and the young as unemployment tends to be greatest among school leavers and persons over 55 years. This also results in a redistribution over the life span.

On balance there is a tendency for unemployment-support schemes to redistribute income from the relatively well-off to the relatively poor — because those who are most likely to be unemployed often happen to be those who are least well-off. The same applies to schemes supporting invalids, the temporarily disabled, widows and orphans, as these contingencies also have a low-income association. The opposite, however, tends to be the case for retirement and old-age pensions, the most costly income-support programmes. The higher-income groups have a longer expectation of life after retirement and therefore will receive pensions for more years than the less well-off.

All these tendencies to redistribute income in particular directions can be modified by appropriate provisions in either the financing or the award of benefits. Thus the tendency for pensions to benefit the rich at the expense of the poor can be counteracted by charging higher flat-rate or higher proportionate contributions in respect of higher incomes; or, alternatively, by paying lower flat rate or proportionate pensions. In practice this is often achieved by two-tier schemes which provide a uniform flat-rate pension as well as an earnings-related pension.

Some of the incidental redistribution effects of income-maintenance provisions, such as those which reduce inequalities between regions and occupations or over the life span, may well be socially as important and desirable as provisions which reduce inequalities between income groups. Income groups are quite heterogeneous in composition, for example a junior doctor or a solicitor's articled clerk may have the same income as a labourer or an agricultural worker.

The establishment of the National Health Service in 1948 which provided free health care (at the point of consumption) for the whole population greatly reduced inequality by divorcing access to health care from the ability to pay and by making it a citizen's right rather than a charity. Since that date the resources devoted to health care, especially in the hospital sector, have increased considerably,[11] and their geographical distribution has become less uneven. Nevertheless there are still marked inequalities in several aspects related to health. The availability of certain health-care facilities, for example dentists, differs widely between different areas; the standard of care provided for subnormal, psychiatric and geriatric patients is on average less satisfactory than that provided for patients requiring short-term care; the morbidity and mortality rates of people in the lower socio-economic groups continue to be greater than those in the higher groups. The reasons for the differential socio-economic mortality and morbidity rates are complex and not fully understood, but there is little reason to believe that they are associated with the quality and quantity of health-care provided. It is much more likely that the differential mortality rates reflect differences in personal characteristics associated with occupations, in life styles conditioned by occupation, and in economic and social environment. Thus it seems reasonable to presume that the longevity of British Prime Ministers is not due to the characteristics of the job, but due to the characteristics of the men who occupy it. It is similarly possible, but by no means certain, that the personal characteristics which enable a man to enter and follow professions such as those of the law, teaching and accountancy also predispose him to an above-average life expectancy. However, it is quite certain that the conditions of certain occupations such as coal-mining affect the expectation of life unfavourably. Also, the fact that the proportion of cigarette smokers in 1972 was twice as great among male unskilled workers (66 per cent) as it was among male professional workers (32 per cent)[12] may influence their respective mortality rates and so may innumerable other habits and life styles which are less well documented and the consequences of which are less well understood.

Even when the facts are well established their interpretation may be in dispute. This is well illustrated by the decline in infant mortality rates — death per 1000 children during the first year of life. There is fairly conclusive evidence that in Britain the rapid decline of these rates in the twentieth century has not been accompanied by a narrowing of the differential survival rates of children from poor and rich families. This has been considered as evidence[13] that the old social inequalities have not been modified in spite of the remarkable changes in the level of the rates.

The same facts can also be interpreted as evidence of a decline in inequality. A simple arithmetical example, shown in Table 6.5, illustrates this point. Between the two periods the mortality for both rich and poor children declined by 80 per cent and in both periods twice as many poor as rich children died. This resulted in more children from rich and poor families surviving. In Period I 6·4 per cent fewer poor than rich children survived while in Period II this proportion declined to 1·2 per cent. It seems perfectly legitimate to consider these changes in mortality rates as a reduction in inequality.

While death is an objective state many illnesses and disabilities are less definite and more subjective. All the indexes which are presumed to be associated with morbidity indicate a much higher incidence and prevalence among unskilled than skilled workers and the lowest rates for professional workers.[14] This applies equally to the proportion reporting long-standing illnesses limiting activity, the number of days lost from work due to illness or injury and the number of consultations with G.P.s.

All these data should be interpreted with great caution. They may reflect, at least in part, other factors than inequalities in morbidity. Higher consultation rates of unskilled workers may indicate their greater need for medical certificates. In this context it is of interest to

TABLE 6.5

Period		Poor families	Rich families	Poor as percentage of rich families
I	Deaths per 1000 births	120	60	200·0
	Survivals per 1000 births	880	940	93·6
II	Deaths per 1000 births	24	12	200·0
	Survivals per 1000 births	976	988	98·8

note that the consultation rate for women in unskilled workers' households is the same as the average for all women. Another relevant consideration is that men require to be more fit in many manual occupations than in white-collar work. A man's state of mind also influences his willingness to go to work when he feels below par. The findings of the *General Household Survey* show that men who are rather or very dissatisfied with their work lost twice as much time as those who are fairly or very satisfied.

It is possible that men who have a positive work orientation get into jobs where absenteism is low, but it is equally possible that men who are in these jobs develop a positive work orientation. These possibilities are not exclusive; they may even accentuate each other. In any case it seems probable that the apparent indications of differential socio-economic morbidity rates do not accurately reflect different states of health.

Causes and Implications of Inequality

The causes which make for inequality in the distribution of wealth and income are not fully understood and are still widely disputed. There are certainly a multiplicity of factors which react on each other. Countries at the same stage of economic development appear to have very similar distributions of income and earnings; changes in these distributions are normally very gradual and only become pronounced during cataclysms. There appears to be a trend for the dispersal of incomes to diminish with increasing standards of living. As these observations are based on data from different sources and on different definitions it would be mistaken to consider their validity as beyond reasonable doubt, but they are the proper conclusions derived from the best evidence available.

Inequalities in income are almost entirely accounted for by two causes: first, the cessation or interruption of earnings due to unemployment, invalidity, unsupported mothers caring for young children, and old age; and, second, the inequalities in earnings. The relative contribution of inherited wealth to the dispersal of incomes is quite small. Economists are attached to the belief that earnings approximate to marginal productivity. However, in societies in which earnings are determined by collective bargaining of groups of workers, each of which is heterogeneous in skill and productivity, by government regulations prescribing non-discrimination by sex and race and by innumerable avowed and disguised restrictive practices, marginal productivity is a concept of dubious validity. In any case the marginal-productivity theory does not explain the factors which make for high or for low productive capacity. There is also a reciprocal relationship:

differences in productive capacity result not only in differences in earnings but differences in earnings also partially explain differences in productive capacity. Thus if there were no rich men to buy diamonds the productive capacity of diamond cutters would be less or negligible.

The characteristics which influence productive capacity are generally considered to include cognitive skills, non-cognitive skills, education, experience, social class, family background, age, health, luck, appearance and Lydall's 'D factors' (drive, doggedness and determination),[15] but there is no concord about the relative contribution of these specific characteristics to the dispersal of earnings among individuals.

One assessment of the relative importance of these factors is the following:

Neither family background, cognitive skills, educational attainment, nor occupational status explain much of the variations in men's incomes. Indeed when we compare men who are identical in all these respects we find only 12% to 15% less inequality than among random individuals.[16]

Jenks's statement refers to the United States in the 1960s and is based on a study of several large-scale surveys undertaken by other scholars.[17] The quantitative analysis of the data on which his findings are based is acknowledged to be of a very high standard at the technical level, but his methodology has been widely criticised. The statement quoted is therefore not universally accepted by social scientists.[18] All the same it is almost certainly more valid than the theories which attribute inequalities in income mainly to differences in educational attainment and cognitive skills.

Jenks's conclusion, that there is nearly as much income variation among men who come from similar families with similar education and similar test scores (I.Q.) as among men in general, contradicts all conventional wisdom but it is well supported by the best available evidence — which is admittedly incomplete.

As all the measurable factors which contribute to variations of income account for only a fairly small proportion of the observed variations, Jenks suggests that the major causes of inequality of income between individuals are differences in luck and non-cognitive skills. Lydall's three 'D factors', health and age are other important causes which make for differences in income.

There can be little doubt that luck — fortuitous events affecting one's interests — plays a very important part in determining an individual's level of income and that it also contributes to differences in the earnings of occupational groups. This is often not fully recognised, as men who are successful by their own standards are inclined to attribute this to skill, industry and merit rather than to mere luck, while those who consider that they have done badly are all too willing to blame their bad luck but are often considered by others as lacking the qualities which make for success. The income of occupational groups whose services can be replaced by machines, better organisation or foreign imports tend to suffer while those who perform services for which the demand either at home or abroad rises rapidly tend to benefit.

The non-cognitive skills which make for higher income are quite heterogeneous. They include the ability to sell life insurance to people who think that they are already over-insured, the ability to encourage others to work and the ability to inspire confidence and loyalty.

Little is known about the effect of income differentials on G.N.P. It is not certain in which circumstances overtime and piece work increase output. There is even less certainty about the extent to which income differentials of varying magnitudes encourage people to undergo training, to accept responsibility, to move to unpopular areas, to put up with unsocial hours and uncongenial conditions and to work with greater conscientiousness and application. It is quite likely that the conventional wisdom exaggerates the beneficial effect of income differentials and under-estimates the effectiveness of alternative measures which could be devised to encourage conduct which promotes output and efficiency.

It is also possible, as was pointed out by Titmuss, that in present-day circumstances a reduction of inequality may be a precondition of economic growth. In societies dominated by large multinational companies and powerful trade unions, a reduction of differences in economic welfare may even be a precondition of the smooth functioning of the economic system. The frustration and sense of unfairness (irrespective of justification) which is experienced by a large proportion of the working population results in low morale and relatively low output. This, it has been argued, might be lessened by a reduction of inequality.

The veracity of these views cannot be demonstrated by an examination of the available evidence, as in all Western industrialised countries the degree of income dispersal is of the same order of magnitude. There is, however, no presumption that a view is erroneous merely because it cannot be proved scientifically.

The traditional view is more firmly established and more widely accepted: a reduction of inequality leads to three consequential changes. First, it would reduce incentives and thus output. That this would happen in some circumstances cannot be doubted; it is the magnitude of the reduction in output which would follow a specific change in differentials that cannot be accurately assessed. Second, reductions in income differentials tend to discourage the appropriate division of labour which is desirable to maximise output. This tendency is further accentuated by high taxes on income. Thus, if both doctors and nursery nurses earn £1 per hour and have to pay 40 per cent tax on their marginal income, a woman would be economically worse off if she practised as a doctor than if she stayed at home looking after her own children. If all incomes were the same some chartered engineers might prefer to work as gardeners and 'do-it-yourself' activities would prosper. Third, a reduction in inequality would result in changes in property values, retail prices and the pattern of production and consumption. Fewer luxury goods would be produced (for example yachts, large houses with big gardens, lobsters) and certain property values (in Mayfair for example) would fall. This would be compensated by increased production of the goods and services bought by those people who would benefit from the income redistribution.

Summary and Prognosis

The broad trend of the various types of inequality is reasonably clear. In this century there has been some movement away from the gross inequalities in the distribution of income and wealth. This has mainly taken the form of reducing the share accruing to the richest without a corresponding increase in the share accruing to the poorest. The major redistribution has happened during the three cataclysms – the two world wars and the Great Depression. In relatively normal times the pattern of dispersal has been remarkably stable. The extent of inequality of both income and wealth has remained quite substantial – the top fifth of income-receivers get two-fifths or more of all personal incomes while the bottom fifth get some 6 per cent; the top fifth of all individual wealth owners account for 60 to 80 per cent of all personal wealth (according to the definition of wealth used).

The differences in life style between the professional and the managerial classes and the great majority of the population has declined sharply over the last few decades. The rate of these changes has been fairly continuous and has been mainly the result of changes in technology and increased prosperity. The gap in life styles between the fifth of all families who are worst off and the great majority of all families has widened.

Inequalities in what has been referred to as 'other differences' have on balance declined and the extension of public health-care services and income-maintenance provisions have worked in the same direction.

The causes which are responsible for the gross inequalities in the distribution of income are not well understood. In the past the importance attributed to education, cognitive skills (I.Q.) and socio-economic background has been exaggerated. Nowadays more weight is attached to luck, certain non-intellectual qualities, experience on the job and to Lydall's 'D-factors' (drive, determination and doggedness). The will to succeed, confidence in the ability to succeed, hard work and initiative are certainly important attributes which lead to higher incomes. Little is known about the extent and causes of inequalities in the state of health of different socio-economic groups.

The future of inequalities in income and wealth will be mainly determined by public attitudes rather than by institutional and structural factors. In all the advanced countries a passion for equality is a minority creed. It appears that in these countries tolerance of a wide dispersal of income above the mean is greater than the tolerance of a wide dispersal below the mean. The desire to eradicate poverty both absolute and relative is more widespread than any wish to reduce the other economic inequalities which exist in society.

Most people desire for their children the best possible, rather than an equal chance, and for themselves the largest possible share of the cake. Collective bargaining, an essential inegalitarian practice which favours the strongest, is in Britain the acknowledged creed of the Labour movement, the trade unions and the militant left. This presumably reflects the views of their members, who are firmly attached to the concept of income differentials. In this context it must be remembered that the level of earnings is subject to the regression to the mean and that many people's place in the income spectrum changes during their working life. Many more people expect (mistakenly) that their place will change in the upward direction.

The scope of altering fundamentally the distribution of income through direct taxation is now recognised to be more limited than was thought possible in the past.

The desire to be, and appear to be, superior is apparently deep rooted in human nature. Income differentials – the essence of inequality – are not merely desired by the relatively successful in order to gain a larger share of goods and services but also as indicators of respect, recognition and standing in society. There is the possibility that the relatively successful might be reconciled to some loss of economic standing by a gain in social standing. A society which attaches more weight to prefixes and suffixes, to stripes on the sleeve and to buttons on the lapel may find it easier to be more egalitarian in matters of substance. At present there is no discernible trend in that direction, but fashions in such matters change.

In the more immediate future there are two non-controversial measures which would contribute to a diminution of inequality: more and better vocational and on-the-job training and a reduction of avowed and disguised practices which restrict entry into professions and occupations. Wider access to high-quality education could also make an important contribution, but there is considerable disagreement about the type of education which would lead to greater social equality in a society orientated to economic growth.

Major changes in the present levels of inequalities which prevail in all the advanced countries are not possible without major changes in attitudes and expectations. Any society which adheres to free collective bargaining as the major device of determining wages and salaries and to free enterprise as the major device of determining investment, production and prices has an inherent tendency to gross inequality. Societies in which public opinion supports a planned incomes policy and a mixed economy would find it much easier to remove some of the present gross inequalities.

Societies just like individuals cannot 'have their cake and eat it'. Reduced inequality has to be paid for by some restriction of freedom and some actual or potential loss of productive capacity, which means some loss in the standard of living.

7 Social Capital

Neil Fraser

I mean by 'social capital' in this chapter those elements in social services which are in the interests of industry and which contribute to future economic development. The classification by Richard Titmuss of one model of social policy as 'the industrial achievement-performance model'[1] could be applied to a social policy which aims to maximise social capital in my sense. Social capital will generally coincide with what economists call 'investment in human capital', that is, policies which increase the productive quality of the labour force, but I think it is also worth including the criterion of improving industry's rate of profit, so as to represent the interests of industry explicitly. Identifying the social-capital emphasis of social services will also mean considering to what extent redistributive or bureaucratic elements in social services are actually harmful to industry.

Because of the nature of social services, their social-capital effects operate to help industry through its supply of labour. A ready supply of labour helps all industry (not just expanding firms) if it prevents competitive wage-bidding and the squeezing of profits.[2] For a very elastic labour supply industry needs an unproductive agricultural sector to gain recruits, or immigration, or perhaps a high birth rate. Social-capital assistance is more likely to be important when these elements are not available, and expanding firms have to rely on labour mobility out of other firms and a limited supply of new entrants. The social services which may enhance labour-force participation or actual hours worked include nurseries, health provisions, certain social-security arrangements and regional policies. Then in tight labour-supply situations social services which affect the skill level of the labour supply are particularly important, that is education, training and services for families as they affect education. The supply of scientists and engineers can have a special impact through the provision of profitable innovations, including ones which circumvent labour-supply 'bottlenecks'. I shall ask why industry seeks state help to create its labour supply and what are the effects of social capital.

Social-capital values have a negative as well as a positive side. Industrial interests are likely to oppose expansions in social services beyond an optimum from the labour-supply viewpoint if some of the cost is felt to be at the expense of profits. Questions of the incidence of public-expenditure financing are inescapable here, and will be looked at in relation to Britain's social services at the end. Social-capital values also connote concern about the disincentive effects of some social policies upon work and the effects on productivity and competitiveness of social policies like safety provisions. The chief values of social policy which contrast with social-capital values are welfare values and redistributive values, both of which seek to widen the coverage of social services beyond the labour force and towards universalism. Their relation with industry is mainly based on compensating for its ill effects.

Social services develop with the support of a mixture of interests. Positive social-capital policies, in particular, often have wide political support and do not need to rely on the meagre attention they receive from business interests (at least in Britain). They are an investment to the worker himself, providing the prospect of a better job and direct benefits. I argue below that further education's expansion in Britain has a social-capital function although it is based on individual demand for student places. It is also clear that policies which keep down wage levels in the short term by increasing the labour supply can get working-class, social-democratic support. A higher profit share is accepted in the short term for the sake of more employment and the prospect of higher wage levels in the future, through economic growth. At the same time effective pressure for more redistributive values probably depends on working-class support. As Ian Gough has argued, 'the strength of working class pressure can roughly be gauged by the comprehensiveness and the level of social benefits'.[3]

It has been argued that all social services are social capital, because welfare benefits to workers and their families act as a 'social wage' and enable employers to pay less in individual wages.[4] This seems to me to assume an unreal responsiveness of labour supply to social services, that is to say, that the absence of each item in the social wage would reduce significantly the labour supplied at the existing individual wage. Wages do not seem to be exclusively determined by supply, but can be influenced by competing demands. In that way industry can supply the subsistence needs of workers, and the future workers whom they support, without calling in the state. However, even if the social wage is not a valid general argument, the social services do support certain low-wage labour, which is a social-capital function. For example, the labour supply of some parents in Britain depends on the 'family income supplement', and in high-cost areas like London much low-wage labour depends on council housing tenants. For cases where an attempt is made to keep down wage costs generally through social spending acting as a 'social wage', I would turn to incomes policies, such as the 'Social Contract' in Britain in 1977.

In this chapter I will look at examples of social-capital policies sought in different situations, with particular attention to the stage of industrialisation and the state of the labour supply. This is insufficient to explain in full social-service policies or their size, for which one would have to bring in the demand for welfare and redistribution. Furthermore, the same factors influence these demands. Industrialisation not only increases industry's need for state help, but also increases the 'diswelfares' of industry (and urbanisation) for which people seek compensation.[5] A scarce labour supply will not only increase the need for social capital but also increases the political power of labour to get the social services which it wants. It should be noted that I do not count as social capital social services which are not in the interests of industry but which are conceded to ward off unrest which might damage industry.

Why State Social Capital?

The first question which one is taught in economics to ask about public policies is why unaided markets cannot achieve the objects of these policies better. I offer here three general reasons why barriers to labour mobility arise when it may be profitable for industry to co-operate with the state:

(1) Many workers have poor access to finance to invest in themselves, which makes wage incentives a costly way to induce them to do it;

(2) Firms have limited scope for investing profitably in their workers because workers may be 'poached' by other firms; and

(3) The costs of location decisions to firms often fail to reflect the degree to which resources in a particular place are either idle or congested.

The first point, the cost to firms of relying on workers to invest in themselves, is a very general one. All aspects of labour mobility can be said to involve investment by the individual worker, in that there are costs against which the potential private benefits have to be weighed.[6]

In the case of education or retraining these costs include earnings forgone during the course, as well as any course fees: when mobility involves geographical movement there are all the costs involved in rehousing; when there are parental responsibilities there may be costs of nursery provision; and so on. The costs for firms are the wage benefits which are required to compensate for these costs. Without social capital, in a market of labour scarcity, they will be high, because it is likely to be only workers from well-to-do families who can respond. Prospective workers without savings would not easily be able to borrow to meet their 'investment' costs because they could not give security. Certainly, individuals would not be able to borrow to pay these costs at interest rates as good as those at which firms make profitable investments.

My second point is best looked at first in relation to education or training. Should firms provide the finance or facilities for the education of their present or prospective workers? If there is free movement of labour, a firm risks having investment in its workers 'poached' by other firms. That is, if free movement of labour establishes a single wage rate for a particular skill, firms will find it cheaper to recruit the workers already trained than pay the extra costs of training them themselves. Hence it is often more profitable for capital as a whole to pay taxes to the state to provide this investment.

However, this argument should be qualified by further reference to the barriers to labour mobility. The costs to workers of changing jobs mean that the same occupations in different firms frequently have different rates of pay. This gives firms scope to invest in their workers profitably. Firms can also increase their workers' costs of changing jobs by the sorts of investment in workers which are not transferable to other firms, for example many occupational pension schemes or the provision of tied housing. Firms are of course not so keen on labour mobility if it means a fast turnover of workers, and there has been quite a development of 'internal labour markets' based on promotion, especially in larger firms.[7] This may seem to contradict the argument that capital seeks social services to enhance the elasticity of labour supply, but in the general interest of firms the latter concern is usually thought to dominate.

I will now turn to my third point, the effect of barriers to mobility on industrial location. Without state action individual firms which locate new developments by the profit prospects to them will often not act in ways to maximise profits or economic development as a whole.[8] If they go to areas of congestion, total costs to industry will rise by more than the individual firm's costs because of the extra demand in the area. But if they go to areas of unemployment, costs to the rest of industry may be lowered if industry is having to bear indirectly some of the costs of unemployment. State social services which help correct a regional imbalance, whether by inducing relocation of workers or of industry, can thus be 'social capital', as they keep down labour costs and enable a higher level of aggregate demand to be sustained for any level of inflation. State house-building is the obvious example of this regional 'social capital'. In Britain examples are the New Towns and the Scottish Special Housing Association. But council housing is not 'social capital' in this way, and indeed rather acts as a barrier to mobility. It may, however, act as social capital for local industry and services. In areas of congestion, particularly London, subsidised council tenants provide a supply of relatively low-wage labour which could not remain without the subsidy.

Social-Capital Policies at Various Periods

I will now examine labour-supply and social-capital policies at various periods, beginning with early industrialisation. Here one immediately encounters the paradox which Habakkuk has investigated,[9] namely that it was actual labour scarcity which seemed to help industrialisation right at the start in two cases – in eighteenth-century Britain and before 1850 in the United States – although both cases clearly benefited from an abundance of labour thereafter. When labour is scarce industrial expansion depends on 'capital deepening'[10] and has to compete with rising wages; but when labour is plentiful industry can expand very profitably through 'capital widening'. Britain's new industries had abundant labour after 1815 due to demobilisation, immigration from Ireland, rapid population growth, and large numbers of rural landless labourers, with the result that real wages were stable for forty or more years. It was when wages started to rise again in Britain that the United States found cheap labour through immigration from Europe. In both countries the emphasis in social policy was the negative social-capital one of reforming the poor law to minimise the interference with work incentives. And in spite of *laissez-faire* ideologies there were small positive social-capital steps looking to the longer-term labour-supply situation, namely public health measures and the Factory Acts to protect children.

   It is in the industrialisation of Continental Europe that a social-capital contribution to productivity is clearly identifiable. Manufacturing there was delayed by British competition, and the cheapness of labour was if anything a liability, keeping traditional industry in being. But in the second half of the nineteenth century manufacturing developed greatly, aided by long-established state education.[11] Of the four kinds of knowledge contributing to economic performance, (1) the ability to read, write and calculate, (2) craft skills,

(3) engineering, (4) scientific knowledge, Landes notes that 'In all four areas, Germany represented the best that Europe had to offer; in all four, with the possible exception of the second, Britain fell far behind.' These advantages gave Germany a lead in Europe in institutionalising technological advance through the use of engineers, applied scientists, cost accountants, and so on. Like the United States, Germany developed assembly-line methods, substituting operatives for skilled craftsmen. Britain was slow to respond to this demonstration of what social capital could do. A national efficiency movement developed with inspiration from Germany, and had its most notable success with the *National Insurance Act* of 1911, which provided health and unemployment insurance mainly for those active in the work force. But education was very neglected in Britain until the First World War (or even the Second World War). In the United States, as in Britain, the Liberal ideology was strong, but there was a movement with quite a lot of support from industry for policies of 'conservation of human resources', in particular workmen's compensation legislation.[12]

Matthews has made the point that by the end of the First World War Britain had capital to employ all its workers but the developing scarcity of labour in the inter-war period was concealed by Keynesian demand deficiency.[13] One might not have expected industry to want social-capital spending. But there was the beginning of regional policies — state assistance to firms to invest where there were unemployed workers, and to unemployed workers to move to where there were job vacancies. And there were policies of rent control and council house-building which, though they derived from working-class pressure, could be used indirectly to support profits — that is, because they would protect families, and therefore the future labour supply, whilst industry was trying to cut wages. However, the country which really used this technique at the time was Soviet Russia. Rimlinger describes the extensive use of social security and social services there to control and develop the labour supply for the needs of industrialisation, whilst wage rates were kept down to provide the surplus for the massive capital accumulation.[14]

It is in the conditions of post-war full employment that there has been the strongest demand for social-capital measures. But at the same time full employment strengthens working-class pressure for redistributive social policies. As a result it is not always easy to say which values are uppermost. Social-capital measures are generally promoted in consensus terms for their contribution to future living standards via economic growth or reduced inflation. There has also been much negative social capital concern with social-service costs, including attempts to highlight it through the E.E.C.[15]

To take first the case of West Germany, support for social capital is clearly shown in this paragraph from Rimlinger:[16]

> The social programmes of both parties strongly favour prevention of illness and the rehabilitation of the disabled, the retraining of workers displaced by technological change, and the upgrading of the labour force in general. By helping the worker help himself, these aspects of the social economic phase of social security policy support the ideal of equal opportunity, which is central in the modern concept of social justice. Also these measures are economically valuable as instruments of an effective manpower policy. The differences between the parties lies in their conception of these measures, whether they are instruments of change or of stability.

But these were not the most important policy measures affecting the labour supply in post-war Germany. The refugees accepted from the east, and foreign workers accepted from the south, were the most important factor permitting fast economic growth — given that demand (at home and abroad) was there. Kindleberger[17] shows persuasively that in the years of ready labour supply West German wages were held down, maintaining profits and investment. A lot of the investment was capital widening, using foreign workers as operatives, so that German workers who might otherwise have been manual workers (including skilled manual workers) could be technicians or white-collar workers.

Sweden, on the other hand, has pursued economic development without much immigration, but has been a pioneer in social-capital programmes. The initiative here apparently came from the unions,[18] who have made sure that redistributive elements and the needs of disadvantaged groups are not absent. The centrepiece, which has been called an active or positive manpower policy,[19] consists of state programmes helping internal labour mobility through widespread retraining and generous unemployment benefits and relocation incentives, plus incentives for firms to invest where there are workers and when there is prospect of unemployment. Sweden's economic growth has been good, though it has been without the fast spurts that countries with widespread immigration have achieved. One might suggest that the social-capital programmes have contributed to this, in similar though less striking ways than immigration, that is by increasing labour-supply elasticities, by counteracting inflation (which should be made lower at any given demand level), and by maintaining profits and thereby investment.

The social-capital spending which stands out in the post-war era in the United States is education. O'Connor has noticed that until the

Second World War industrial corporations there trained the greater part of their work force themselves.[20] Since then there has been, as he says, 'a rapid expansion of lower level technical education and the establishment of a vast system of higher education by local and state governments'. The emphasis is on a marketable skill for all youths leaving school. However, there is a reservoir of unskilled labour, chiefly in the service sector, which is kept out of the big corporations by union and management practices. This 'dual labour market' means that the emphasis for growth in the corporate sector is on research and development for new products and capital-deepening methods (like automation), emphases to which the education system lends much support.

Social Capital in Post-War Britain

The objectives of social services since 1945 have not been publicly linked to the labour supply and economic growth in Britain to the same extent as in some other European countries; but the link has been made and has influenced social-service developments. It was made particularly after 1960, when economic policy ideas started to turn to making the most of labour resources. British industry was diagnosed, from inside and out, as short of qualified manpower (managers, engineers, certain skilled manual workers), 'over-manned', and short of profits because of 'wage push' and the cost of bidding for labour. Industry sought extra labour from immigrants but found that route blocked, and throughout the period has been adding married women to the labour force. The government's contribution was a mixture of policies involving various departments, including the social services. They are reviewed in an O.E.C.D. study in 1970 called *Manpower Policy in the United Kingdom*[21] which covers education and training, labour mobility as it is affected by the employment service, cash benefits and housing, regional policies and incomes policies. But the effect of changes in social services on economic performance remains a very controversial subject.

Education's most important social-capital contribution since 1945 seems to me to be the expansion to cater for professional and technical white-collar skills. Eric Robinson has commented that 'after the war the most spectacular development in English education — the phenomenal expansion of the technical colleges [that is further education] was the result not of political decisions but of steady pressure from progressive employers and other employees'.[22] Where there was political support it reflected a similar objective: witness Sir Edward Boyle: 'it was always easier to get a bit more on the building programme for further education than for other things because of the Treasury doctrine that this affected economic growth most'.[23] The growth has been particularly in full-time higher education, where there were 114 per cent more students in 1972–3 as compared with ten years before (made up of 82 per cent more university students, 120 per cent more college of education students and 248 per cent more advanced students in full-time further education college courses).[24] The part-time route to advanced qualifications (H.N.C. and professional qualifications) is also retained in further education colleges, which have roughly equal numbers of full-time and part-time students at the higher education level.[25] And for full-time students these colleges have pioneered sandwich courses to give a very close matching to industry's needs.

A study of electrical engineering factories provides evidence about the use of qualified manpower in research-based industries.[26] The proportion of employees in those factories with higher qualifications was surprisingly small (in 1966; 4½ per cent had higher education science or engineering qualifications, and a further 2·2 per cent had O.N.C.s or 'A' levels. Furthermore, there was not a close relationship between occupational levels and educational qualifications, suggesting that many of those staff were not directly using the knowledge and skills which they had been taught. The demand from the electrical industry for qualified manpower was such that it provided salary differentials giving rates of return to employees of 11 per cent for a degree (as opposed to 'A' level) and 17 per cent for part-time study to H.N.C. level (as opposed to O.N.C.).

The provision of places in education after the compulsory school-leaving age has been largely planned, as in the Robbins Report, on the basis of student demand, not manpower forecasts. But the needs of industry are still crucial to that basis, as employment prospects (which are shown by the rates of return above) probably prompt much of the student demand. Indeed it is wrong to identify the needs of industry as being for precise numbers with particular skills, for there is much scope for substitution between manpower with different qualifications (which professional bodies of course seek to deny). There is a strong economic component in the common criticism that English education is too specialised, pursuing a depth which is not needed by industry at the expense of failing to provide competence in, for example, mathematical skills.[27]

The social-capital effects of general schooling are much harder to identify. Education does of course provide a selection system for employers, and many changes to education are made in the name of improving that, with the objective of 'equality of opportunity'. But the belief that streaming and specialisation bring forward the 'scholarship boy' has now been widely challenged by a belief that the economic effects of these characteristics of British education may be negative. As to the direct effect of what is learned in school on productivity in industry, I would confine it mainly to the professional and technical skills already discussed. It is very debatable if improvements in general schooling can claim much credit for the rising numbers acquiring educational qualifications, as compared with the effect of changes in employment prospects, parental incomes and grants. And it must be remembered that over 50 per cent of school leavers have no 'O' levels and 40 per cent no C.S.E. qualifications. These children now get more schooling, in that before 1944 they would have left school at 14 and they now leave at 16, but the effect on their performance at the unskilled and operative jobs to which most are confined must be slight.

It can be argued that education will not yield its full potential in social-capital terms without complementary expenditure by parents on their children: expenditure which the state can support through a 'family policy'.[28] Policies such as generous family allowances, or maintenance grants for older pupils, which are redistributive and (potentially) productive too, have not been developed in Britain as they have in Continental Europe. Moves in that direction here have been regularly sacrificed in public expenditure. But Britain does have a high and growing proportion of mothers who augment their family budget by working themselves.[29] This of course adds to the labour supply, and has led to a large public demand for nursery facilities to support it. The expansion of nursery schools in the 1970s can be seen as a response, although the form adopted is less geared to the social-capital demands than are the day nurseries, which are not being expanded.[30]

In training for craft skills there has been much state activity since 1960, although without reaching Swedish levels. In 1964 the *Industrial Training Act* arranged for firms in each industry to pool their apprentice training costs, with a view to increasing the numbers being trained. The government sponsored the institutional arrangements for this (Industrial Training Boards), and offered greater use of further education colleges on a 'day-release' basis,[31] but it was run by the industries themselves. The scheme has been criticised for not removing the shortages and for not assisting the development of newer skills in the newer industries.[32] For training workers for industries new to them the government has relied on a separate scheme, now called the Training Opportunities Scheme, which uses both its own training centres and the further education colleges. This provides intensive half-year courses training to a craft skill level, and is being extended rapidly in the 1970s.

I will pass now to social security and the needs of industry. In 1965 and 1966 measures were introduced which were directly justified because they would make workers accept redundancy more readily. These were redundancy payments and earnings-related supplements to unemployment (and sickness) benefit. The idea came, according to Heclo,[33] from 'officials inside Whitehall and economists outside', and was taken up by the National Economic Development Council, which has union and employers' representatives, and the new Labour Government formed in 1964. Demands for such labour-market policies did not come from either side of industry, as they did in Sweden.

Having given examples of social-security expenditure arising for labour market reasons, we ought to ask if it is ever reduced to force people into work, as Piven and Cloward[34] argue is the case with local public welfare in the United States. The centralised British system is not subject to the same pressures from local employers of low-wage labour. I do not think the work controls in the system increased with full employment, and one control, the 'wage stop', has recently been removed. These controls are nevertheless real. There are penalties for leaving work of one's own accord and unreasonably refusing work offered, limits to the duration of the earnings-related supplement (six months) and unemployment benefit itself (one year), and also a lower rate of supplementary benefit to which the unemployed are confined. Benefit rates are not comparable with the vast majority of wage rates, and when the latter are low, employers are assisted in still getting workers by the Family Income Supplement. However, at the same time as there are all these work incentives, overlapping means tests can provide a massive disincentive to work and earn more. The Conservative Government in the early 1970s tried to find a solution to this problem, the tax credit scheme, and so illustrated the daunting expense of getting rid of means tests (for it would have achieved little in that direction).

The obstacle to labour mobility which is most often mentioned is the localised basis of council housing in Britain.[35] The main efforts to minimise this obstacle, apart from efforts to dissuade councils from insisting on residence qualifications, have been on the one hand continued house building and on the other the raising of rents (as in the *Housing Finance Act* of 1971) to ease the pressure of demand. The advantages of rent pooling is the main argument used for preferring local authority to 'nationalised' public housing. But one may question any idea that firms do not do quite well out of the present system. Firms have enough political muscle to persuade local authorities to build for their incoming workers. There are local authorities as well as New Town building to induce firms to settle, and in high-cost cities like London many firms can pay low wages only because their workers come from subsidised local-authority housing.

But in spite of these social-capital elements in social services, it has been lately more often argued that the interests of industry are in reducing expenditure on the social services. The core of this argument, as it has been presented recently,[36] is a claim that workers have shifted

much of the tax burden of the extra public expenditure on to industry
by higher wage demands designed to maintain the real value of
take-home pay. This squeeze of profits has reduced industrial
investment, and industry has had to seek relief in subsidies, in a 'Social
Contract' agreement with the unions, and in deflation to reduce the
bargaining power of labour. The consequent reduced growth in national
(especially industrial) output has only made the battle over its
distribution more severe. Industry's struggle to reduce costs, aided by
the social-capital moves to ease the path to redundancies, the deflation,
and international recession with which they coincide, have created
large-scale unemployment. With the lack of profit opportunities
preventing industry using so much available labour, the problems of
labour supply might appear solved. But it has been claimed also that the
use of manpower, especially qualified manpower, by the public sector
harmfully reduces the supply for industry, particularly for the time
when growth is resumed.

Table 7.1 (column 3) shows the striking increase in public
expenditure in comparison with G.D.P. since 1954. The increases for
some social services over the same period were higher than for public
expenditure as a whole — education grew 265 per cent, social
security 187 per cent and the National Health Service and housing each
168 per cent. It is worth noting that some services very close to the
needs of industry have also increased very fast — for example, roads
270 per cent. Defence is the biggest item making room for the fast

TABLE 7.1
Composition and growth of G.D.P., 1954 to 1974*

	1954	1974	Percentage growth 1954—74
Public expenditure	32·9	51·3	168
of which transfers	9·2	21·8	308
Public resource expenditure	23·7	29·6	110
Consumers' expenditure	67·9	63·8	61
Private investment	8·7	12·4	145
Balance of trade	−0·3	−5·7	
G.D.P. (at market prices)	100	100	72

* Columns 1 and 2 are percentages of G.D.P. at current prices. Column 3 is
percentage increase between 1954 and 1974 in costs deflated by a G.D.P. (market
prices) deflator.
SOURCE: *National Income and Expenditure* (1964—74) tables 1, 58; and
National Income and Expenditure (1965) table 48.

growers — its cost was the same in 1974 as in 1954 in constant G.D.P. price terms.[37]

Table 7.1 also shows that public expenditure on transfers has grown much faster than public resource expenditure. This is very important in considering the impact of public expenditure on industry, because transfers support, rather than reduce, consumers' expenditure and private investment. As a result the two together are almost the same percentage of G.D.P. in 1974 as in 1954 in spite of the public expenditure growth, although, as can be seen, this is very much with the assistance of borrowing from abroad (Table 7.1, columns 1 and 2). The social services which are mainly goods and services expenditure are education and the health service, whereas social security is transfer expenditure. Much of the growth in transfers was in the last year of this comparison, through subsidies to keep down prices.

In line with total public expenditure the income-tax burden on the working population has grown visibly. For example, a married man on average earnings paid a tenth of his earnings in income tax in 1960, but a quarter of his earnings in 1975.[38] Furthermore, Turner and Wilkinson have persuasively demonstrated that the beginnings of the acceleration in inflation in the mid-1960s coincided with slower growth in take-home pay for wage earners and faster growth in public expenditure.[39] Spending on education, health and social security were growing at 6 to 7 per cent a year, the average manual worker's gross pay was rising at 2·8 per cent a year, but after tax the same worker's net pay was rising only 1 per cent a year (all in real terms).

But we need to consider the 'social-wage' argument again here, and ask if the value of the output of social services might be a substitute for the additional tax burden to the average wage earner. There are two reasons for rejecting this argument, one specific to this period and the other general. The first concerns the demographic trends of the period, which have led to a rise in the ratio of the population of non-working ages to working ages from 49 per 100 in 1941 to 67 per 100 in 1971.[40] Although such trends are inevitably a cost on the working population, they are liable to lead to disbelief in the 'value for money' of the instrument for meeting them, the social services. The trends are fortunately on the point of turning in a favourable direction; but the second point may well be unchangeable. This is the limited scope for social services to increase productivity because the quality of much of their service is judged by the number of staff. This gives a rising cost per unit of output compared with industry, which is able to offset part of its salary and material cost increases through technical improvements. In addition, the share of costs taken by salaries is very high in the social services. These factors, which are collectively known as the 'relative price effect', are illustrated in Table 7.2. This shows that the increase in

TABLE 7.2
Relative price effect in education and health, 1954 to 1974

Total percentage growth at 1970 prices in current expenditure on goods and services
(a) Deflated by G.D.P. (market prices) deflator
(b) Deflated by deflator for public authorities' current expenditure on goods and services

	(a) Cost increase (per cent)	(b) Volume of resources increase (per cent)
Education	259	165
Health	156	71

SOURCE: *National Income and Expenditure* (1964–74) tables 14, 58.

costs for these social services, on which their tax burden is based, is much greater than the increase in their use of resources, which is also (it is assumed) their output increase.

The increase in use of resources by education and health as shown in Table 7.2 is nevertheless considerable. It can also be illustrated by the rise in the proportion of the labour force employed by the two services, which was from 7·7 per cent in 1959 to 12·7 per cent in 1974.[41] Private industry clearly sees this as a threat to its labour supply and, because of the cost of outbidding the public sector, as a threat to profits. As a result we are likely to see not only more attempts to direct this spending in social-capital directions, but also attempts to find productivity increases in social services (that is, the hope of the same output with fewer staff).[42]

I conclude from this that we should see the rise in social service expenditure as only a part of the heightened struggle for resources[43] which has brought about the decline in industry's profitability since the war. The context for this is the scarcity of labour for industry whilst full-employment policies were pursued which strengthened labour's position in seeking higher wages and more benefits from public expenditure. The struggle to restore profits uses positive social-capital policies plus restrictions to other aspects of social services. But more important for the attempt to raise profitability are the abandonment of the policy of full employment, the Social Contract between government and the unions which inhibits wage inflation and direct subsidies and tax concessions for industry. Social policy is involved, however, in the Social Contract, which includes the conscious pursuit of social benefits and living-cost subsidies as components of a 'social wage'. Now that industry has identified the explosion of public expenditure as a cause of its own shortage of resources, it may well not discriminate clearly between social-capital and other social-policy elements in this expenditure and both will be under attack.

8 Demand and Need

Della Adam Nevitt

> By necessities I understand not only the commodities which are indispensably necessary for the support of life, but whatever the custom of the country renders it indecent for creditable people, even of the lowest order, to be without. A linen shirt, for example is, strictly speaking not a necessary of life − [but] − in the present time, through the greater part of Europe, a creditable day labourer would be ashamed to appear in public without a linen shirt. (Adam Smith, *The Wealth of Nations* bk 5, ch. 2, pt II, Discussion on Taxes upon Consumable Commodities, 1776.)

> In examining social or normative definitions of need the social scientist can help to bring them into the open, reveal contradictions and loose ends and show the different functions played by law, regulation, policy and custom. (Peter Townsend, *The Fifth Social Service* (London: Fabian Society, 1970) ch. 1, p. 9.)

Almost 200 years elapsed between the publication of the first of the above quotations and the second; during that period economics has greatly increased our understanding of the theory of choice and the relationship which exists between concepts of need, necessities and demands. The works of economists have not, however, been fully absorbed into the literature on social policy and administration, and the quotation from *The Fifth Social Service* owes more to early pre-scientific works on economics than to the work of great nineteenth-century authors such as Jevons,[1] Wicksell,[2] Marshall[3] or Wicksteed.[4] Twentieth-century economists working in the field of demand theory have been almost completely ignored in the emphasis given by social administrators to 'law', 'regulation', 'policy' and 'custom'.

The danger of using any of these four terms as a proxy for 'demand' is that it divorces law, regulations, etc. from the economic base which gives reality to the laws which are introduced, regulations which are enforced, policies which are formulated and customs which are created over time by the constant repetition of certain behaviour patterns. Educational policies, for example, are a reflection of either individual or group demands. These demands will sometimes be for universal education over a particular age group, sometimes for highly selective provision for certain social classes or age groups and sometimes for particular occupational skills. Whatever the detail of an educational policy and the laws and regulations which enforce it, demand and supply functions will determine the actual provisions made, and over time these provisions will themselves create 'customary' needs, or, using Adam Smith's terminology, 'necessities'. In this chapter I shall use the most simple microeconomic analysis to relate Bradshaw's taxonomy of social need to demand and supply theory. For completeness I shall discuss both individually purchased goods and services, and publicly provided social services. The former are 'social needs' in so far as they enter into discussions on wage levels and the determination of social-security and other income-maintenance benefits; the social-need element in the public provision (free at point of consumption goods) of goods and services requires no special explanation as the social acknowledgement of a 'need' must be assumed whenever governments provide a service, although a minority of citizens may not necessarily agree with a government's definition of every need.

When the word 'demand' is used in this chapter it means a schedule of prices related to various quantities of a good or service which an individual, company, commune, government institution or agency wishes to purchase. The demand schedule is a function which is determined by the incomes and tastes of 'consumers'. A consumer may purchase goods for himself or for other people (for example a parent buying on behalf of a child, a teacher on behalf of a pupil, and so on). When demand is brought together with supply, a market price is determined; this price may reflect indirect taxes, subsidies or the consequences of redistributing incomes from rich to poor through social-security policies, or from poor to rich by the existence of monopolies, regressive taxation or other non-egalitarian policies. *Effective demand* is a demand which has been met; demands which at one period in history have been 'unmet' may be met by social policies which redistribute incomes or establish an agency which purchases the required goods on behalf of those who cannot buy them on the open market. The agency then distributes the goods free or at a subsidised price to everyone (for example health services in Britain) or to selected people (for example dwellings to families eligible for a local-authority tenancy in Britain). Social needs are demands which have been defined by society as sufficiently important to qualify for social recognition as goods or services which should be met by government intervention. These demands may range from pure service goods, such as the demand for the establishment of a system of justice, to the demand for the provision of holiday facilities for elderly persons. If a 'social need' has not been recognised and converted into a 'public demand', it is because the 'taste' or the 'income' of society are not regarded by politicians as sufficiently favourably inclined to that good to justify its inclusion in the category of demand goods. It is then necessary for those who favour the particular good to make it into a 'social demand' by (*a*) increasing the public's 'taste' for it by explaining its full importance, and/or (*b*) showing the public that national income is sufficiently large for society to incur the expenditure required without forgoing other more highly desired goods or services.

There is no clear dividing line between 'luxury' and 'need' goods or services. Both are sub-sets of the wider set of demands and can only be fully defined in relation to the society under examination, although certain goods such as salt, water or oxygen are incontrovertibly 'necessities' in the sense that no living creature can survive without these essential goods. However, the modern use of the word 'need' has little to do with survival and relates to a concept of goods which are demanded by many people and 'should' be made available to everyone, either through a government non-market scheme which distributes the goods directly to those classified as in 'need', or by income distribution and/or redistribution. Luxuries, on the other hand, are things which many people demand but in respect of which the government has not intervened in the market. Goods and services can of course be transferred from a 'luxury' to a 'need' category and vice versa.

Individually Purchased Goods and Services

The goods and services falling into this category may in economic terminology be classified as 'consumer demands'. Need goods and services would then be a sub-set of the general set covering all consumer demands. In this context demand for any one good depends upon the willingness and ability of the consumer to purchase the good in question. Ability depends of course upon the income of each individual and the price of all consumer goods. The willingness of consumers to exchange money for a particular good depends upon the taste of the consumer for that one good, relative to the strength of his taste for other goods, including the retention of his money.

In order to obtain the downward-sloping demand curve defined by economists, certain assumptions about human behaviour must be made. These assumptions are normally grouped under the general assumption of rationality, which is tautologically defined by the following five assumptions each of which is necessary for the derivation of a downward-sloping demand curve.[5]

Assumption 1

There must be an ability to make a choice. That is, given both good A and good B, the consumer can consciously choose between A and B and decide that:

> A is better than B
> or B is better than A
> or that he is indifferent as between A and B.

The indifference condition must not be a symptom of an inability to decide between A and B, but a clear decision on the part of the consumer that A will do as well as B for a particular purpose, or, at the margin of choice, a little more of A is just as acceptable as a little more of B.

Assumption 2

There must be consistency in selection. If a consumer says that A is better than B, and that B is better than C, he cannot then say that C is better than A.

This consistency rule is frequently absent in the 'choices' made by very young children and the choices of groups of heterogeneous people gathered into one institution or organisation. In local government, for example, one group of councillors may select A, another B and a third C. Corporate and other systems of planning are designed to bring A, B and C together so that the whole council can make a consistent selection from the three possibilities; in this way the 'corporate' nature of a local authority is stressed and an attempt made to introduce the same degree of rational behaviour as one commonly finds when one individual is making choices (that is listing priorities).

Assumption 3

In order to obtain a continuous demand curve, both A and B must be desired by the consumer. This means that if a consumer selects A, he can be persuaded to switch to B, if B is gradually increased by additions of B so that the consumer will become indifferent as between A and $B + b + b$, etc.

Assumption 4

More of any commodity is better than less of it. Thus '$A + a$' must always be preferred to A This assumption is useful when considering efficiency problems since most of us would be willing to agree that for any given effort (or expenditure) a greater output is preferable to a smaller one.[6]

Assumption 5

The more that a consumer has of anything, the less he wants more of it. This is the reason why, when one good is substituted for another, economists assume that the marginal rates of substitution fall with each increase in the stock already held.

This assumption is particularly important in considering human behaviour in multi-commodity markets. Decisions about expenditure are very seldom concerned with 'all or nothing' purchases but with a little more of some, a little less of others and the continued purchase of the customary amount of other types of goods. When the concept of diminishing marginal rates of substitution is applied to goods defined as necessities, it means that at the margin consumers will shift their purchases marginally from one necessity to another and not that they will be totally deprived of one necessity as their incomes fall or prices rise. A routine example of such changes in purchases is the seasonal adjustments housewives make in the purchases of vegetables; as each crop is harvested and becomes relatively more plentiful and thus cheaper, it is purchased in preference to other dearer green vegetables no longer in season.

One major exception to the rule of marginal adjustments is housing space which is often let or sold on an 'all or nothing' basis. With this commodity it is usually impossible to make a marginal adjustment to the amount of space occupied, and this may explain why eviction is a much more common family disaster in our society than, for example, acute malnutrition. However, even with housing space, adjustments may be made to the amount consumed in the long run either by movement from one house to another or by letting one part of a dwelling.

The assumptions made about 'rational' demand behaviour are highly relevant to the concept of 'need'. If more is always better than less, but the more we have of a thing the less we want more of it, it will follow that as people get richer and their demands fan out to cover a greater variety of goods, the customary collection of goods designated as 'needs' will become more numerous. In general, needs can be expected to expand at the same rate as demand; in the extreme case when all income is distributed according to need the two sets of goods would be identically equal, but in all other circumstances individually consumed 'need' goods would be a sub-set of demand.

The determination of the sub-set of need goods will depend upon the supply and demand functions of each good or service when incomes are not distributed strictly according to need. To explain this it is convenient to start with the assumption that need goods can be identified by reference to a set of objective criteria which are unrelated to supply and demand conditions. These objective criteria would be used to identify and list the needs of each individual and we would have a set of equations of the following form:

$$N_j = q_a n_{aj} + q_a n_{bj} + \cdots + q_a n_{nj},$$

where N is the total need of the jth individual and each $q_a n_{aj}$ is the jth individual's need for commodity or service n_a, and the q_a coefficient gives the quantity to which each individual is entitled.

The problem is to agree the quantities and goods which will be entered into each equation on the assumption that neither supply nor demand shall be taken into account. Given this assumption there appears to be only two extreme alternatives which could be used to give precision to each qn; the first is to assume a Utopia in which each individual obtains what he wants subject to some educational process which will induce the citizens of Utopia not to want that which will injure their neighbours. The alternative, equally extreme solution is to assume a subsistence-level economy in which each individual has enough to maintain life over a given span of years, but no more. As soon as we move from these two extremes, supply and demand functions are brought into play.

Consider, for example, the statement that 'all individuals should have good n because 80 per cent of people are willing and able to buy this good in the market place and it is unjust that 20 per cent are too poor to buy n'. Assuming that the reason given for the failure to purchase the good by the minority is correct (and not due to differences in taste and priorities) the following assumptions may be made about the supply and demand conditions for the industry producing good n. Demand has a low elasticity because the good has no close substitute, and relative to many other goods it is strongly demanded. The mere fact that 80 per cent of people consume it suggests that it is one of the things which Adam Smith would have recognised as a necessity which is *customarily* consumed. On the supply side the industry must be a large one such as agriculture or one that enjoys considerable economies of scale in making some modern product such as wireless sets. In both cases supply could expand in a year or so, if demand for the product increased still further through a redistribution of incomes which allowed the poorest 20 per cent of individuals to consume the product.

This fairly straightforward example of a 'need' good may be matched by considering a good which is only consumed by 10 per cent of the population. Such a restricted consumption implies a fairly high elasticity of demand for the good and/or a very inelastic supply. An example of such a good might be education in a country with no government or extensive voluntary provision. Teachers and schools take a long time to produce, and if education were classified as a need good under these circumstances it would be many years before universal education of an acceptable secondary- and higher-education standard could be reached.

For this reason, when drawing up a list of 'need' goods it is necessary to take into account the supply and demand conditions of each good or service which is entered into a need matrix. Prices as well as quantities must be entered into such a matrix because price levels give, in a very convenient form, vital information about relative supply conditions. In the matrix given in Table 8.1 goods which are suggested for classification into the sub-set of need goods have been divided into four groups:

A. Goods with low elasticity of demand but elastic supply;
B. Goods with elastic demand and elastic supply;
C. Goods with low elasticity of demand and low elasticity of supply; and
D. Goods with elastic demand and low elasticity of supply.

The goods contained within each group can be further subdivided into those which are 'inferior' goods (that is those upon which expenditure falls as income rises) and goods for which consumption rises with incomes.

The matrix has been partially completed and is only intended to illustrate the idea of a matrix of socially acknowledged need goods. In an ideal world (with the aid of computers) such matrices would be drawn up each year at budget (and new prices and incomes policy) times, and decisions on income distribution would be made in the light of this information. Each individual would appear once within the matrix and the sum of all individuals' needs would equal aggregate

TABLE 8.1

Goods proposed for a 'need' matrix of individually purchased goods and services

Goods: Individuals	Group A Goods n	Group B Goods o	Group C Goods r	Group D Goods s
a	$p_n q_n$	$p_o q_o$		
b	$p_n q_n$		$p_r q_r$	$p_s q_s$
c etc.				

NOTES: Group A goods — low demand elasticity but elastic supply.
 Group B goods — elastic demand and supply.
 Group C goods — low elasticity of demand and supply.
 Group D goods — elastic demand, low elasticity of supply.

Goods in each group:

In A there are n different types of goods and services, each with a different price. Example of goods in this category are: salt, bread in Britain, rice in China, burial services.

In B there are o different types of goods and services. Examples are household crockery, most clothing and furniture.

In C there are r different types of goods and servies. Examples are dwellings and gold wedding rings.

In D there are s different types of goods and services. Examples are cultural facilities such as provision of operas, paintings by famous artists and precious stones.

Individuals:

All individuals should appear in the matrix, but for convenience households instead of individuals may be the unit to which resource allocation is made.

socially acknowledged need. If such matrices were drawn up, two policy errors could be avoided. The first is the over-recognition of some individuals' needs and the under-recognition of the needs of others for whom no pressure lobby had been formed. The second error which would be avoided is the designation of a group of goods, socially acknowledged to be needed, so large that its cost exceeds the proportion of G.N.P. which society has agreed to spend on them. This proportion cannot be set in isolation from other socially desired expenditure such as investment expenditures, government current expenditure on publicly provided goods and services, the balance between national imports and exports and the political willingness of the population to pay taxes and reduce non-need consumption in order to increase the consumption of goods socially designated as need goods. Each of the above variable elements in the allocation of national resources will act as a constraint on the expansion of socially acknowledged need, and will frequently make it necessary to prune back need which has at an initial stage been entered into the 'need' matrix.

The pruning process might proceed by first re-examining each of the need goods to make sure that none have been inserted into the matrix without due regard for economy and social welfare. Group *B*, for example, may contain the 'need' for the services of a motor-car, and on second thoughts it might be regarded as better to specify a greater quantity of public transport and to omit private transport from the matrix.

The second pruning procedure would be an examination of the short- and long-term costs of supply of each need and the estimation of the costs of supplying various outputs. For the goods of groups *A* and *B*, where supply is elastic, we can expect to obtain an increased output of a given percentage for less than a similar percentage increase in price. It will therefore be relatively inexpensive (in terms of real and money resources used) to expand the output of these groups of goods. With groups *C* and *D*, where supply is inelastic, costs will rise by a higher proportion than the quantity supplied. It may be for this reason that even if the need goods in group *C* are generally acknowledged to be 'true' need goods, they may not be met or included in a 'need' matrix. When societies switch expenditure towards goods with a low elasticity of supply, unit costs of supply increase and pressure tends to develop for a moderation in the rate of increase in expenditure. This is most clearly seen in the housing field but also arises in medical care. The pressures which are exerted need not be purely political; in the development of a large-scale housing industry, for example, imports may rise in excess of exports; or the long investment period may mean that consumers feel pushed into a situation in which there is a promise of jam tomorrow, but insufficient bread for today. This tends to make for a revision of socially acknowledged needs lists and it perhaps explains why some 'needs' which seem somewhat peripheral to the concept of necessities are met, while others more central to the idea are only partially recognised.

In the above discussion it is hoped that need goods have been established as a sub-set of the greater demand set of goods and services, and that goods cannot sensibly be designated 'need' goods without some reference to the supply and demand functions which determine production and consumption. Need is all too often used carelessly to denote a collection of goods which are without price tags, and the concept becomes little more than a form of wishful thinking. When 'need' is totally divorced from the demand concept it seems only to express a 'want'; when it is separated from supply conditions, at best it expresses the hope that all goods so designated will have an infinitely elastic supply and at worst the idea that 'need' goods can be obtained for nothing.

In 'A Taxonomy of Social Need',[7] need for social services was subdivided by four definitions: 'normative', 'comparative', 'expressed' and 'felt'. In the socially acknowledged need matrix, the normative element appears through the insertion or exclusion of a good, but in the matrix the decision to insert or exclude a good depends upon the price of the good as well as the value judgement that (supply and demand conditions allowing) it would be a good thing if the commodity were consumed by the individual(s) to whom the good (or a sufficient income) is to be given. Comparative aspects of need are given dominance in the socially acknowledged need matrix because *all* relevant comparisons can be made before need goods are designated. Felt needs are those aspects of need which causes a good to be put forward for consideration; society may reject or accept felt needs according to the conditions of supply and demand. Expressed needs are the economists' effective demands in the matrix. Each good entered into the matrix is thought, by those who approve the collection of goods chosen for inclusion, to be demanded.

If incomes were so distributed that individuals had enough income to purchase all the goods and services 'needed', it must be supposed that in general they will buy the 'need' goods. However, there may not be a complete fit between what is defined by government to be needed and what is demanded, because each individual has his own priorities, and it would be perfectly proper in a free society for a consumer to reject a designated need good in favour of a non-need good. For this reason even if incomes were ideally distributed, a sample survey of household expenditure may uncover some households not purchasing 'need' goods.

Publicly provided Goods and Services

Much rather unnecessary mystery surrounds the need for goods and services which are publicly provided. Heavily value-laden statements on the 'need' for more and better public services, whether in the health, housing, education, social-security or personal social-service fields has led Williams to designate this area of study as 'needology'.[8] The metaphysics of the needology schools of thought are particularly clearly exposed in Townsend's passage in *The Fifth Social Service* where he appeals to a concept of exogeneous objectivity when he suggests that neither (*a*) the opinion of users or suppliers, nor (*b*) conventional social views offer a sufficient basis for planning social services.

> Social policy [he writes] would be viewed too much from within, psychologically and institutionally. Services would be judged too much in terms of objectives already defined than of those which have yet to be defined, too much in terms already recognised, subjectively and socially than of those which have still to be recognised. Standards and needs have to be judged also from an *external* standpoint. While ultimately it may be difficult to substantiate a true objectivity, nonetheless this goal is worth striving for.[9]

This passage contains two features with which issue may be taken. First, it explicitly rejects human choice in the selection of priorities in favour of some non-human agency of selection. It is as if there were principles of need, similar to physical laws such as gravity. Apart from the most basic need for nourishment there are no overriding physical or sociological laws which will predetermine the identification and selection of needs. The only general and not very helpful rule which might be laid down as a guide for needologists is that the political expression of a need is a function of people's expectations about government behaviour; this is in turn a function of experience.

The second and possibly more serious error contained in the passage quoted above is that it assumes that the supply of needs will be infinitely elastic and will therefore respond without price change to any increase in demand; but this is patently impossible. In the first section of this chapter, I identified need goods consumed by individuals as a sub-set of demand goods. Publicly supplied goods are also of course a sub-set of demand goods and services. The only significant difference between the two is that in the case of individually purchased goods the individual makes the choices; in the case of publicly provided goods the government or an institution or agency makes the decisions. When, for example, a government decides to build a lighthouse, a demand has been expressed for a lighthouse to be situated in a particular place and to perform an identified function. This decision differs in no important economic respect from the decision by an owner occupier to add a garage to his house. If one is recognised as a demand the other must be similarly recognised. However, in the case of government two problems arise; the first is that governments very seldom have a sufficient income of their own to meet all the demands made upon them and they must therefore impose taxes. There is a strong probability that there will be some opposition to any increase in taxation and some tendency for those who most benefit by government expenditure (net of tax payments) to support expenditure, while those most likely to suffer the tax burden (net of benefits) will oppose it. This conflict generates a great froth of political rhetoric, for and against each item of government expenditure; in these games of political power, needologists support their arguments for more or continued expenditure with what economists would label the 'taste' assumption that lies behind every demand function. The public are exhorted to change (reduce) their 'taste' for private consumption and to expand their taste for publicly provided goods and services.

Even if consumer taste is successfully altered and a large political majority agrees to raise taxes, reduce private consumption and expand government demand, supply conditions may be unfavourable, and as government demand increases scarce factors of production which are required for the new services may cause average unit costs of supply to rise. In the long run the whole economy will adjust to long-run political changes which introduce permanent changes in the relative strength of desire for (*a*) individually purchased and (*b*) publicly provided goods and services.

The division of goods into those which are individually purchased and those which are publicly provided is convenient for purposes of exposition; but they are not independent of each other. In many goods a straight substitution occurs from one to the other, as for example when public provision for nursery schools is made and the private use of child-minders declines. Interdependence also exists in the relationship between the reduction in individually controlled purchasing power which occurs when taxes are imposed and the increases in purchasing power which occur when governments distribute incomes through transfer payments and the payment of wages, rents and interest to the factors of production used by the government. Even when the government operates on a balanced budget, changes in the distribution of income which occur through government actions, such as increasing pensions or introducing rent rebates for lower-income householders, will increase the demand for more essential goods consumed by poorer people and decrease the demand by the better-off for less essential goods. This is one of the reasons why the price of food and other goods purchased by low-income families over the last few years has risen faster than the price of many manufactured goods which are normally purchased by families with above-average incomes.[10]

The interrelationship of one part of an economy with all other parts means that while society may express the will to move to a more desired distribution of national resources (if political agreement is reached about the desired distribution), little progress can be achieved in reaching the target distribution if supply and demand functions are ignored. If current issues are perceived solely in terms of social justice and economic constraints are regarded as unreal barriers erected by those who wish to hinder or prevent social reforms, changes may be introduced which will create distributions of resources which are as much or even more unwanted than the original distribution. This is seen particularly clearly when one feature of government policy generates unemployment and under-utilisation of capital equipment in some industries, which are then subsidised to avoid high levels of unemployment. The problems of decline in some industries will of course be greatly increased if at the same time other industries are inflating their costs by trying to meet demands for which suitable real resources are not currently available.

It is convenient to think of government demand in the form of a matrix in which the price and quantity of all goods and services supplied by governments to individual citizens is recorded. Conceptually this is the type of matrix which underlies the work of Nicholson,[11] but because he is more interested in the net tax/benefit position of different households, his conceptualisation contains figures for net gain or loss in money terms. This automatically nets out the supply and demand function and encourages the idea that, given the will, transfers of government expenditure could quite easily be made from less to more demanded goods. For rational decision-making (that is the selection of activities which will achieve preselected objectives) in the government sector it is necessary to have supply and demand models of each good or service provided, and the distribution of those goods to individuals. Only in this way can we avoid the trap of imagining that some government goods have an absolute priority and must be supplied at any cost. A topical example of the way in which a change of supply conditions can lead to a reduction in the quantity of a service demanded can be found in the immediate response of education authorities to the Houghton Report.[12] As soon as the Secretary of State for Education and Science accepted that report it was clear that 'economies' would be made in the use of teachers and that a great incentive had been created for the re-examination of staff/pupil ratios. As in the case of the individual consumer, government demand is a question of marginal adjustments to changing circumstances and in particular to changes in the costs of the factors of production. Since teachers have become relatively more expensive than other factors, we may now expect a shift in expenditure from education to, for example, housing in areas of relatively high unemployment.

In these two sections I have emphasised that 'need' can only be a useful concept if it is equated to a demand by governments or individuals for goods and services. So long as prices and quantities are omitted from estimations of 'need', the concept can have neither theoretical nor empirical value, and it properly belongs not to the social sciences but to the vocabulary of political rhetoric.

The Estimation of Demand for the Social Services

The rejection of demand theory by students of needology appears to stem from a profound suspicion of the market model of an economy. The virtue of demand theory is the cause of its rejection by those who are motivated by high ideals and a strong sense of professional commitment or compassionate altruism. How, they ask, can it be possible to count the cost when the provision of treatment for the sick, care of the aged or the creation of a justly egalitarian society is under discussion? The narrow materialistic view of economics as the pig-philosophy was thoroughly examined by Robbins in his famous *Essay on the Nature and Significance of Economic Science.*[13] Having explained that economics is a science concerned with that aspect of behaviour which arises from the scarcity of means to achieve given ends, he rejected the notion that economists were primarily concerned with a particularly low type of conduct. He gave an illustration of the way in which an economist would be able to analyse the changes which would occur in a community of sybarites which were reformed after a visit from a preacher with the oratorical powers of Savonarola. Robbins writes of this situation:

> Surely economic analysis is still applicable. There is no need to change the categories of explanation. All that has happened is that the demand schedules have changed. Some things have become relatively less scarce, others more so. The rent of vineyards falls. The rent of quarries for ecclesiastical masonry rises. That is all. The distribution of time between prayer and good works has its economic aspect equally with the distribution of time between orgies and slumber. The 'pig-philosophy' — to use Carlyle's contemptuous epithet — turns out to be all-embracing.

Instead of using the illustration of sybarites becoming ascetics, we might consider a population of capitalists becoming supporters of a communist or 'welfare state' society. All such socio-political changes will change demand and supply schedules as the demand for education, health care, housing facilities, a better environment, and so on increases. At the same time the demand for very large houses would decline as incomes and wealth were more evenly distributed, and an elitist demand for educational establishments would fall as more people accepted the social desirability of 'comprehensive' schooling.

However, it may be said that some method must be used to bring the wants of the people to the attention of decision-makers. Professionals or concerned groups of consumers acting as 'experts' might then be regarded as channels through which medical, educational and other 'needs' were sifted and drawn to the attention of decision-makers, who would then reject or accept some, or all, of the needs put forward and convert them into demand schedules. In this case the concept of need is being used (much as the nineteenth-century concept of 'utility' was used) as an ill-defined shadow lying behind the demand function. In the theoretical development of demand theory of the 1930s, utility was found to be an unnecessary encumbrance.[14] Need as a concept may have a similar history and gradually give way to the more precise and hence immensely more useful concept of demand.

This would not of course mean that much of the present work associated with studies of need would not continue; but the purpose of such studies would be much more clearly identified as an 'advertising' operation in which the objective was to change the attitudes of society to selected social problems so that instead of viewing certain individuals as, for example, delinquents, they were viewed as individuals in a market situation which had frustrated demands for adequate and securely held accommodation. Such studies would stress the association between poor housing conditions and delinquency *and* the ineffectualness of the individual's demand function in prevailing supply conditions. Another type of study might start from a value assumption such as the one that a civilised nation would provide access to adequate housing for all citizens, and would then concentrate analysis on those aspects of current demand and supply functions which were meeting or frustrating the fulfilment of that objective. Such studies would move from the current situation via analytical models to medium-term predictions of future supply and demand functions.

Conclusion

If needs are only goods and services without price tags, there is little that social scientists can do with the concept. When needs are defined with reference to prices for various quantities the concept becomes indistinguishable from demand. If, for reasons of tradition and familiarity with old terms, the concept of need is retained in studies of social administration, need should be seen as a sub-set of goods and services for which there is a demand.

The withdrawal of the term 'need' does not in any way imply a reduction in regard for the intangible human qualities of compassion and altruism which have always played so dominant a role in the writings of social administrators. It means only that we openly acknowledge that the achievement of a just and compassionate society requires alterations in demand functions, not the mere accumulation of statistical data about the availability or non-availability of a randomly selected group of goods and/or services, which are more or less ardently wanted by an arbitrarily chosen group of potential consumers.

9 Needs and Outputs

Bleddyn Davies

The importance of developing valid measures of needs and outputs is undisputed. Without such measures, the social-policy analyst can make only a limited contribution to the case for spending on social policy and can make fewer suggestions for using resources effectively. The crudity of the measurement hampers the development of studies of efficiency in service provision. It makes it impossible to estimate what benefits are produced from different combinations of resources. It makes the central-government control of local authorities more arbitrary, and prevents social-service agencies from monitoring their own success. It makes some simple questions difficult to answer, and makes other questions impossible to answer at all. It allows the political process to tolerate bad policy on major issues. Theories of territorial justice must remain primitive until needs and outputs are properly measured.

At root, the reasons why most needs and outputs remain either unmeasured or inadequately measured are as much that insufficient time and effort have been devoted to the analysis of the concepts and their measurement as that the measurement is often difficult, sometimes dangerous, and usually expensive. It will not be possible to argue convincingly for more and better measurement until sceptics can be convinced that the concepts are clear, that conditions in which measurement is practical and valid have been specified, and that these conditions are probably satisfied in a broad range of cases. This chapter is about the concepts and these conditions.

The first section discusses the measurement of output in the social services. The second section discusses the logic of the need judgement, and the measurement of need in 'need studies' and the compilation of need indicators. The third section discusses the conditions in which output and need can be measured and criteria by which evidence for such measurement should be evaluated.

Outputs

The concept 'needs' is closely related to the concept 'output' A statement about needs is one about 'priorities', about objectives or benefit streams and their relative importance. The concept of output concerns the achievement of objectives. It is the sum of the number of physical units produced, each unit being weighted by a valuation of it.[1] Clearly the values should be compatible with judgements about objectives and priorities. Therefore it is not surprising that it is those studies which have attempted to measure output (though sometimes calling it by other names such as 'standards') which are often those which contribute to ideas about needs as a concept and to the development of instruments to measure needs. Because it is they who have developed the concept 'output' and ways of measuring it, the economists have contributed greatly to the development of 'need' as a concept. It therefore makes good sense to discuss the measurement of output before dealing more specifically with need.

The measurement of output has proved difficult in all services, not only social services.[2] Indeed there are many areas for which there is little agreement about the nature of output. However, progress has been made as economists have become more interested in evaluating the effectiveness of public services, particularly in the measurement of the outputs of health and education.

The data base of output indicators

It is useful to distinguish three types of measure: indicators based on *levels of provision, throughput*, and the effects of services on the *attainment of their objectives.*

Level of provision How indicators based thus should be interpreted depends on the level of aggregation of the analysis. The same indicator can be tantamount to an indicator of input or physical output, depending on the implicit model underlying its use. But even if it approximates to output, it takes no account of variations in the differing contributions to welfare of each physical unit of output. Such contributions can be unequal either because of their intrinsic heterogeneity (because they are of uneven quality for instance) or because homogeneous units have different effects on the recipient (perhaps because the more the recipient obtains, the less he values an additional unit). One has therefore to evaluate the appropriateness of the use of such indicators in each context — to ask whether the argument is such that the provision is an 'input' or 'output', whether the units of provision are intrinsically homogeneous, whether they all contribute much the same to 'welfare'. Like some nursing dependency scales, indicators may be quite elaborate in form but be input indicators used for measuring output, and so implicitly deny the relevance of substituting inputs for one another in the production of what are the true outputs. Since such substitutability almost always exists, their value may be very limited. Other indicators which use input resources as their unit of measurement may be based on the outcome of a process of optimising the use of inputs, and so are a direct transformation (and therefore the equivalent) of an indicator that measures units of outputs. They do not make the usually untenable assumption that inputs are not substitutable; but if their method of operationalisation depends on the existence of a process of optimisation, whether optimisation really takes place must be investigated.

Throughput A second type of measure is based on work-load or throughput — number of visits, patients, cases or residents. Feldstein's classic study of the relations between inputs and outputs in British hospitals was based on an indicator of throughputs,[3] the number of cases in each of several broad disease categories, as has most subsequent analysis of hospitals. The mix of inputs is not part of the definition of the throughput indicator, so that their use in evaluation does not prejudge the issue of what is optimal. But such indicators assume each of the units of output in each category to be homogeneous in its quality. Moreover, they take no account of the differences in the contribution that each of the units makes to social welfare. When forming an indicator of the output of a manufacturing industry, the economist weights units of outputs by the price these units fetch in the market, on the grounds that relative prices reflect social values. In services not sold in the market, it is necessary to find some analogous method of doing this if a true output indicator is to be obtained. Feldstein took as the valuation the estimated marginal cost of different kinds of case, assuming that the system allocated its resources optimally between types of case so that the valuations of the marginal case of each type was similar.[4] Of course he was perfectly aware that such an assumption was far from valid. Indeed he had published several papers that showed this to be so. He made the assumption because he could not find a better way of handling the problem.

Our inability to find such superior methods – often because of which data are collected by professional bodies and the government – forces us to assume some rather unreal and very undesirable worlds. For instance, the D.H.S.S. *Census of Residential Homes* for 1970 is a unique collection of data on inputs into residential care. It lacks data which measure the main outputs of residential care as social-service policy defines them, even the effects on dimensions of the self-perceived quality of life of the residents themselves. Suppose we treat the number of residents in each dependency category as output – that is, make the type of assumption so often made in the literature on hospitals or education systems. The only quality indicators in the collection are for inputs. The production relations models then imply a world in which the objective of residential homes is just to provide the basic minimum standard of care that the central government's social-work service sets out to enforce. The models would attribute any input above the minimum required to accomplish this to the inefficiency of social-service departments, however effectively such additional inputs added to relevant aspects of residents' quality of life. The model discounts some of the main objectives of social-welfare provision. Yet they are worth computing. For instance, they show what are the minimum combinations of resources used to cope with any mix of residents, and indicate the substitutability of inputs in doing so.

If used with discretion and a real understanding of the context, and if hedged around with caveats so that their results could not be misinterpreted by the reader, they form a way of answering some of the useful questions from the only data available; and they clarify issues which must be faced before the expensive task of collecting new and better data can be undertaken. Most of the work using indicators of output measure based on throughput has only a limited usefulness, but is undertaken because no better alternative is feasible. What is important in assessing whether or not to accept the argument based on them is that by implying what are the objectives of the service, indicators also imply a normative model of the role of the service in its broader social context.

Benefits from services Not surprisingly, the development of more content-valid and reliable output indicators is one of the most important objectives of research, not only by economists but also by psychologists, sociologists and others. Reliability implies reproducibility. Content validity implies that an indicator measures what is intended, and most of what is intended. Content validity and reliability are matters of degree. The achievement has been modest, but sufficient to raise hopes. Frequently used are the standardised tests developed by psychologists for a variety of purposes in health and education. The comparison of test scores before and after a quantity of service is received is the basis for assessing the output of that service. Some of the economists of education who have done so with most success are Bowles,[5] Hanushek,[6] Levin[7] and Michelson.[8] It has been applied to estimate the relationships between resource inputs and university courses. For instance, Attiyeh *et al.* produced the entirely credible result that students who spent twelve hours studying a programmed learning text learned practically as much economics as did students in seven weeks of a conventional course of elementary lectures.[9] Similar to the use of test scores in education has been the use in the evaluation of health services of tests of mortality, morbidity, physical fitness (as by Mushkin)[10] and functional incapacity (like that developed by Garrad and Bennett).[11] For some purposes even crude mortality indices are useful. For instance, the prenatal mortality rate is held to be useful for limited evaluations of the maternity service, though it certainly does not cover all the important welfare consequences of alternative provisions. Again, *Towards a Social Report* (U.S. Department of Health, Education and Welfare, 1969) included an indicator of life expectancy free of death-bed disability as a general health indicator. The O.E.C.D. proposes a similar indicator for each of the member countries, as well as life expectancies at various ages. The best yield scales are not far short of the ratio level of measurement, so that the improvement in performance of such indicators due to one combination of inputs rather than another could be assessed by comparing the number of units difference in the score attained, and benefit—cost ratios could in principle be computed using them. The indicators have in common the assumption that there is a simple relationship between the change in test score and the social value of the output. This is also the case for many other indicators of physical output, like a weighted count of publications as an indicator of the research output of universities.[12] The same applies to such crude indicators as the probability of the survival of placements for evaluating success of foster care,[13] or the probability of leaving as a result of a further offence or absconding as an indicator of the failure of probation hostels.[14]

Many economists have tried to do better by making more explicit the basis of the social valuations that weight physical units in their indicators. Both health and education economists have used weighting systems based on life-time earnings. Part of the intellectual rationale for this are the judgements that the major influence on the private demand for education and health is its expected contribution to life-time incomes, and that investment in health and education yields returns to society in higher growth, and that the contributions of individuals to this also are broadly reflected in their life-time earnings. Allowance is often made for divergence of social from private benefits. Clearly the rationale is rather more elaborate than this, and is slightly different for health and education. Nevertheless, it remains a sweeping judgement, and one with value assumptions that not everyone would accept. The literature using it is voluminous.

One example of its use in health was by Weisbrod.[15] An example of its use in education is Verry and Davies,[16] who based their indicator of the teaching outputs of British universities on estimated expected life-time earnings. Implicit in the procedure was the assumption that consumption benefits of the process (and external social benefits not reflected in the individual's earnings) were much the same among the units of analysis. Since Verry and Davies were implicitly comparing institutions within subject groups, this seemed reasonable — although it could be argued that studying at Sussex might confer greater consumption benefits than studying somewhere less attractive. But it would seem less reasonable to apply the same assumption to estimating the benefit-cost ratios of taking a Ph.D. in Arts at Sussex and an H.N.C. in Drainage working in a lonely garret and attending evening classes in a draughty college in Greater Sleetandsmog. (Of British cost-benefit studies, possibly Morris and Ziderman[17] make the most far-flung comparisons.) Weighting by life-time earnings is based directly on the professional judgement of economists about what are the most important welfare consequences of receiving the service.

Who defines 'output'?

Academic or professional The adoption of expected life-time earnings as the basis of the output indicator is based on the academic's own judgement about what are the most important welfare consequences. It is this judgement which is the source of the weights attached to physical units of output in the process of aggregation into an over-all indicator. The weighting systems for many such output indicators are based thus. The professional or academic. chooses the. range of consequences to be treated as outputs, and specifies the criteria which settle their relative importance in the indicator. In such indicators he may sometimes compromise by including client perceptions about the consequences that he has defined as salient, but the judgement is ultimately his. In most attempts to measure the outputs of the social services, the source of the weighting judgements has been the academic, though sometimes the academic attempts (with more or less success) to base the judgement on the assumptions of the relevant profession.

Recipients or citizens There are two ways by which the weighting might be based directly on the preferences of recipients. First, preferences can be ascertained directly from clients and potential clients, or citizens in general. One is likely to obtain data of very limited value unless one forces respondents to consider limitations on what can be achieved. For instance, in answers to separate questions in the same survey, respondents will both choose larger quantities of output (perhaps stating a preference for more spending on services) and choose lower costs (perhaps stating a preference for lower taxes). It is necessary that preferences be elicited in a way that forces the respondent to simultaneously consider costs and benefits. Moreover, it is highly desirable to be able to measure the preferences at a high level of measurement — the Likert scale may indicate the relative intensity of the preferences of an individual, but it is not claimed that it yields interval scales. Techniques of asking about preferences in surveys have been developed which attain both objectives.

Clark describes the use of budget pies in conjunction with tables that show the rates of conversion of money into performance.[18] Respondents are asked to divide a circle into three or four sections to correspond to their budget preferences in the light of the conversion tables. An interesting example of the use of the technique was that used by Ostrom.[19] Slightly more elaborate is the use of pegs (to represent money) with a peg-board laid out so as to present alternatives. Respondents are asked to allocate a budget of pegs or chips between up to fifteen services. The technique has been substantially developed since the pioneering work of Chapin and Weiss.[20] Tests suggest that the methods yield sensible results.[21] In the United Kingdom the technique has been applied particularly to evaluating community preferences in environmental and transport planning, and fixing of rent levels of public housing,[22] but clearly they are two that must be used with even more discretion than types of question that appear to yield less information. In particular, some uses of Social and Community Planning Research priority evaluators depend greatly upon pictures (in conjunction with the prices of attaining that degree of environmental quality that the pictures are supposed to indicate). It is not obvious that people read the same environmental conditions into a picture. For instance, Ostrom found that respondents who lived in the same street vary substantially in the light levels they set for a box when asked to indicate the light levels of their street. What meaning can be attached to respondents' preferences when they cannot even remember the most basic features of a situation with which one would expect them to be thoroughly familiar?[23]

The second way of inferring preferences is to look at how citizens had modified their behaviour to suit their circumstances — *revealed preference*. The whole generation of post-war economists has been much less willing than most to base their judgements on people's statements about their preferences. They judged such statements to be a less adequate indication of true preferences than how people actually behave in the variety of circumstances they faced. This stance is by no means unique to economists. Among sociologists, Homans, and among psychologists, Watson and Skinner, took much the same view. Most cost—benefit analyses therefore base their evaluation on data which indicate what costs people are prepared to incur to derive welfare, just as goods are valued by what prices people are prepared to pay to obtain them. There are areas in recreation planning — for which credible attempts have been made to derive valuations[24] — but their application to hypothetical circumstances can be as, or more, unreal than deriving weights by direct questioning. Economists now seem more willing to recognise that the careful collection of data on preferences by direct questioning can be of use in evaluating potential benefits. Many recognise that their position has been extreme. The change in view is exemplified by Sen's anecdote about two behaviouralists meeting at a conference. One said to the other 'I see you are very well. How am I?'[25] Oscar Wilde's character who knew the price of everything but the value of nothing might well have been an economist of the revealed-preference school.

A wide variety of techniques has therefore been developed for providing weights for output indicators — indeed a much wider variety than space allows us to mention here. Although the expense of collecting data for the measurement of output often virtually predetermines the choice of some bases for indicators rather than others if evidence is to be handled at all in the short run, in principle there is a wide enough repertoire of measurement techniques from which a choice can be made. What is important is to develop good criteria for making the choice. The design of the output indicator not only implies what the objectives of the service are, as we saw from the choice of indicators for residential homes; they imply also a normative theory of the organisation in a political context. This is a set of postulates about who should make judgements about what consequences of the services are important, as well as their relative importance. This is an issue to which we shall return.

Need

The basic theory of the need judgement

The reason why the measurement of output and the measurement of need is so related is that need is essentially a cost-benefit judgement, while output is in principle the stream of net benefits – the same stream of benefits taken into account in the cost-benefit judgement. It is this failure to keep constantly in mind the cost-benefit nature of the need judgement that has made economists suspect the concept. As Feldstein argued,[26] professionals so often talk about 'meeting needs' when it would make for a clearer analysis if they talked about 'optimising the use of resources'. As he pointed out, professionals have a tendency to identify needs with current professional practice, quoting with approval Brian Abel Smith, who wrote that 'It is only a matter of time before traditional medical care becomes regarded as "good" medical care.'

Any need judgement is based on acceptance of relative valuations of the welfare consequences of alternative interventions in relation to their costs. This perception is most elegantly argued by Culyer, Lavers and Williams.[27] An account of their argument will clarify the concept. They postulate a world with only two commodities, health and education. In this world, decision-makers know the outcomes for indicators of the state of health and of the state of education of any allocation of the available resources. It is the job of a political body, whom they designate 'the Minister', to assess what alternative combinations of states of health and education would produce equivalent over-all welfare. Their concept of need is a measure of the number of units change in the state of health that the Minister would be willing to allow in order to obtain a unit increase in the indicator of the general state of education. This is an 'opportunity-cost' perception. It reflects both the cost of more health in terms of less education and the relative values attached to different states of health and education. In their two-commodity world, the value of the state of health forgone is the marginal social cost of the improvement in the state of education. They agree that this can be described either in terms of the other desired output forgone, or in terms of the value of inputs required to increase the state of health.

Their argument is illustrated in Figure 9.1, which is taken from their original exposition. The diagram is analogous to the indifference-curve diagrams of economic textbooks. The two axes measure states of education and health. One set of curves is *convex* to the origin, like indifference curves, and expresses social judgements about the welfare equivalences of different combinations of states of education and health. Their convexity reflects the not unreasonable assumption that the more health a community enjoys, the less it will value increase in health in relation to other things. The welfare obtained from a curve further from the origin is greater than that from one nearer the origin. For instance, given the state of health, a curve marked W_3 yields a higher state of education than that marked W_2. It is the slopes of these

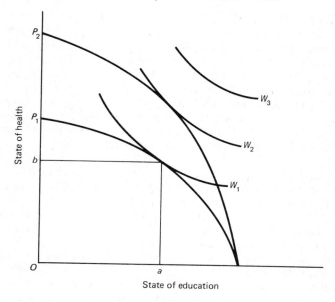

FIG. 9.1

The optimal choice of states of health and education with different technologies

curves that measure the loss in the state of education gained by the increase in the state of health, and so the 'intensity' of need for health in relation to education. The curves that are *concave* to the origin show what combinations of states of health and education it is judged could be achieved with various allocations of resources between the two services.

Let us suppose the combinations that can be produced are as shown by a concave curve P_1. Under such conditions, the highest level of welfare achievable is that shown by the curve W_1; and this is just achievable if the state of education Oa and state of health Ob are produced. It is sometimes useful to think of 'need' as a welfare shortfall — a gap between the actual level of welfare and one below which intervention is appropriate. This would be measured on the diagram by the shortfall in one of the dimensions of the over-all states of welfare compared with the level of that dimension of welfare defined by the optimum. The choice of an optimum defines the margins at which a need for intervention is argued to exist, and which those assessing individual cases should apply. Since the total quantity of resources that are made available is the outcome of the assessment of the costs and benefits available from interventions in these compared with other sectors, this optimum provides the appropriate reference point for judging the extent of welfare shortfall. If a case presented levels of welfare which exceeded the combinations shown on the iso-welfare curve, there would be no argument for the allocation of resources to helping them.

Suppose that the Department of Education and Science had set an arbitrary standard in excess of *Oa* to be achieved for education. Its achievement could only be at the expense of a lower state of health, and a lower state of welfare over all. In practice the standard would have been defined in input or performance terms, but this makes no difference in principle. It is clear from the model that such targets should only be set as a result of a careful process of choice between the alternatives. Feldstein and Culyer *et al.* quote from the social-policy literature to show that those whose focus is one set of services very often ignore the opportunity costs for others. In this the economists see themselves as fighting the same tendency to develop tunnel-vision as some organisation theorists. What the economist calls 'sub-optimisation' and Etzioni calls 'goal displacement'[28] can mean substantially the same thing.

Of course such rhetoric may well do an injustice to the common sense and political *nous* of those whom it quotes and pillories. Often the arbitrary standards that the economists are criticising have the merit of seeming both sufficiently concrete and modest in their implications for the welfare of recipients to have a widespread political appeal, and therefore to be used as a criterion of success. The main use that is made of them is to strengthen bids for resources and help to set identifiable goals for organisations. But unquestionably the risk of tunnel-vision is real, and there is a clear advantage in having an explicit concept of need that is part of a normative model of resource allocation based on optimising behaviour.

If circumstances change, the targets must be revised. This could occur because of changes in priorities. The government may fall, and be replaced by one which values health and education differently. In this case, the slopes of the curves would change, and so should the allocation of resources. Alternatively, there might be a change in the levels of health and education that can be jointly produced from the resources available. Such changes may occur for various reasons. Technical progress in health-care methods may make it possible to produce a higher state of health from any allocation of resources. The new production possibilities may be those described by the concave curve P_2. Again the government should reallocate its resources and reset its standards. Since the total amount of resources available is unchanged, it can now achieve better states of both education and health. (This follows from the convexity of the iso-welfare curves and the concavity of the production-possibility curves.) The best allocation of resources would result in a greater improvement in the state of health than in the state of education, since health is now cheaper in relation to education than before.

The same argument would apply if P_1 and P_2 referred to two countries. If it were cheaper to produce health in one region than in the other, if it cost the same to produce education in both, and if the judgements about equivalent welfares were similar, the country in which health was cheaper would achieve a higher state of health if resources were properly allocated. Other things being equal, the imposition of a similar health standard on both regions might lead to the achievement of a lower state of welfare in one or both countries than if standards were tailored to the relative costs of producing the two states in each country. Such a situation may arise not just because there might be impenetrable mountain ranges between the two countries across which knowledge about the new technology could not travel; they might equally arise because of variations in relative prices between the two countries. This implies an important question for the theory of territorial justice: states of welfare at what level of generality should be equalised between areas? It is valid to substitute health for education to take advantage of differences between areas in relative costs of producing them if it is a more general concept of welfare that is judged most important for territorial justice. If territorial justice in health itself is sought, one can substitute only at a lower level of generality. If territorial justice is separately sought for each of a number of dimensions of quality of life for each broad client group, much narrower opportunities exist for substitution to take advantage of variations in relative prices between areas.

The argument has so far postulated a political body controlling the allocation of national resources. A more realistic case would be a political body allocating resources between public and private spending and between sectors of public expenditure. However, in this case it must be emphasised that the criteria are over-all social costs and benefits not just the costs and benefits to the agencies involved. Moreover, governments can control resources other than their own; public expenditure is not the only method of social intervention. A government might achieve its ends by legislation and other means. Majone uses an almost identical model to discuss the control of environmental pollution by means of direct regulation, the imposition of efficient standards and the provision of incentives by means of effluent charges.[29]

The ideas of this section can be summed up in a few sentences. First, the need judgement is essentially a cost—benefit one. For this reason it should be sensitive to those features of the context which reflect changes in cost and benefit streams. If such judgements are to be made accurately, understanding is required about: (i) the relationships between inputs and outputs – the consequences for welfare of alternative allocations of physical resources – and the relative prices of these resources; and (ii) a legitimate basis for weighting the relative importance of the welfare consequences of interventions. Such understanding is, of necessity, quantitative. This understanding is quite compatible with probabilistic knowledge, but the probabilities must be sufficiently high for reasonable predictions to be made. Changes in production relations in the relative prices of resources or the relative weightings attached to different welfare streams could alter the optimal need judgement. This need judgement can either be expressed as an estimate of the benefit forgone in the use of resources in one way rather than others; or (since precisely the same information is required and is the outcome of precisely the same model of decision) it can be measured as the quantity of resources implicitly allocated by the judgement.

Need studies and need indicators

Need studies Although the cost–benefit nature of the need judgement has long been recognised, need studies conducted in the social services rarely take into account a wide-enough range of factors necessary for a sound cost–benefit judgement. This is true of such studies in housing, the personal social services, education and other policy areas. The studies of needs for the elderly and chronic sick rarely probe the alternative streams of welfare consequences that follow from the application of different services. For instance, few of them investigate the consequences for shortfalls in subjective well-being of receiving different packages of services. Indeed, they assume that there is no choice to be made between alternative ways of achieving a desired set of welfare consequences. They have therefore contributed little to an understanding of the 'technology' of the social services as systems of substitutes and complements, the relationships between services as inputs and different kinds of outputs. By not doing so they contribute far less to our knowledge than is required to apply to the context the logic of resource allocation; since without this understanding the central-government department or the social-service manager at the local level cannot select the best combination of services to suit local circumstances.

Circumstances relevant to the selection vary greatly. The surveys implicitly assume that they do not. For instance, they assume that the relative costs of providing additional units of each service vary in the same proportion in all areas. This is not the case. The relative costs of providing bricks and mortar and key professional manpower in an overspill housing estate (Kirkby for example) and in an outer London suburb or Brighton are entirely different. Again, the costs of making unanticipated adjustments to the supply of different services differ greatly between areas. Social-service departments should not be aiming to provide a uniform pattern of services, even when they are faced with uniform patterns of needs. But the patterns of needs are not uniform – the populations of different areas have quite different characteristics salient to need judgements; not only do they differ with respect to their personal characteristics and contexts, that are important in determining the contribution of any input of services to their welfare, but also the characteristics of their social settings differ greatly. The social networks to which they belong, and the social structure of the locality in which these networks are placed, so vary as to present quite different pay-offs to different forms of intervention. Cultural differences are important; for instance, the benefit of receiving a free school meal to a child and his family is affected by much else than the family's assessed net income which (virtually) alone forms the criterion of eligibility or need. There is substantial variation between areas in the proportions of families earning less than various levels of assessed income who also have such characteristics as they feel poor in relation to various reference groups; that they have special features (like lacking a mother or father) that causes them to have a lower level of material well-being than their income suggests; or that they appear to be sensitive to various forms of stigma associated with receiving the service. The benefits to be derived by fixing any one eligibility level of net income therefore differs between areas.[30]

Again the need study typically neglects the relation of the social-services system to the broader context of priorities in public intervention and relation between public and private resource allocation. The cost–benefit ratios of social-welfare intervention in relation to other uses of resources vary between areas, so that the total amount of resources which should be allocated to social welfare varies. Therefore the studies fail to take into account yet another essential feature of the need judgement. Most of the need studies can relate only to a Utopia with the odd characteristics that there is no apparent scarcity of resources, but there are nevertheless clearly bounded expectations and ideas about what welfares and 'diswelfares' are intolerable. In the context of a cost-benefit judgement, clearly bounded assumptions of this kind can be made only with knowledge about the total quantity of resources available.

Therefore the body of research into need does not incorporate important features of the theory of the need judgement. Indeed, this body of literature is not firmly rooted in any body of logical analysis about the principles for allocating resources. Valuable as it has been in the political and administrative process, the absence of a clear intellectual basis has left us bereft of the evidence we need — despite the expenditures of large sums of money on the collection and analysis of data.

Need indicators Much the same applies to the development and use of need indicators. Those who have designed need indicators have neglected the implicit cost-benefit nature of the need judgement as much as those who have designed the need studies. They have neglected that the need judgement is almost always about the allocation of resources — albeit sometimes resource allocation by indirect means, such as the regulation of others. The designers have therefore failed to recognise that one criterion of a good need indicator is that it should clearly reflect a judgement about the allocation of resources arrived at after considering the evidence. Moreover, the way the need indicators are used often betrays a failure to deal with one essential aspect of the context; that there is substitutability between resources, so that in different circumstances of costs and needs, different combinations of service provisions are appropriate. The degree to which the use of indicators has shown a sensitivity to the substitutability of services has been crucial to the quality of the policy argument. Indeed, the scholarly acumen of many of those who use need indicators has been less than those who have developed need studies. A weakness of the former has been that applied sociology has not been enlightened by applied economics; it has been social-policy analysis hopping heroically forward on one leg. In the latter, the work has been illuminated by neither, and the analysis has lacked any obvious means of forward locomotion.

The definition of the need indicator must be compatible with a concept of the need judgement. In the last section, we showed that the need judgement could be measured either as the quantity of one form of output that would be sacrificed in order to obtain a unit of another (when the relevant cost and benefit streams had been considered), or as the quantity of resources that would be allocated to produce the pattern of outputs implicit in that judgement. If the need judgement is the estimated amount of resources judged to be appropriate to allocate to a potential recipient with certain need-related characteristics in the specified circumstances, a need indicator is an estimate of the amount of resources appropriate to some (defined) population. It is the sum of the resources judged to be appropriate for each individual in that population. If v_i is the value of the resources judged appropriate for person i, and n_i is the number of client units similar to person i with respect to need-related characteristics, the need indicator can be defined as $\Sigma_i(n_i v_i)$.

Need indicators have so far only been used to compare the needs of populations of territorial areas for a service or system of services; this is an arbitrary limitation. It merely reflects their origin in the study of territorial justice.[31] It is useful to have need indicators for all those circumstances in which one would be able to compare need judgements. One should be able to use indicators to compare the need of the populations of areas for one or a system of services. One should also be able to use indicators to compare different client groups within the same area, or different client groups in different areas. Similarly, one should be able to use them to compare the needs of populations for different services. The definition of the need indicator that we have just presented is a total population weighted by the resources judged appropriate to each of its members. One can sum over whatever population is appropriate to the problem in hand. The formula allows summation to be carried out over quite different populations. The conventional type of need indicator is therefore only one case of a general form. The concept of need indicator we are here advocating is as general as the concept of need itself. Most important, it is firmly rooted in the theory of the need judgement.

This is a very different concept of the need indicator from those derived from social-malaise studies, indeed, its intellectual origin is quite different. It is significant that perhaps the most impressive of the pioneering studies in this country that developed the indicator of social malaise was undertaken by a town-planning department.[32] Its intellectual origin lies in the sociology of the city, the social-area analysis of Burgess and the Chicago School.[33] The social-malaise study is based on theories about the determination of the characteristics of areas within the city, and latterly on theories about the determinants of deprivation in 'markets' of crucial life chances.[34] The emphasis of the social-malaise study is more on the classification of areas than on the derivation of indicators. It is not based on a normative theory of intervention. It is therefore only loosely related to prescriptive theories about the allocation of resources. In contrast, a need indicator of the type described by our formula is based very explicitly on such normative theories — in fact it is based on entire ideologies, such as that which underlies the operation of the personal social services as systems of substitutes and complements in the meeting of needs.[35] The nature and level of generality of the two types of indicator make them useful for quite different purposes.

Need studies and need indicators: an overview The literature is considerable.[36] Stephen Hatch and Roger Sherrott[37] and John

Edwards[38] draw attention to important dangers — albeit dangers that were discussed in the first study to (explicitly) use need indicators. However, much of it so accepts the conventions of the need studies as to reflect in full their lack of salience to those aspects of the theory of the need judgement that most clearly reflect its cost—benefit nature.

This is true of Bradshaw's interesting taxonomy.[39] What makes the taxonomy and Bradshaw's discussion of it of interest is not that it presents a theory of the need judgement, the need indicator, or the need study, but that it touches on the ways in which the need studies and indicators fail to present data which is the outcome of an appropriate optimisation process. He also advocates pluralism in the sources of judgements. For instance, he proposes that the analyst may be more confident if he bases his decision not on one but on a number of sources of data for judgement, although none of the sources reflecting the outcome of an optimisation process — a proposition whose validity we shall not discuss here. Among other things, Bradshaw discusses the inappropriateness of some of the sources of value judgements implicit in need research, the inescapability of making judgements about the cultural influences on people's expectations about the quality of their lives, and other factors important to a 'theory of demand' for services.

Bradshaw is right to place his discussion in a broad context — to imply that a theory of need implies a model of optimisation, and so argues about the political, organisational, and intellectual bases for judgements. The exploration of the bases of judgements in the political, organisational and intellectual characteristics of contexts is essential; indeed, it has hardly yet begun. Such a discussion is enormously demanding, and has not been systematically attempted. It takes us into difficult territories of a large number of subjects. If it requires a disciplinary biped to develop a theory of need thus far, it would require an unusually athletic and well-co-ordinated centipede to develop it fully. The following section adopts an amoebic approach.

Needs, Outputs and Optimisation

The central paradox of this field of intellectual endeavour is that in order to provide a basis for estimating needs or outputs, it is necessary to have evidence of what judgements would be made in conditions in which actors optimised. Yet the study of needs and outputs would be of most value when behaviour falls far short of optimisation. In this (and the next) section, we explore the conditions required of evidence thrown up by the political processes and organised interventions themselves for it to be the basis of the measurement of needs and outputs.

Estimation of individual preferences

Abstracting for a moment from the issue of whose judgements we are discussing, we need a body of techniques which makes it possible to describe how much of one output a judge is prepared to sacrifice in order to gain an additional unit of another. In other words, we need to be able to plot the iso-welfare curves over the relevant range. It is insufficient that we are able to describe the outcomes of one judgement. If they are to be of much use, it is necessary that these judgements should be 'reliable' in the technical sense — that repeated measurements made under the same conditions will give the same result. This requires that we develop a theory of measurement for that type of output, a theory that explains unr⸱liability in that context and shows how it might be avoided. One should not be pessimistic about the chances of achieving a satisfactory degree of reliability. An example that is interesting because one would have anticipated serious problems of reliability is the measurement of dimensions of psychological well-being among the aged. For instance, the Life Satisfaction Index developed by Neugarten *et al.* with five dimensions — zest for life as opposed to apathy, resolution and fortitude, congruence between desired and achieved goals, positive self-concept and mood tone — has proved remarkably reliable.[40] Of 855 paired judgements 94 per cent showed exact agreement or near-agreement within one step of the scale. Again the scale seemed to satisfy the criterion of validity. A comparison of the ratings by the interviewers with those of clinical psychologists yielded a correlation of +0·64. Shorter versions of these scales likewise achieve an apparently impressive degree of validity. This scale has been extensively used and further developed, particularly by Adams.[41] He showed the scale to work for old people from communities different from the urban and rural areas for which it was originally developed. Bigot later used basically the same scale on a British sample.[42] Such scaling techniques have been further developed by (among others) the authors of the Life Satisfaction Index, yielding scales with a considerable inter-judge reliability. This area illustrates the development of a theory of measurement in only one policy area; examples can be multiplied. That we require a body of techniques which allow us to describe the rating of outcomes validly is not the most restrictive of conditions, even when outcomes are of different levels of probability.[43]

The second question is whether there is sufficiently widespread agreement about what are the principal 'outputs' and what are the crucial dimensions of 'need' or welfare shortfall. Some would argue as a matter of empirical fact that there is rarely agreement about what constitutes outputs. For instance, Glennerster writes:

the objectives of social policy in general and in particular are in dispute. The literature in social policy is largely concerned with disagreements about the appropriate boundaries and rationale of social intervention. It is the very stuff of political debate. Nor can it be argued that disputes only occur about marginal changes . . . social services are typically concerned with areas where either the final objectives are in dispute or where there is disagreement on what weight to attach to the several outcomes. Where agreement does exist, it usually focusses on means, not ends. The recent proposal to introduce universal part-time pre-school education is a case in point. It was supported by those who hoped that it would help to break a cycle of multiple deprivation, and by others who believed that this was a profoundly mistaken belief. It was supported by those who wished to see more mothers go out to work, and by those who thought that such an outcome would be socially damaging. It was supported by those who hoped for a more equal society, and by those to whom this was an anathema. It was supported by parents who wanted social benefits for their children, and by those who wanted them to learn to read earlier and do better academically. This is typical of most extensions in social welfare. Nor is it the case that in an *established* social service the 'providers' — social workers, local housing officials or teachers — are agreed about their objectives.[44]

It would be foolhardy to claim that there are only rarely circumstances in which most of those involved would broadly agree on what are the most important consequences of policy interventions. Yet it would seem to overstate the case to assert that there are few sectors of policy in which there would be considerable agreement about what major consequences of interventions should be taken into account in assessing the success of the policy. In Glennerster's example, most of those who believed that it was profoundly mistaken to think that part-time pre-school education would break a cycle of multiple deprivation would nevertheless consider this to be an outcome important enough to be worth recording. Again, perhaps both those who wished to see more mothers go out to work and those who thought that this would be socially damaging would see that consequence to be of salience to the assessment — indeed it is arguable that differences in judgement about the *consequences* of mothers working may well underly much of the disagreement about this. Again the egalitarians and anti-egalitarians would both be interested in the consequences of the policy for social equality, and parents would be interested to know about the social benefits for their children and know whether they read earlier. Thus, even in the notoriously complex field of the evaluation of educational provision, and for a form of intervention for which there did not yet exist an on-going operating ideology which reconciled the interests of those who influence the field, it is clear that there would at least be agreement about what would be some of the important consequences. In more and better established sectors of intervention, there would probably be more agreement about what would be the most important consequences. Of course we are not here arguing that there would be consensus about the *weights* that we can put on different outcomes; that is a different matter. We are certainly not arguing that the *values* that influence these weights are the same – in arguing that agreement in values is necessary for synoptic planning, Lindblom[45] and those that have used his argument are doing battle with a straw man.

Predicting production relations

A second requirement is that it must be possible to estimate what combinations of output can be produced from those resources available over the range relevant to policy discussion. We do not know the degree to which this condition is satisfied. This is so for two reasons: first, the collection of special data is expensive in money and skilled labour, and there are too few sectors for which there exist data which could be re-analysed to yield valid indicators of outputs; second, too few of the research workers with access to usable data are able to exploit the new and complicated modelling techniques needed to estimate subtle production relationships. There are examples in which technical errors at one stage of an analysis are compounded by technical errors at subsequent stages, with the result that it is extremely difficult to interpret results. For instance, it is not uncommon to attempt to improve the validity of indicators derived from survey data by using factor-analytic techniques. These allow the analyst to derive new indicators from the original data. Sometimes the form of factor analysis chosen and the technique used to rotate the factors are inappropriate. For instance, it would probably be wrong to assume that parental interest in reading books was uncorrelated with parental education. Yet data from large and expensive national surveys have been factor analysed to yield variables of this kind using techniques which assume such variables to be uncorrelated. These variables have subsequently been used as independent variables (quasi-inputs) to explain achievement scores.

It will be remembered that in Figure 9.1 the production-possibility curve was concave to the origin. It is important that the form of the models recognises that producing the two or more outputs together might make the production of any one of them cheaper than if they were produced separately. The use of such complicated forms is very rare indeed. Indeed, very few of the studies explore the possibility that the effects of the variables are non-linear; that is, a change by one unit in a predictor variable will have a different effect on outcome at different levels of that predictor variable. Few indeed explore the possibility that the existence or scale of the effect of a variable may depend upon the presence or level of other variables; yet these are contexts in which we have every reason to believe that causation is complicated by such relationships. Perhaps not enough time has yet elapsed for there to be much evidence about how predictable are production relations. The computer revolution which made feasible complicated modelling, and the growth in the social sciences that is slowly increasing the number of people trained to use them, are both too recent.

What cannot now be argued is that such production relations can never be predicted in any circumstances. However, there may be some reluctance to acknowledge this. Some appear to believe that the relationships between inputs, quasi-inputs and outputs are *too variable between cases* for it to be possible that strong general relationships exist. As it stands this argument is technically fallacious. It is quite possible for a causal relationship to be powerful on average, although the causal factor might appear to have only a weak effect in many cases. A relationship is a statement about what on average exists. There may be great variability about the average, yet the independent variable may on average have a large effect on the dependent variable. There is a more subtle version of this argument. It is that the resources may have a substantial impact on a dimension of outputs in the expected direction for some, for others no impact at all, or an impact in the opposite direction, or an impact on quite a different dimension of outputs. Jencks suggests that this is one reason why there is not a clear and consistent set of relationships between such things as school size, class size, ability grouping and curriculum.[46] He found that equalising the quality of elementary schools would reduce cognitive inequality by 3 per cent or less.[47] 'The most plausible explanation for these findings is that school resources have small inconsistent effects on achievement .... Teachers with high verbal scores help certain students to develop their verbal skills but inhibit others.'[48] He argues that it is never possible to predict much about such differences in relationships in advance, although it is always possible to invent explanations after the relationships have been discovered.

But is there anything surprising about this? The observation of regularities, their explanation and the subsequent testing both of the regularities and of the explanation is of the very essence of the process of developing causal argument. That the application of similar resources to people of different characteristics has different consequences should surprise no one. The fundamental production unit of a service is the person: it is the person who reacts to produce the welfare consequences of the service. The models must be based on individual data and incorporate those characteristics which contribute to this individual response. That a body of theory does not permit this is an indication that it is superficial. Examples abound of such relationships, and attempts to incorporate them in bodies of theory whose objective is to explain individual and group differences. Mothers vary in their probability of being sensitive to the potential of the status of receiving free school meals for stigmatisation.[49] Elderly residents who are able-bodied are stimulated by (moderate amounts of) engaging activity. Those who already tend to be slightly confused may be made more confused, as John Townsend and Ann Kimbell suggest.[50] Clearly production relations are not simple; anyone who expects them to be so is usually doomed to disappointment.

Are they *too complex* to be described? Interactions between factors in the production of each output are certainly highly complex; factors that influence one output also influence others; and threshold effects and non-linearities are common. It is true that the researcher seeking to use techniques which reflect the complexity of the situation he is modelling can quite easily find himself constrained by gaps in the technical modelling literature.[51] However, the modelling repertoire available is not so inadequate that most of the problems cannot be handled adequately by those who have mastered it.

Third, some appear to believe the *production relations are changing too quickly* for relations estimated for one period to be of much interest in the next, although they believe that production relationships are estimable at one time. This is frequently the case, but is certainly not always so. Indeed, one often wishes that this were more frequently the case. For instance, what is striking about most old people's homes or geriatric hospitals that have been in operation for a decade or more is how slowly the material and social environment and the production relations of many of them change. The following could have been written at any time during the last thirty years:

There seems to be a lack of direction and information about the functions of the geriatric service and the facilities which it should provide. The nature of the work of a geriatric department appears to be understood only partially, with a result that in some areas this service has concentrated only on acute illness in the elderly and in other areas only on long-term care of patients. In general there is a failure to realise that a geriatric department not only serves the needs of the community, but also the needs of other hospital departments. .... Just over one half of the hospitals for geriatric patients in these regions were built before the beginning of the twentieth century, and only eighteen per cent since 1950. .... The outdated premises used for geriatric patients often provide accommodation quite unrelated to the needs of the population of their area .... They are sometimes not provided with lifts, sufficient toilets with adequate space to provide even custodial care with the minimum of dignity. For lack of toilets and space, patients have been seen using uncurtained commodes four in a row .... The work of staff is constantly hampered by lack of space and facilities.

These quotations are taken not from the report of research conducted in the early 1950s, but from the *Annual Report* of the Hospital Advisory Service for the year 1974.[52] There has been as little sign of change in the production relationships as in the physical and social environment. This should not be surprising. What really count in the production relations of service institutions are the quantity of resources and the role expectations of the staff having closest and longest contact with clients. Such staff are often much less sensitive to broad changes of values than are more senior staff whose professionalisation has been more thorough. The same must be the case for some types of hospital. For such services, production relationships are sufficiently stable for reasonable estimates to be made and used.

This is not to argue that circumstances are usually such as to make it possible (and worthwhile) to estimate production relationships — merely that we should not allow our prejudices to suggest that it is never or rarely worth making the attempt.

Sufficient Consensus about the Weighting of Outputs

Many would see this as a (if not *the*) crucial issue. They would argue that social action is often impossible if an attempt is made to precisely explicate ends and their relative importance — that agreement can often be found about means in circumstances which make it impossible to find agreement about the weighting of ends (or the values which influence the weighting of these ends). Indeed many argue that it is very rare to find consensus about the weighting of ends in social policy. The quotation already made from Glennerster (see p. 147) is a good illustration.

However, the absence of spontaneous, pre-bargaining consensus about the weights to be put on ends, or even the absence of a willingness to express an agreement about means as an implicit weighting of ends, is not in itself an overwhelming difficulty. For instance, H. A. Simon's 'behaviour alternative model' puts more weight upon value judgements at the end of a process. One reason why the absence of consensus about ends — but merely an acceptance of the ends implicit in agreement about means — is not an overwhelming problem is that there are conditions under which it is in the interests of people to accept a settlement on an issue which does not perfectly reflect their preferences for reasons which do not imply that the political process as a whole is acting to the benefit of some at the expense of others. Pareto optimality demands that production or distribution should be reorganised if someone's welfare can be increased without harming anyone else; so that action is possible if losers are compensated by gainers to the satisfaction of the former. Thus a citizen may be willing to accept a policy he does not like because of compensation in some quite other sector. This is the strong (Pareto) form of the compensation principle — that losers are compensated by the gainers.

There might well exist a widespread feeling that action should take place in some circumstances if the losers *could* be compensated by the gainers. The potential losers may feel that they should be prepared to make some sacrifice for the common good and accept without obvious direct and immediate compensation a set of outputs not to their liking. For instance, in a society whose citzens value a pervasive sense of social justice, the better-off may be willing to accept the redistribution against themselves to a degree that they might consider socially unjust because this redistribution was decided upon by a political process regarded as legitimate. In these circumstances there is not agreement with the weighting of ends in any sense other than a willingness to accept them since the process by which they were derived is regarded as legitimate. Acceptance at this level is almost a condition of citizenship. It may be motivated by the not altogether altruistic desire to support a political process which on the whole is a positive-sum game, rather than risk transforming it into a zero- or negative-sum game through their intransigence. They may feel that this transformation would cause losses to themselves in the long run, as well as to the community in general. The importance of social policy in maintaining a sense of legitimacy of the political order is widely recognised by writers of different schools. Boulding (in his *Collected Papers*, vol. II) went so far as to argue that 'integration' is to social policy as the 'economy' is to economic policy.

For reasons such as this, a high degree of 'spontaneous' consensus about ends may not be a necessary condition for using evidence that arises from the outcomes of the political process as a basis for weighting indicators of need; though taken with other circumstances, such consensus strengthens the case for doing so. It is as easy to exaggerate the degree of dissent about some issues as it is to exaggerate the degree of consensus about others. In the example quoted by Glennerster, we may ask what proportion of those who supported the proposal to introduce part-time pre-school education was a more equal society an *anathema* (our italics) rather than something that did not deserve much weight? What proportion of those who wanted from it social benefits for their children were not at all interested in them reading earlier? How far would those who disagreed about the merits of mothers going out to work have found it easier to agree about the merits of mothers doing so in more precisely specified circumstances? How far is apparent dissent about ends really a reflection of differences of judgement about production relations, about the consequences that follow from an intervention? Perhaps the degree of diversity in the weighting of ends is not always all that great. Perhaps, moreover, bipartisan political debate may as often tend to exaggerate this diversity — making a unimodal distribution of preferences appear bimodal — as it does the opposite. It is of the essence of bipartisan political debate that, on occasion, opportunities should not be lost to embarrass the opponents — to undermine the *diffuse* support for the government though the opposition may gain little *specific* support.[53] Agreement about means when consequences are more predictable implies agreement about ends. The unwillingness to weight the ends precisely can often be due more to the need to rationalise outcomes in terms of different ideologies — to manage more effectively the demands of supporters by describing the advantages of the consequences in terms which will appeal to them. That the political debate results in agreement about means rather than ends, and that there is an apparent lack of consensus — even an apparent bimodality in the distribution of preferences — is no assurance that the outcome can provide no basis of evidence for need and output measurement. Conversely, apparent consensus can exist for bad reasons, and the weighting of ends implicit in the agreement can be a misleading basis for measurement. We must search for better criteria than the degree of consensus if we are to develop a set of principles to apply when assessing how far current practice provides a good basis for the development of indicators.

Demand and organisational and political influences on outcomes

Patterns of existing consumption of services are partially determined by those demand influences whose effects are stable for a time and not quickly amenable to changes in supply policy, and the supply response of providing organisations in their demand environment (and so the political framework which controls the supplying organisations and helps define their tasks). One of the basic conditions required for a process to yield good evidence is that suppliers are so organised as to exploit to its maximum the efficiency of the technology of the interventive area. These technologies seem usually not to be merely, or even largely, the products of the political and organisational characteristics of the suppliers — though such factors lead to the neglect of some choices of technique. It would seem that basic technologies — repertoires of interventive techniques, and the consequences that follow from their use in similar circumstances — are much more similar in advanced countries than the service organisations that apply them.

Although such technologies are often flexible, one must not under-estimate the degree to which their application imposes demands on the formal organisation of suppliers in a context which makes logical the choice of some mixes of techniques rather than others. What choice of technique is appropriate usually depends upon the environment as well as on the technology. There are many circumstances in which there is no optimal form of organisation applicable across the range of environments found within even one country. For instance, although the writings of the Brunel Institute of Organisation and Social Studies may aim mainly to describe the anatomy and physiology of alternatively organised social-service departments rather than to create a normative theory of social-service department organisation, one is certainly tempted to infer from its work that a geographical model may be more appropriate for some environments while a functional model may be appropriate for others. It is no accident that Hereford and Worcester and East Sussex are possibly the two authorities with the most explicit commitment to the geographical model. It might well be that, left to their own devices, areas whose populations are sparser might well choose to combine functions in a way that is not legally permitted in England and Wales. For instance, one might envisage that health and social services might be administered by the same organisations in some contexts, as they are in Northern Ireland. The reasons for doing so could include the need to reconcile economies of large-scale provision (a technological factor) with sufficiently local provision (entailing a balance between the technologically determined benefits of specialisation and variations in the costs that must be met to achieve a given standard).

The response of the supplying organisation to the environment in the context of a technology is much influenced by the weighted sum of responses of the organisation's members.[54] Several factors are important. First, it is important to have a span of functions for the organisation appropriate to optimise the choice of technique, since 'cross-overs' complicate processes and invite goal displacement. Second, corresponding to a hierarchy of decisions imposed by the technology of greater generality in their consequences for supply and greater longevity in their effects, there must be a hierarchy of decision nodes in the formal organisation. Examples are decisions determining the future supply of capital, human and physical, in contexts where there are economies of scale to be reaped through specialisation. That organis-ation structure can prevent the reaping of the benefits that come from such potential economies is clear; compare British and American local government. A second example is the way in which the new fashion for corporate management tacked on to an organisation whose structure and traditions are fundamentally alien to it has as yet been unsuccessful in securing the best use of interventive policies, so that choices of interventive technique by social-service departments have been dis-torted by demands imposed by policies with more pervasive effects. This may be seen in the reports of community development projects.

Third, the supplier must be so organised as to develop and deploy professional skills of the variety required by the technology. Bureau-cracies usually consist of separate but interacting and competing social structures. Professional groups are the nuclei of many of these, particularly in organisations among whose activities is the provision of social services.[55] The implications for the characteristics of organisations are apparent from studies like those of the Aston group[56] or Hage and Aiken.[57] The characteristics of the organisation must be such as to enable the functionaries to have an appropriate influence on those decisions for which the efficient use of the technology demands their expertise.

Fourth, organisations must have a structure which affects the degree of flexibility of the technology and the predictability of the demands made on it in the market. Again there are strong parallels with commercial organisations.[58] Writers on this complement the political-science literature that attempts to define those contexts in which what Lindblom calls 'partisan mutual adjustment' (P.M.A.), decentralised and fragmented forms of decision-making, best enable responsibilities and tasks to be matched to the cognitive and learning capacities of individuals.[59] That conditions are such that P.M.A. is the most effective form of organising decision-taking in a context is not in itself a reason for rejecting the outcomes of the decisions as evidence for measuring needs and outputs. What Braybrooke and Lindblom are arguing is that in some (indeed they argue *most*) circumstances, optimisation is actually best achieved by P.M.A. — by comparing and evaluating increments only, by considering only a restricted number of policy alternatives, by considering only some of the important consequences of any given policy alternative, by adapting ends to means as well as means to ends, by returning again and again to the same issue over time (rather than attempting to discover a permanent solution), by identifying social ills that seem to call for remedy rather than pursuing policies that lead directly to a well-defined future state, and by making a large number of persons make decisions that influence outcomes.

The key issue is the degree to which it is possible to define what constitutes rational decision-making by the criteria of a normative model of resource allocation, and the degree to which the mode of decision-making actually adopted is indeed rational. As Self argues, 'rationality' consists 'in no more than a belief in systematic treatment of the relevant data, together perhaps with a bias (which arises naturally from a systematic approach) towards widening the frontiers of analysis'.[60] Actors in a P.M.A. situation frequently act 'rationally' by this criterion. Moreover, surely Dror is correct to argue that organisations frequently choose the balance that they strike on an issue between the rational comprehensive and successive limited comparison models.[61] The optimising organisation may choose one solution for some issues but not for others. The outcomes of either may be a good basis for the evidence needed. What is important is to recognise the degree to which the organisation is facing the issue, and choosing the appropriate mode. Here the criteria suggested by Self are useful;[62] namely that the comprehensive approach can work if the problems are similarly perceived by sufficient people, if interests can be more effectively reconciled by comprehensive planning, and professional techniques can be made to support the interests of comprehensive planning.

The most important supplying organisations operate in a broader political context. In particular, the political context can influence the balance of influence of interest groups even within the organisation. It can also influence the goals the organisation sets for itself and how these develop. An interesting example is the degree to which changes in the external political environment, notably the development of micro political activity and its acceptance, have changed the balance of power of interest groups over the planning decision. Interest groups, administrators, and others in the political process given power by a system, will often accept change only with reluctance. Majone quotes the case of American attempts to control environmental pollution.[63] Administrators were reluctant to adopt the most effective techniques of control because they would have curtailed their freedom. He argues that economists had shown that effluent charges were superior to other tools of environmental policy. Yet both in Europe and in the United States environmental legislation continued to rely almost exclusively on inferior tools. This he ascribes to the pursuit of selfish interests by pressure groups representing industrial polluters, environmental pressure groups (which participate in the setting of standards and therefore acquire power which they can 'trade' in order to attain their ends) and legislators and administrators (for whom the setting of standards leaves more room for manoeuvre than charging for the shifting of responsibilities to lower levels of government, administrative discretion and bargaining). Decisions about charging are too ambiguous and visible. The failure to attain the desired level of environmental quality leads too directly to pressure to raise charges. They make it impossible to hide the costs of pollution control, or to transfer them to the weaker and less organised groups in the community. It would be naive to pretend that the goals of organisations are not distorted by the self-interested actions of officials.[64]

American political scientists have written extensively about the way in which pluralist political processes manage demands on the system in such a way as to maintain political stability. They are not always such as to explicate issues in such a way as to maintain a sustained dialogue about issues, even those that are general in context and recur through time. This is so even when they are major issues. They quite frequently operate so as to limit the influence over decision-making to a small proportion of those most affected. In doing so they leave too much discussion of the weighting of outputs to professionals and others in the organisations. Land-use planning during the 1960s is one example of a policy area in which this was the case.[65] The William Tyndale enquiry shows that the same might equally apply to education. Glastonbury has shown that it applies to the social services,[66] and Sinfield describes some of the consequences of the tunnel-vision of professionals.[67] I believe that it applies also to the Rate Support Grant – the Layfield Committee has now reported – and school-meals policy.[68] The political machinery must be such that politicians may exercise political leadership. Whether or not they can do so depends on many other things also, including the existence of a broad range of policy analysts in the area.

Some writers largely ignore the impact of consumer demand on outcomes. In particular, the British sociologists who focus on those they see as the 'urban managers' under-estimate the importance of client demand (and generally the way in which variations in the environment inhabited by the organisation affects its responses). There is abundant evidence of the power of demand – for instance, of the way the choices council-house tenants make increasingly constrain the investment decisions of authorities.[69] The responsiveness of school-leaving to the labour market and expected rates of return on investment in education shows the same to be true for education. Evidence for need judgements that reflect demand must take into account the degree to which that demand is influenced by factors that should not influence needs. The difficulty with a demand-based need concept is that factors that should not be embodied in need or output indicators have a powerful effect on demand. First, demand is to a substantial degree supply-determined. Supply is needed to transform a *weltschmerz* into a demand, or the pattern of supply determines the form a demand will take. Second, the transformation of the subjective perception of a welfare shortfall into a demand depends on such factors as knowledge about the service. Third, the perceived potential of the context for the stigmatisation of recipients, and perception of the seriousness of the welfare shortfall, have to be balanced against the 'transaction costs' of exercising the demand — completing complex forms, finding the right agency, often by a process of trial, referral, and error, travelling to and from offices, and waiting for attention in them. Such perceptions vary in a complex way between groups of clients.[70] Elaborate theories of demand are necessary if we are to base indicators of demand and need on demand evidence.

The Policy Context: The Characteristics of 'Policy Paradigms'

The third section of this chapter stressed the importance of two issues. Under what conditions is an attempt to measure needs and outputs worthwhile? What are the criteria by which we can judge the validity of evidence about demand or supply as a basis for the measurement? The discussion therein related to both. However, the discussion was general. What is missing is a discussion of the contextual insight which provides the actual basis for answering the questions implicit in what has gone before.

The contextual insight reflects an imagination unique to the analyst — a 'quality of judgement' sharpened by imaginations developed in contact with the strands of literature and experience on which the analyst has worked. But it is at least influenced, if not dominated, by an individual interpretation of a 'policy paradigm'. It is the policy paradigm more than anything else which makes possible the application of the general criteria to the specific context. By policy paradigm I mean the entire constellation of beliefs, values, assumptions about cause and effect, appreciations about the techniques of intervention, and beliefs about the consequences of alternative actions, which are substantially shared by the community of actors which influence outputs in the political and bureaucratic process. Although generally vague and containing innumerable contradictions, it is something recognised by most if not all the actors in the political and bureaucratic systems. I call them 'paradigms' so as to stress the analogy with Kuhnian scientific paradigms — to make explicit that we are discussing ideologies, social constructs.

The policy paradigm exists because it fulfills an essential function. It provides, maintains and develops the basis for social action. Sharpe, who has recently used a concept which is similar but not identical to this concept of the policy paradigm, writes: 'It is impossible for representative bureaucracy to work without [a policy paradigm].'[71] It is essential if technical inputs are to be contributed effectively into bureaucracies employing professionals with a delegated discretion to influence outcomes. Since it structures the perceptions of both the factual and the value elements that are in practice so hard to disentangle in most areas of intervention, it provides the base-line for decision-making — structuring the expectations about consequences and costs of alternative courses of action in the conditions of imperfect knowledge, uncertainty, and the type of interdependence of actors in the pluralist power context that Lindblom describes in developing his model of partisan mutual adjustment.[72] The paradigm helps to structure problems, so contributing to their solution. Indeed it provides exemplars to assist the problem-solver. It helps to define what types of evidence are needed to make more satisfying the basis for action. Professionals teach the paradigm to general administrators, and thus to politicians and interest groups.

The characteristics of the paradigm most salient to the two issues distinguished in the first paragraph of this section are intellectual, political and organisational.

Intellectual

Certainly one condition is the degree to which the paradigm is elaborately articulated. The paradigm requires articulation in two ways: first, it has to be articulated in a language which will help a sufficiently broad range of interests to accept the structuring of problems and possible solutions; second, it must be so articulated that existing professional and other scientific and bureaucratic skills can be mobilised to serve it. Knowledge and intellectual techniques developed for other purposes can only be successfully mobilised if the intellectual components of the paradigm are made explicit; and the desire of professionals and bureaucrats to exercise power within job contexts can only be realised with legitimacy if the professionals and others possess esoteric understanding and a mastery of complex skills. One aspect is the impressiveness of both the conceptual structures used and the degree to which they have been exposed to the 'test' of evidence. Particularly important is how well theories seem to explain salient outcomes, and how well the tools which depend on the intellectual components appear to achieve the policy objectives implicit in the paradigm — at least those where success or failure are visible. These criteria closely parallel those which determine the continuing credibility of scientific paradigms. Many intellectual reasons for the collapse of policy paradigms are very like those of the collapse of scientific paradigms.

Political

To interest groups with political influence, the policy paradigm must appear to lead to actions that are at least as satisfactory as any other likely policy. How far a policy wins the acceptance if not the support of organised political interest groups, rather than 'voice', is crucial; though of course such mobilised political interests can be compensated for their diswelfare in this area by positive benefits in another. Again we see how important it is that a paradigm is well-articulated and successfully purveyed both to a broad public with a general interest in government as well as to parties with a specific interest. Selling the paradigm to the general political market provides the diffuse support which will give the paradigm the significance to decision-making that comes from a general perception that action that reflects it contributes to the public interest, and so a role in maintaining their position while managing demands (in the Eastonian sense).[73]

Some such precondition would be acceptable to all political writers, I think, even the most cynical. It is quite consistent with a view of politics similar to that of Michael Oakeshott, and expressed in the quotation made in Heisler's chapter in this book. The absence of a destination makes the Oakeshott view more cynical than the Lindblom model, which recognises that actors have objectives.

The British social-policy-analysis tradition grew from Fabian origins. Such analysts certainly do operate principles and formulate objectives compatible with them. Therefore the analyses question whether the beliefs and assumptions of the paradigm square with evidence. The best studies so explicate the paradigm as to show its internal contradictions — contradictions in the applications of values, and in the presumptions about cause and effect. They mobilise evidence so as to clarify relationships and correct assumptions. They attempt to apply a value system that is consistent with the result of the analyses of the relative quantitative importance of the competing causal arguments. Similarly, they try to allow for obvious imperfections in the political market: to apply a basic sense of equality to a situation where the distribution and mobilisation of power is unequal.

Organisational

Paradigms can hardly exist in a satisfactory form when organisational structures — bureaucratic, or political like governments or pressure groups (including professional and client associations) — are unrelated to policy ends. A major reason for the concentration of normative theorists of territorial justice on the improvement of the structure of organisations is a belief in the importance of organisational structure for the development of the paradigm. Indeed it is arguable that they have been more interested in this dynamic aspect than they have in more static arguments developed by H. A. Simon and his disciples. that it is necessary to subordinate organisation to the requirement of the social objectives that they serve. But through time the intellectual, political and organisational factors are interdependent to a degree that would make it wrong to separate them in the analysis. The intellectual development of the paradigm is greatly dependent on organisational factors in a world where the sponsorship of analysis is largely (and increasingly) corporate — as Webb argues.[74] The intellectual basis likewise contributes to the political appreciations. The political conditions contribute to the possibility of organisational development. The organisational development in turn contributes to the capacity of the actors to adapt the intellectual propositions of the paradigm smoothly to changes in the real world and to changes in perceptions of that world.

Thus making the judgements about evidence requires the application of general criteria to a policy paradigm. The policy paradigm must be explicated, some of its contradictions exposed and its testable propositions discovered and examined against evidence. Only then can reasonable judgements about the two issues be made.

Conclusions

Techniques exist for collecting the evidence needed for measuring both outputs and needs, though these have yet to be adapted to the special features of each social-service context. The economists have long since developed the concept of 'output', and the concept of 'need' also has been given a precise meaning and a context in a general argument about the allocation of resources. However, the measurement of outputs has not always been compatible with arguments about how resources should be allocated in the social-service contexts in which it has been undertaken. Similarly, need measurement, both in need studies and in the form of need indicators, has not adequately reflected the central logic of the need judgement. But the really difficult problems are to assess whether conditions are such in a specific context with which the policy analyst is faced that it makes much sense to attempt to measure needs and outputs, and whether the evidence that can be collected could be such as to yield valid indicators. Ultimately this is a matter of the analyst's judgement in the light of some general criteria whose application to the context is aided by the analysis of the context's policy paradigm. In basing the assessment on the scrutiny of the network of forces that influence actual need judgements, the social administrator would be doing much the same as the economist, who assesses whether the prices yielded in a market will secure an efficient allocation of resources mainly by examining the network of forces which influence outcomes in that and related markets. What economics provides but social administration lacks is a body of theory that suggests questions for this examination.

10 Cohesion or Disjunction in the Planning of Public Policy?

J. D. Stewart

There is no final answer to the debate over cohesion or disjunction in the planning process. The argument for cohesion is normally set in the terminology of comprehensive planning.

The case for comphrehensive planning in government is easily made. It rests upon the interrelationships between the problems, issues and needs confronted by government and upon the interrelationship between the activities undertaken by government. The housing problem is related to the social problem, which is related to the educational problem, which cannot be separated from the economic problem. Planning for one set of problems in isolation is too limited because of the impact of other problems. The case has been made and will be remade.

The case for comprehensive planning is only frustrated by its impossibility. No planning process can encompass all the interrelationships. To achieve comprehensive planning by planning comprehensively is impossible. To match in the planning process the complexity of the world in which the planning process is set is a task that can never be completed.

That is the case for disjunction in planning or in action. It is possible, and to an extent it works. If the interrelationships of a complex world cannot be matched in a planning process, then the problem must be simplified by disjunction. If the world cannot be planned, perhaps education can be planned, or if not education, then at least the school-building programme.

But the debate continues. Simplification, although necessary, can always be challenged. The case for cohesion remains. The problem is to give expression to it, for it is only in comprehensive planning that it can be given final expression and that is impossible.

To explore the dilemma that follows from the recognition both of the necessity of disjunction, and yet the desirability of cohesion, is to explore one facet of the dilemma of the governing relationship that links government to that which is governed.

The complexity of the world cannot be matched by government. Government must act by simplification. That is inherent in the governing relationship.

Government simplifies in many ways. It simplifies first and foremost by isolating. It isolates problems or issues and treats them in particular ways through particular units of government. It may isolate by area. The jurisdiction of a national government or a local government runs within boundaries. A local authority is concerned first and foremost with the problems in its boundaries.

It may isolate by some other defining characteristic. It proceeds by specialisation. Government to do its work fragments itself. Indeed it defines its work by the elements. It is concerned with education. It is concerned with health.

Within departments of government geared to health or education, units, sections and divisions carry further the process of specialisation and fragmentation. An education department is divided into sections. At local-authority level those sections may be primary, secondary, further, special, sites and buildings. Problems and issues are isolated in these sections. In this way the complexity that is the world is reduced. Problems and issues are reduced to the size and shape of the units of administration. The structure of the administrative system is a simplified model of that which is to be governed.

Isolation is not complete. It is reduced by cross-processes of conflict, collaboration and co-ordination. But those processes are based upon and reflect the units which conflict, collaborate or are co-ordinated. The focus of the units and the processes dependent on them is limited by the isolation of the unit's perspective. Isolation is not to be regretted, only recorded. It is necessary to the achievement of government action. The particular structure can be criticised, the strength and weakness of the cross-processes can be discussed, but whatever shape is taken by the structure that structure must to an extent isolate. Even the linking processes carry their own isolation. Financial co-ordination carries its own limitation and its own isolation. The administrative structure cannot match external complexity.

Second, government simplifies by routinisation. Every problem and issue cannot be considered as unique. Many have to be understood as one of a class or a category: that which is unique in many problems has to be ignored; that which can be categorised or classified has to be stressed. Government operates largely through procedures, for to operate otherwise would be to stop government.

Whether it is the clerk in the office fitting oddly shaped problems into neatly shaped boxes, or the courts in their majesty fitting cases to general laws, government involves relating the individual to the general. Only in this way can government be carried on in complex societies. Only in this way can formal equity be ensured. For although equity may be held to require consideration of each case or issue in all its uniqueness, formal equity requires the application of rule. Government simplifies by dealing largely in formal equity.

Third, government simplifies through its assumptions. In a changing world it is still simpler to assume that there is no change or that change can be ignored. In a complex world it is still possible to act by assuming simplicity. In an unknown world it helps to assume that what is not known is not relevant. In this way government can be carried on. Government cannot endlessly search for certainty. Every government organisation operates through imposing a little certainty upon a world that is uncertain.

Simplification is justified because it works. Simplifying assumptions, routinisation and isolation enable government to function. Simplification is not to be regretted. It is foolish to regret the necessary, especially if it works.

But simplification does not always work. The problem is that it is turned into a crisis because old rules cannot encompass it; the unforeseen that leads to disaster that could have been foreseen; the department that destroys what another department builds – all these are known and documented. In extreme cases the shrieks can be heard even through the on-going administrative process. The process is changed. A new pattern of simplification is adopted, which takes account of the shrieks. It is still a simplification, but at that point at least – the shrieking point – it may fit the world better – for a time.

It surely need not be necessary to wait for the shrieks. There are signs before that. Before the shriek there is the complaint, the petition, the letter to the M.P. Before that there is the awkwardness in the office as a case is fitted to a routine. There are always symptoms.

The hope is that the machine, that is the political-management process that we call 'government', can respond before the shriek. There is the hope that it could respond to the shout, to the complaint, or even to the awkwardness. There is the hope that government should be a learning, responding organisation.

It is right that there should be the hope, but it is right too to realise that the hope will never be fulfilled – completely. To learn and to respond to the wind in the office files, the rumour in the grapevine that links street to office, is a goal but it will never be finally attained. Government depends upon simplification. The alternative is not the completely responsive organisation, since that implies a knowledge of complexity and an ability to respond that is beyond the capacity of government.

To seek the unattainable in action is to strain the organisation so that it fails to achieve even the possible. Government can be improved but there are limits to that improvement. Simplification, although it can distort, is necessary. Without it government ceases.

To say simplification is necessary is not to say that what is, is all that might be. To assert the necessity of simplification is to define a necessary condition for government; it is not to defend any given pattern as necessary for government. Improvement is – or may be – or should be – possible. The improvement, however, will not replace simplification. It will not enable the government machine to consider all problems, issues and needs in all their interrelationships; it will not avoid the routinisation of many processes of government; it will not be based on perfect knowledge; it will remain simplification.

Although simplification has to be accepted and distortion seen as inevitable, present simplification and present distortion do not have to be accepted. Distortion can be lessened – although it may only be lessened at a cost. The prevalent system of government distorts significantly by stress on one dimension – the functional dimension. A world in which cross-linkages are as important as that which is linked is simplified by government into functional divisions. Some simplification is required by government, but not that simplification. The cross-linkages that are the world cannot be matched in government, but the principle of cross-linkages can be matched. Government which is built upon the functional dimension can encompass other dimensions. The picture of the world that has both warp and weft will still be a distortion, but at least it may be a recognisable distortion.

To propose a further dimension to functionalism is not to destroy functionalism but to use it. Reformers who challenge the principle of simplification are doomed to failure. They must use the principle of simplification, but must be ready to add complication – perhaps by adding a new dimension, with its own simplification. The government process cannot be challenged outright. Its very strengths can, *must*, be used.

The dilemma posed by the necessity of disjunction and the desirability of cohesion is but a special example of this dilemma that is inherent in the governing relationship. In that relationship are linked the necessity of simplification in that which governs and the reality of complexity in that which is governed.

Planning in government is conditioned by its fragmentation. At each level of government concerned with social policy new processes of planning are developing. The new health authorities are required by the Department of Health and Social Security to develop health planning. The same department called in 1972 upon social-services departments to prepare ten-year social-services plans.

Each functional department at national level and each functional department or functional authority at local level plans its own activities and the development of those activities. The functionalism at the centre supports and is supported by the functionalism in the locality. Education department and the Department of Education and Science support each other in a functional world. The hierarchy of health stretches from district through area and region to the D.H.S.S. That functional principle dominates the planning procedures. There are cross-linkages in government. They are the linkages that are required by sharing of resources. Conflicting demands upon limited resources have to be resolved within government. That, by itself, does not add a new dimension to government if the choice remains between broad functional areas.

Functional planning has been attacked as disjointed planning in a world where problems interact. The case has been made. It barely needs remaking. In our society its echoes are everywhere. The problems of education lie outside the schools. The social problems of an area are the aftermath of economic decline. The physical aspirations of the high flats are matched by the neuroses of the inhabitants. The urban motorway has advanced into and retreated from our city as the problems of transportation solved have been more than matched by the new problems created. Multi-deprivation has been stressed. The issues and problems of our society cannot adequately be stated in terms of limited functions.

The critic can often see an easy solution; but it is a solution that merely changes the form of the problem. A particular failure to link activity A with activity B or problem C with problem D can easily be solved by emphasising that particular interrelationship; but emphasis is given at the expense of under-emphasis. The particular criticism is soon met — at the screaming point — if the screaming is loud enough. The machine re-adjusts but does not change. It reacts to the screaming point. It does not anticipate the next screaming point.

So the machine itself must change. New processes and new structures are proposed that can encompass the complexity — or can approach it.

There is talk of the social content of structure plans. There were experiments in community-development projects sponsored by the Home Office. There are three inner-area studies sponsored by the Department of the Environment. Urban guidelines were set out in other studies. Collaboration is sought by health authorities and local authorities. Recent years have seen the development of corporate planning in local government. Corporate planning was an aspiration to comprehensive planning – the activities of the authority seen as a whole in relation to the needs and problems it faced.

The aspiration to comprehensive planning reflected felt needs. The problems were real. The case was made. Yet comprehensive planning will not be achieved. It will not be achieved because it is impossible. That much is clear. To plan comprehensively requires of any unit of government that it:

(1) identifies all the problems and issues it faces and their interrelationships;

(2) determines the values it wishes to pursue in resolving those problems and issues;

(3) considers all alternative ways of realising those values; and

(4) considers all the effects of those alternatives.

It is too easy to show the impossibility of such planning. All problems and issues cannot be identified. All interrelationships cannot be plotted. Government cannot resolve all the values it pursues. All alternative ways of realising those values cannot be found nor all effects known. Government operates in a world of bounded rationality. It simplifies.

Comprehensive planning systems in name are often new patterns in simplification. They do not achieve cohesion. They merely impose new patterns of disjunction. P.P.B.S. systems (planning, programming and budgeting systems), which represent one approach, cast government planning into comprehensive forms based on the main objectives of government. Under each main objective were developed the main programmes of the government unit, descending through sub-objectives in hierarchies that appear as divisive as the functional divisions between or within departments they were designed to replace.

In some of the programme structures developed in local authorities, one finds such broad programme areas as 'leisure and recreation', 'social welfare' or 'education'. The cynic might be forgiven for wondering if the apparently comprehensive planning process represented by P.P.B.S. was a change from the functional planning it replaced. Comprehensive planning in urban government gained its drive from stress on the interrelationships that are embedded in the complex life of the city. A road is not a means of transportation alone but a dividing and a joining factor in the social fabric. A child in a school is influenced deeply by the social and physical environment in which he lives. Problems, it was asserted, do not fit neatly into the little boxes that make up the fabric of government.

Yet the initial instrument for comprehensive planning in urban government did but little to enable government to take account of these complex interrelationships that lie between programme areas. This may appear to be because the programme areas selected were in many cases merely a reformulation of previous departmental divisions. An education programme area may differ marginally from an education department in what is enclosed within its boundaries (for example, it may exclude certain leisure activities provided by education departments), but the broad base of the programme area closely corresponds to the broad base of the activities of an education department.

But even if the programme areas defined by local authorities (or by central government) were formed on a different basis from that of the traditional department, it would not have resolved the problem of the practicality of comprehensive planning.

Programme areas can be defined in many ways. They can be defined in terms of client groups: children, the elderly, the young married, and so on. Programme areas – or areas for planning – can be defined geographically. These are alternative models of the government's understanding of the world. They have a value in that. They do not by themselves represent comprehensive planning. They do not encompass the interactions which comprehensive planning must encompass if indeed it is to be comprehensive.

The models of comprehensive planning that have been proposed are not, in fact, comprehensive planning. They are now simplifications proposed as alternatives to the present simplifications. But to argue against all is not to reject more and certainly not to reject other. The impossibility of considering all problems does not mean that the present problems considered are correct. It does not follow that because comprehensive planning is impossible, no change in government to meet the case for such planning is possible or desirable. Because all problems cannot be considered it does not follow that more or different problems cannot be considered. More problems can be considered. Different problems can be considered. The model of comprehensive planning challenges the limitations of fragmented planning – even though the model cannot be realised.

If it is impossible to carry out comprehensive planning by planning comprehensively, is it then possible to carry out comprehensive planning by not planning comprehensively? Paradoxically the answer might almost be 'yes', not seeking to achieve directly, but indirectly.

Government plans along its dominant dimension – the functional dimension. The particular set of functions reflects the dominant view of the main issues faced by the organisation. It maps an understanding of the external environment and of the relationship of government to that environment. That map has only one problem and that if it is the dominant map; it excludes other maps. Alternative maps are required — not to achieve the same dominance as the functional map — nor even to overthrow its dominance; they may only require to challenge it or at least to add to it.

Comprehensive planning is likely to be achieved in part — and that after all is all one can expect — by adding other dimensions to the functional planning process. Planning will not be comprehensive — but it will comprehend more.

The activities of government and their interrelation to the environment can be mapped on more than one dimension. The areal approach has value if added to the functional approach in societies where the dominant organisation and hence the dominant perspective of government in planning is the functional perspective.

The areal perspective provides a counterbalance to the functional. The development of a regional tier of administration within the machinery of central government for which developments in recent years provide a basis is one possibility. The development of areal management within the machinery of local authorities provides another possibility. These areal perspectives need support if they are to be effective. That means political support — there must be political weight behind the perspective. It also means information sources. An areal perspective made up of no more than the perspective of functional departments can hardly be said to add a new dimension to the organisation.

The areal approach adds another dimension to the organisation and provides a possibility of perspectives that differ from the functional. The tension between them can itself make planning wider in scope.

However, perhaps another approach is possible — an approach which could strengthen the areal approach as well as the functional approach. It is to recognise that a wider scanning of the environment than government normally undertakes is possible if the precision which government normally seeks is abandoned.

It is to use the building of imaginative futures, the search for rumour, the clamour of the alternative viewpoint. It is to use all those sources of information that most organisations operating functionally reject as irrelevant to the organisation's responsibility. They are passing, changing and evolving elements.

Such viewpoints do not amount to a comprehensive viewpoint, but they enable more or other to be comprehended. They permit a wide-ranging scanning to supplement the detail. Comprehensive planning is impossible, if by that is meant that all is comprehended in all its detail. It is, however, possible to achieve a wider perspective if detail is for the moment sacrificed. What is impossible is to combine width and detail in the same vision. Such a wide-ranging scanning can challenge the certainties of the organisation's functional perspective. (This approaches the more encompassing strategy of Etzioni's mixed scanning strategy, which distinguishes 'contextuating decisions' from 'bit decisions'; cf. A. Etzioni, *The Active Society*, pp. 283–306 – see 'Notes and References', p. 240.)

It is an attractive concept. It recognises the reality that comprehensive planning is impossible while still remaining desirable. The problem remains as to how it is done. It could, for example, be argued that the *Public Expenditure Survey* or even a local-authority budget gave just that – a broad perspective on government activities. But that is to misunderstand. Such documents do give an overview of activities undertaken by government. They are built up from activities. They add nothing to the activities. They give no new perspective.

This perspective on the organisation's activities is required. It can be cast in one form or another. It is already there. It can perhaps be improved – as perhaps a programme budget does – that is all. It gives us no new perspective. Wide-range scanning, if it has a role, turns outward from that with which the organisation is already engaged to that which the organisation perhaps is not aware of.

A review of problems faced, or issues not faced, is perhaps the role of this wider scanning. No statistical analysis projecting forward that which is already known to prove that the problems will remain the same – only there will be more of them – will meet this requirement. The review will not be based on the perspective of the organisation but be designed to bring in perspectives from outside the organisation. Problems that are relevant to government but which cannot be perceived by the existing organisation may be perceived – interrelationships that are present in the world that is governed, but are not perceived inside the organisation. These are what are looked for in such an overview. It provides that which the detailed routines of the organisation cannot provide.

Such reviews can be undertaken by the developing complex of research units, think tanks, policy review staff, corporate planning units, which are a growing part of the apparatus of government. The growth of such units is in response to the demand for the alternative perspective – often inadequately expressed.

They do not all provide it. Some seek to match the contribution of the functional and in the end they do just that. Their justification lies in challenge and for that they require political support for a time — perhaps not longer less the alternative perspective becomes routinised and ceases to challenge.

Of course such units must be capable of more detailed analysis — if only to gain organisational force. Such analysis goes under many competing or complementary titles — cost-benefit, programme analysis and review (P.A.R.), operational research — and so on. That detailed analysis must involve an examination of issues on a cross-functional basis. Such analysis can only be undertaken on a limited range of problems and issues. To do more is to become involved in the routines of government. The alternative perspective has to be maintained.

Disjunction* is inevitable in government. It has to be recognised. Cohesion is reached towards, never achieved. The comprehensive ideal is a false ideal if conceived in the detail appropriate to the particular. It cannot be specified in detail.

Government can comprehend more but not all. It can comprehend better if it recognises more than one dimension — perhaps the areal dimension as well as the functional one — and if it has the possibility of a wider-ranging perspective than is possible to functionalism alone.

It may be easier to achieve cohesion by supplementing disjunction than by trying to abolish it.

Some of the more useful literature in which this debate is pursued is mentioned on page 240.

11 The Organisation of Professional Work in the Social Services

George F. Thomason

Perspective

In recent years a good deal has been written on the subject of organisation in the personal social services, much of it responding to the recommendations of the Seebohm Committee Report and the subsequent reorganisation of the service in accordance with the terms of the *Local Authorities Social Services Act* of 1970. Much of what has been written has tended to accept the 'inevitability' of bureaucratic orgainsation for the service, and to consider the extent to which organisation on these principles will either produce conflict with professional principles or prove acceptable to a profession (of social work) which may have founded itself on a consonant 'rationality'. Writers like Rowbottom[1] and Kogan and Terry[2] conclude that the tensions likely to arise are so marginal or peripheral that they can be reduced easily enough by attention to management or organisational style, devoted to the creation of maximum devolution and maximum flexibility in the definition of work roles. Implicitly, therefore, the bureaucratic organisation and the professional organisation coincide at the point where bureaucracy is at its most flexible, and professional organisation (perhaps) at its most structured.

This chapter takes the view that to start with assumptions about the inevitability of the bureaucratic form in modern society is to prejudge the whole question of whether efficiency can be achieved by any other organisational means in those circumstances where the basic 'work to be done' by the enterprise in question is work which arises only out of human problems or human needs which are presented to the system by individuals who may have only very unclear ideas of what their needs or problems really are. Such 'work' cannot be very precisely defined *a priori*, and can only be measured in actuarial terms, and for these reasons scarcely presents to the bureaucratic administrator a firm foundation for his administration of that work.

Consequently, it seems worthwhile to begin consideration of the organisational problem in such services by looking at the work which has to be done and at the kind of demand which such client-borne problems are likely to make of the people who constitute 'the workers' in the enterprise. When we have some answers to these questions, we have some basis for asking whether the bureaucratic form of administrative organisation has anything or enough to contribute to the solution of the problem.

The Mission

The major contribution of the Seebohm Report[3] to this consideration lies in its general, and relatively idealised, statement of the *mission* of the personal social service. The Report recommended that there should be established 'a new local authority department, providing a community-based and family-oriented service which will be available to all'. It then went on to detail some of the 'services' which would thereby be provided:

> The new department will reach far beyond the discovery and rescue of social casualties; it will enable the greatest possible number of individuals to act reciprocally, giving and receiving service for the well-being of the whole community. [It] will have responsibilities going beyond those of existing local authority departments, but they will include the present services provided by children's departments, the welfare services provided under the National Assistance Act, 1948, educational welfare and child guidance services, other social work services provided by health departments, day nurseries, and certain social welfare work currently undertaken by some housing departments.

It is largely a matter of history that the main burden of this recommendation was that previously separate services and activities should be brought together — integrated — to improve the nature of the service rendered. The emphasis thus moved from specialisation to generalisation of the help provided, and therefore also from specialist workers to generic social workers capable of 'covering' the whole spectrum of need, albeit with specialist back-up.

As these recommendations came to be put into effect, the personal social services became organised around the concept of a 'team' of workers, usually related to a geographical area, which further emphasises the desire to provide at the leading edge of the service a *general* coverage even if the depth of expertise sought in that service must also call for some degree of specialisation of knowledge and skill. Such consequences may be regarded as entirely consistent with the spirit of the Seebohm conception of the mission.

Nevertheless, to suggest that a service of a certain order of excellence will be available to all is in a particular way an idealised expression of a service mission. What will be made available, in reality, will be a service which is as intensive and as extensive as society (national or local as the case may be) is willing to afford at that point in time. That, in turn, is determined by political judgement (however that may be supported or influenced by special pleading by lobbyists and others) but not by any concept of effective demand (as the economist would employ that term). The question of how much of a 'free good' or 'free service' should be made available at any given time is therefore one which can only be resolved by a value judgement of some sort — and it therefore follows that people who hold different scales of values will tend to resolve the question in different ways. If, therefore, there might prove to be a high degree of consensus in society as to the general mission of a service (as in the Seebohm terms above), there might contemporaneously be a considerable degree of dissensus as to the amount of the service which ought to be made available.

Just recently, with central-government cuts in allocations to various services, this distinction between an 'effective' and an 'efficient' service[4] has been brought into sharp focus. Many of the social workers, who might well subscribe wholeheartedly to the statement of mission to be found in Seebohm, have been led, in protest, to demonstrate against the cuts proposed in the personal social services, and many of those who manage the service, and who might equally well subscribe to the Seebohm Report statement of mission, have been forced to argue for a 'realistic' appraisal of the service to be offered in the present economic climate. This administrator/professional conflict cannot be placed at the door of 'organisation'; in essence it is a political question, and as such it supports the proposition that the definition of mission is a matter for political decision.

The Work to be Done

Nevertheless, the kind of expression of the mission quoted above does indicate something of the kinds of work which have to be carried out (even if the quantities derive from the political decisions just referred to). First, there is that work which is associated with the 'generic workers' of the 'team', and historically this work has been divided into specialisms associated with children, welfare and mental health. It is here that the 'family-orientation' referred to by Seebohm is to be found, and the work is therefore essentially diagnostic of the problems brought to the agency's attention and prescriptive of solutions (which may involve the services of other agencies and workers). In this area, too, are to be found those 'professionals' who most readily spring to mind when the question of the organisation of professional work is raised in this context; nevertheless, it must be borne in mind that (in England and Wales, 1973) less than half of the workers involved are formally qualified as 'professionals'.

Second, there is that work which is associated with non-residential, day care and service, usually divided between centres for children of nursery age, adults, the mentally ill, the elderly and the physically handicapped, and the provision of help in the home. The service provided here is partly family-orientated and partly focused on the individual and his or her needs for care, instruction, and so on. In these non-residential centres there are a number of 'professionals' in evidence, but these include professional instructors and nurses, as well as social workers *per se*; in the home-help area, however, where over a third of the total employees in the local authority social services are to be found, the workers would normally not be accorded the epithet of 'professional worker'.

Third, there is that category of work which is associated with residential care and instruction. The work in this area is in some respects identical with that provided in the non-residential area, but there is a necessary addition of work of the 'hotel' type arising out of the residential nature of the service provided.

Whilst the workers in these areas do not account for all of the 222,000 workers in the local authority personal social services, they are the ones who carry out the primary tasks for which these services were established. The remainder are mainly administrative and clerical staffs, and maintenance and domestic staffs, who provide a necessary support to these activities of the 'front-line' workers (whether they are professional or non-professional). The latter are the ones who are engaged to handle such problems as the clients bring into the system, and whilst the activities involved may be distinguishable from one another because of specialisation, there is a sense in which they can all be linked together as being concerned to help clients deal with their various problems.

Isolate and Reciprocal Roles

Perhaps the most important characteristic of the work roles which arise from the solution (or attempted solution) of client-borne problems of this general type is that, at the point and time when the helping role is actually being exercised, the worker is generally isolated. The client brings the problem (whether initially to the member of the area team, or subsequently simply to ask a domestic for help with a very specific problem) to a worker in the system, and in the nature of the presentation of the problem that worker must in isolation (that is on his own) effect some resolution, even if it may be a temporary one. Whilst it would be idle to pretend that every problem which is thrown up for solution in this general way is of equal weight or difficulty, it is worth at least beginning with the recognition that most such problems do require the worker to act on his own, or on his own initiative, *and* that that requirement is not imposed only on the professionals.

That said, however, we must also recognise that in many of these problem-reducing situations, the real or final resolution of the problem will depend upon a number of workers bringing their skills to bear on the problem in parallel or in series, and that for this reason many of the roles which can be identified are also in this special way reciprocal ones. This aspect is emphasised in the creation of 'teams' in the service — whether area teams of social workers, teams within day centres or shift teams within residential centres. There is a clear sense in which, even when the worker may have to act on his own initiative in dealing with particular problems, he is also carrying out a role which is supportive of, or reciprocal to, that of another worker, possibly with very different skills, in the system.

These two characteristics of the work roles in the service situation are distinguished here because they appear to carry particular implications for the organisation of the service. On the one hand, the workers involved must be, or be made, capable of exercising initiatives when acting on their own in dealings with the client; on the other, the manner in which that initiative is exercised must be so constrained that it does not, for example, undo the work of someone else who is seeking (with possibly different skills) to deal with some other aspect of the same client's problems. (This, after all, was one of the motivations for the Seebohm Report's main recommendations.) Of course it could be contended at this point that what has been said in this section about roles in the personal social services could be said about roles in any system of purposive activity.[5] The difference lies in the peculiar constraint that is imposed upon this kind of system by the fact that the problems which such a system is seeking to reduce are client-borne and related to personal well-being; for that reason, mistakes or inadequate co-ordination must produce culturally unacceptable consequences.

Discretion and Co-ordination

The 'organisational' consequences of these characterisations of the social workers' roles focus upon the discretion associated with them and the manner in which co-ordination is effected.

It may be put that the main reason why most writers on professional organisations perceive the existence of administrator/professional conflict is that these two types of role must compete for the allocation (and the control) of discretion. In order that the professional worker may carry out his (isolate) role adequately, he must be possessed of sufficient discretion (or authority) to decide on the appropriate course of action. But the administrator's role is itself defined in terms of determining the means, modes and methods by which the workers in the system will act to realise the mission of the enterprise, and this in turn means that the administrator's role must operate to reduce the discretion which can be left to the worker to decide for himself.

The discretion allocated to any worker can never be complete or absolute; but the problem which arises in organising professional work develops from the choice of method by which its constraints are imposed on the exercise of this discretion. On the one hand, such constraints can be introduced via the socialisation of the worker: one of the functions of professional training is to inculcate, not only skills, but values relevant to professional judgement, and it is the latter which help to ensure that the professional (carrying out his role in isolation) will decide, within the range of his discretion, in ways which are consistent with the realisation of a professional mission. On the other, they can be introduced via the situationally determined rules through which the enterprise seeks to mould judgements in the interests of securing the mission of the enterprise. The choice is, essentially, between the occupational or professional code and the organisational rules.

Although it ought not to require emphasis, it remains necessary to emphasise that these codes and rules are not really concerned with the same types of problem. The archetypal model of professional socialisation is one which is founded on the belief or assumption that professional work is carried out by workers with identical roles which are nevertheless discharged in isolation. For this reason the function of the professional code, whose values are transmitted in training, is to ensure that the conduct of the professional worker is such as not to bring the profession into disrepute, and it is certainly not to provide the professional worker with a set of values to guide his conduct within an organisational system. What the code does serve to do is to provide the organised professional with an excuse for rejecting the rules of organisation as being inimicable to the discharge of his (isolate) professional role. Nevertheless, it may be hypothesised (in the absence of any detailed empirical study of this issue) that some professional codes (and perhaps more particularly the codes associated with the 'lower professions' of teaching, social work and nursing) contain more guidance on group and organisational conduct.

If this were indeed to be the case, there would then be grounds for the assertion that the conflict between professionals and administrators in social-work agencies is somehow mythical, or that 'in any case, Social Services Departments exist to promote values that the professionals — the social workers in this case — wish to promote [because] the objectives are incorporated into the organisation's objective'.[6] Rowbottom does not go this far, since he restricts his comments to 'total conflict', but it may be an insufficient characterisation of the problem to suggest that in exercising personal judgement the professional worker must accept 'certain boundaries or constraints which are set from above more or less broadly and more or less explicitly'.[7] In so far as there is overlap, there may be conditions for the avoidance of conflict, but can it be assumed that the boundaries or constraints associated with efficiency are always acceptable to those whose values derive from effectiveness criteria?

Concern or Contract?

The code which is developed to guide the caring professionals may conform to the abstract models which have been well-discussed in the literature on professionalisation,[8] in that it represents a *rational* codification of scientific knowledge applied to the appropriate field. Nevertheless, there is always built into such codes an element of human 'concern' for the client, which owes more to sentiment than to science and more to passion than to rationality. This feature of the caring professions may be accorded too little weight in discussions of the professional/administrator tension; the caring profession's foundations may lie as much in communal as in societal systems, and therefore as much in sentimental as in contractual ties.

To the extent that this is so, it may be as useful to regard the professional's response to bureaucratic administration as founded in the communal—societal distinction as in the confrontation of two variants of the organisation of rational legal authority (the bureaucratic and the professional). If the foundation for the conflict is in the latter, then there is likely to be a considerable overlap between the values of the two sub-cultures, but if it is in the former the extent of overlap is likely to be extremely small, and mutual accommodations are much less likely.

Given the distribution of trained professionals in the labour force of the personal social services, this point of distinction may be of particular significance. For even if the professionals themselves fall into the one category, the larger group of non-professionals might be expected to have greater affinity with the other. In so far as members of modern societies are socialised in the values of the bureaucratic society, this is likely to be untrue; and in so far as non-professionals might be considered to be more prone to instrumental orientations towards their work, it may also be untrue. But there is the evidence of casual observation (although not to the best of my knowledge data from empirical research) to suggest that non-professional workers in the caring services tend to subscribe to a similar (if uncodified) ethic of dedicated service to that followed by the professionals themselves.

In considerations of the value of the bureaucratic model as a supplier of principles of organisational design for the social-services departments, it is clearly of some importance to have some kind of answer to this question about worker orientations. The bureaucracy is to be regarded as a device for ensuring that when mission and tasks call for a labour force which is made up of 'strangers' (not already or independently linked together by ties of sentiment), the necessary commitment can be secured on the basis of formal contract. It therefore presupposes, first, that the sentimental ties are not present (when in fact they might well be through a professional ethic, or something similar), and, second, that a willingness to respond to 'contract' is present (when in fact the labour force may not possess such predispositions). Thus, in the sort of language used by Etzioni in the different but related context of compliance relationships, it may be necessary to determine what the real position is in the personal social-service departments, if only to avoid incongruency between the imposed and expected foundations of commitment to mission and task.[9] This has particular consequences for what constitutes acceptable personal authority and for what will be allowed to pass for the rules governing the work.

The Professional/Administrator Solution

Many professional organisational arrangements seek to effect a compromise which helps to bring about this consequence of acceptable rules; this takes the form of placing senior professionals (persons who may be assumed to know the code and to have internalised its values through long practice) in the key administrative positions — such as that of director of social services. Where, indeed, this is the key role, it can be expected to function to absorb the 'uncertainty' which will arise at the interface between the efficiency-pursuing organisation and the effectiveness-orientated professional workers. However, this compromise may belong to a situation which is now rapidly disappearing.

For not only have the social-services departments been 'reorganised' in accordance with Seebohm: local government has also been restructured in pursuit of objectives identified in the Redcliffe-Maud Royal Commission Report and the *Local Government Act* of 1972.[10] This, taken in conjunction with the Maud (1967) and Bains (1972) Reports,[11] has introduced a number of new concepts into the system.

In particular, emphasis is now placed upon 'management' (as distinct from the more widely accepted notion of 'administration') of local-authority activities, and this process is now to be carried out by teams of chief officers operating within a framework of consensus in reaching their decisions. What in effect this means is that in particular the decisions about the allocation of resources are to be made by teams of chief officer/managers (albeit in association with elected representatives), and this might be represented as a move to push these significant management decisions down to a level of organisation which was previously permitted to administer the system on the basis that those allocation decisions were 'givens' in the situation. This change of function at the chief-officer level — from administration to 'management' — is likely to throw the 'compromise' solution into jeopardy by virtue of the new emphasis on responsible allocation decisions within a requirement of consensus.

The senior professional under these circumstances is forced to accept and apply the values of an efficiency-orientated system to decisions about professional work resources. In order to make this possible, it has proved necessary to provide 'management training' to such senior officers — in many such fields and not alone in the local authorities — and the clear implication of that training process is that there are not only skills but new value systems to be learned before such officers can deal adequately with the new roles thrust upon them. Of course it is also true that those professional workers who are currently being trained for their professional work roles are also being subjected to a modicum of training in 'management', but whilst they may, in the process, acquire some managerial judgemental norms and some motivation to judge in this way, their older colleagues who did not have this dubious advantage (of management training) are unlikely to possess either norms or motivation, and the level of uncertainty to be absorbed by the new chief executive managers may be so great that the split in values will appear below them in the department, rather than above them, as may well have been the case previously.

Rules for Conduct in Organisation

It may be argued that it is because the professions have rather persistently refused to change the professional-as-individual-practitioner model to make room for a code of professional conduct in the context of co-ordinated professional activity, that the bureaucracy has been adopted as the only or the main model to guide design of professional service organisations. For where the professional cannot, or can no longer, carry out the individual practitioner role (and this applies as much to hospital doctors as to social workers) there is a need for some acceptable set of rules governing the conditions of co-ordination of different activities or the reciprocity inherent in the 'reciprocal roles' already identified. If the profession does not provide these rules, then they must be developed elsewhere – and elsewhere is very likely to mean within a structure of bureaucratic administration.

This is essentially what the bureaucracy is efficient at. As Steggert has summarised it, the bureaucracy represents a set of principles which ensure the provision of 'a system in which responsibilities are assigned and authority relationships are established most rationally and most efficiently'.[12] As such, it clearly fits the requirements of an efficiency-orientated mission. Furthermore, 'classic bureaucratic theory posits a strict and well-defined hierarchy of authority functioning on the basis of clear cut chain of command principles'.[13] This feature helps to ensure that the system will seek to depend upon formal rules as the mechanism for structuring judgement and relationships.

Of course the model of bureaucracy is sufficiently generalised for it to be possible for a large number of particular variants to be developed. A large number of writers have from time to time concerned themselves with the theoretical propositions which might apply at this level of choice. They have employed varying terms to describe the broad dimensions of the choice – monocratic and developmental bureaucracies; mechanistic and organic management systems; bureaucratic and collegial administration; and bureaucratic and professional (or project) organisation. In their different ways, however, all of these seem to be seeking to find an alternative to the model in which two features are present: first, the high degree of centralised control which associates with the logical application of the principle of hierarchy; and, second, the consequential rigidity of definition of behaviour or action of those caught up in such an arrangement. In seeking to establish the nature and extent of such choice, however, there is no intention of offsetting the (bureaucratic) organisation with an anarchistic non-organisation, a feature of the debate which allows Rowbottom, for example, to argue that the problem to be resolved organisationally is one of 'style' not structure,[14] and Katz to suggest that all 'recent sociological theories of complex organisations are a series of footnotes to Weber'.[15]

What is implied by this notion of 'style', and what is usually built into the second of the alternative 'patterns' of bureaucracy listed in the preceding paragraph, is flexibility – in the definitions, the rules and the relationships. For example, roles are relatively loosely defined to permit the widest possible discretion to the worker, rules are precise but kept to a minimum consistent with co-ordination of activities and control of performance, and relationships are often characterised in the 'friendly' if 'correct' terms often associated with the professional–client relationship itself. This is, in essence, where overlapping can be discerned between the values of the professionals and the administrators. But none of this detracts from the coercion which must derive from an efficiency-orientated mission, nor from the inherent tensions which must develop between the roles which derive from that mission and those which involve direct service to the client.

Thus the burden of the argument to this point, and the consequences for organisational design, might be summarised as follows:

(*a*) there is a problem associated with the definition and maintenance of the mission of a personal social-services department, and if this problem has been disguised by the recent redefinition in which some workers had a say, it is likely to reappear in the form of a demand for a continuing voice — organisationally, some mechanism must be provided for this to happen if commitment is to be maintained;

(*b*) there is a second problem associated with the development of an acceptable set of rules to govern the relationships between workers committed to client service, when those workers must be organised in teams, and if these rules are not developed by the professional workers themselves, then they must, perforce, be worked out by someone else — such as the administrators;

(*c*) there is then the consequential problem which arises in that event, namely what kind of discretion must be allocated to the administrators and what kind to the professionals themselves, given that not all situations and contingencies can be covered 'by rule'.

These are concerned with each of the three levels of decision usually identified in complex purposive organisations, and therefore with three 'levels' of the organisational problem:

(*a*) the level of 'corporate' decision, usually involving the 'ultimate' authority to decide, and concerned with the setting of objectives and the making of policy — in public-service organisations this is a function difficult to assign because of the manner in which national planning and local planning become intertwined;

(*b*) the level of 'administrative' decision, concerned essentially with the determination of the methods and means by which the objectives are to be realised and the policy standards maintained;

(*c*) the level of 'executive' decision, where the rules which arise from (*b*) are made to fit the peculiar operating circumstances of the enterprise.[16]

Determining the Mission

The determination of a public-service mission must, ultimately, be a matter for the public; in essence this means that such decisions will reflect the workings of the 'democratic process'. This cannot mean, however, that, say, the workers in the service can have no say in the decision process. Such a conclusion could only be justified if the democratic process could be said to give every individual member of the society an equal voice in decision-taking, and patently this is not the case. In a situation where policy decisions respond to the arguments of organised pressure groups expressing a particular point of view, is it sensible or realistic to suggest that the workers in the service, no matter how well organised they may be, should be denied any rights to voice their arguments? Outside the 'governmental' context, society is moving round to the view that the organised workers should be provided with an avenue of influence: then why not within that context?

In the case of personal social services, the recency of the Seebohm Report has tended to obscure the need to tackle this problem. The Report put together the views of many 'pressure groups', including the social workers themselves, and provided thereby a statement of mission to which most could give assent. As time passes, however, the 'founders' objectives' are likely to transmute into the 'objectives of the ruling elite' unless some device is provided for channelling alternative views to the point at which such decisions are taken. Recent experience suggests that, in the face of cuts in financial allocation (a modification of the mission by government), the workers in the service consider that the only device they have available to influence this elite is the 'demonstration'. It may be asked whether this is a sufficient provision?

The major alternative to this which has been adopted in the past has been the mechanism of joint consultation – and in all the recent reorganisations the employer has been exhorted to develop this arrangement for mutual influence. Even when the exhortations are heeded, however, a major problem remains. Joint consultation is enjoined upon the 'employer', who, in the present context, can only determine the specific objectives of the service within a framework of given purposes and financial constraints. Thus joint consultation at the local-authority level, like management at that level, can only operate within a restricting framework of decision already taken by Parliament and the Ministries. In spite of the volume of words uttered on participation, very little has been said about participation at this level of managerial decision by governments, except in the context of devolution (and as far as one can judge this is not envisaged as anything other than a breaking-up of central government – with all its prerogatives – into small change).

As a consequence of this, local (government) joint consultation must start with an acceptance that certain important decisions about mission are already taken and are to be taken as constraints. Such participation as joint consultation permits is therefore confined to participation in the taking of those decisions which are open to the local authorities to take. However, there is a strong presumption that these decisions are also the product of a 'democratic process' which is sacrosanct, and therefore in reality all that joint consultation at this level can achieve is a possible modification of the advice which the corporate managers (the teams of officers) give to the elected committees as to the specific objectives or priorities which might be pursued. This is a far cry from what is envisaged in promised legislation on the way in which commercial undertakings shall be run in the future.

If, therefore, it can be argued that, from this point of view, democratically elected governments are different, and cannot be subject to check by interest groups, the resolution of this question in that context might entail the development of a system of representation of various interest groups on a corporate planning body; to some extent this is already done, but on the assumption that the senior professional (for example the director of social services) provides the most efficient way of representing the professional interest. This may be less tenable in itself in the present context, and in any case it does little to improve the opportunity for learning unless the consultative arrangements within the department itself are extremely efficient. However, as will be argued below, the function of this kind and level of consultation ought to be different from what is envisaged here, which is the opportunity for representatives of the various worker interests to participate in the formulation of planning advice to the elected representatives – a sharing, that is, by the team of the officer's role in respect of corporate planning.

Diagrammatically, this conception may be depicted as in Figure 11.1. The corporate planning function is there regarded as the ultimate responsibility of the elected representatives but the advisory responsibility of the corporate team of officers. Both central government, through legislation/regulation and advice, and the local community, through the elected representatives, must operate to constrain the decisions which this ultimate authority is required to take. Nevertheless, two other categories of person may be seen to have a role to play.

First, the heads of departments (whether or not they are part of the corporate team) in their boundary positions between 'the corporate planners' and 'the workers' must have some opportunity to contribute informed or expert opinions to the former, and some special planning advisory machinery may be necessary to permit this to happen.

Second, the representatives of 'the workers' may need to be provided with machinery to enable them to carry out a similar function. It should, in this context, be emphasised, however, that this representative status is not associated with decisions about wages and conditions of service, nor with the administrative rules: what is envisaged here is the contribution of representative opinion from within the service on the priorities amongst the objectives to be pursued by the enterprise.

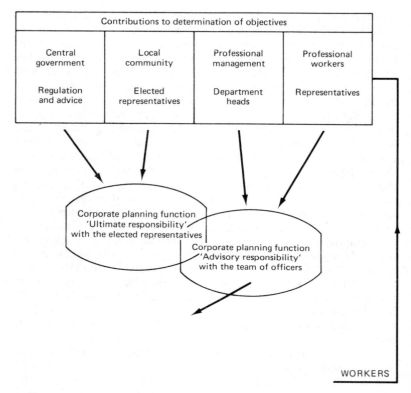

FIG. 11.1   *Emergent decision-taking structures: corporate decision-taking*

Making the Rules

It is at the level of rule-making within enterprises that the professional/ administrator conflict is seen to develop. The rule-making process is what is usually seen to be the particular preserve of bureaucratic organisation: bureaucratic principles are concerned with the manner in which 'experts' may be brought together in a purposive way even when they have no prior affinities or alliances to cement the relationships between them. The professionals, on the other hand, appreciate that the rules which are made in this way will severely constrain them in carrying out their isolate roles within a co-ordinated framework, and tend for this reason to offer resistance to the bureaucratic processes of rule-making.

As we have already argued, one of the ways in which this problem has been tackled in the past has been to place reliance upon the senior professional in an administrative role to protect the discretion of the individual professional role. Currently, this notion has been extended in the form of giving the senior professional membership of a team of officers which is required to reach its decisions unanimously. From one point of view this might be said to give the senior professional a veto on decisions which do not accord with professional values, but from another point of view it might equally be said to place the senior professional in the position where he must accept a 'greater good' than that of his profession alone.

Furthermore, this solution to the problem is further bolstered by the requirement of 'consultation' within each specialist work area (whether it is professional or not). In fact, this tends to take the form of organisation designed to secure 'consensus' amongst 'the workers'. This is most clearly specified in the Brunel University *Working Papers on the Reorganisation of the National Health Service*, where the consultation between professionals is depicted as 'between equals' and that amongst other workers follows the more conventional lines of joint consultation within a hierarchically structured department.[17] As in the other case, this may be regarded from one point of view as an arrangement for allowing worker influence on administrative decisions, but from another as a device for 'selling' the administrative roles to the work force.[18]

It may be accorded that both of these intentions are in themselves laudable enough; but it may be questioned whether this formalistic structure provides the best means of their realisation in all the circumstances of the professional organisation. Joint-consultative machinery as a *permanent* piece of communications organisation serves more the interests of the administrator in standardised mechanisms, than that of the professional for pragmatic solutions according to the circumstances. Joint consultation presupposes the existence of a hierarchy of decision authority, and is really a product of the bureaucratic form of organisation, some of whose disfunctions it seeks to reduce. If the worker interest rests on a denial of the authority of the administrator to make the rules to govern the conduct of the professional in his work role, the administrator's imposition of an arrangement for two-way communication rests upon a false assumption.

Organisationally, therefore, this problem may call for some variation on the matrix organisation theme,[19] rather than for a line-and-staff,[20] or a consultative hierarchical organisation.[21] In this conception, all the workers in the system will form a pool from which allocations may be made, from time to time, to generic or specialist roles. Provided that this allocation is not made on a rigid, once-and-for-all basis, the systematic rotation of workers from one to another in response to interests may contribute to a process of organisational learning in which individuals may at one and the same time learn something of the organisation's problems and contribute to the rule-making process by which it is sought to reduce them, and the kind of line-and-staff tension which Dalton discusses may be avoided.[22] (See Figure 11.2.)

This may need to blur the distinctions between both 'line' and 'staff' positions, and between the 'administrative' and 'executive' sub-systems. There will be a need for administrative co-ordination — for example by assistant directors — but only to ensure that the constitutional rules are followed in establishing the instruments of administrative decision-taking and performance monitoring. Like the elected representatives in the corporate planning system, they will carry the 'ultimate' responsibility for seeing that the decisions are taken, and that they are taken in accordance with the 'constitution' of the department.

But these permanent administrators may need to draw their staffs from the professionals as a 'pool' of labour who will then be engaged as either 'line' or 'staff', generic or specialist, according to the operation of the rotational rules or on the basis of self-selection according to interest. Such job-interchange, which can be developed within a system

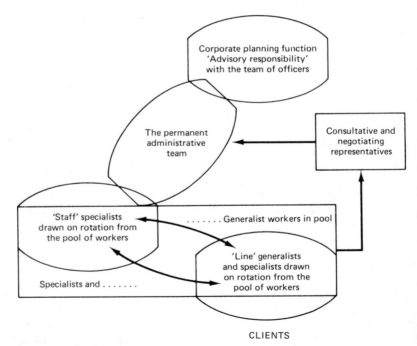

CLIENTS

F.IG. 11.2   *Emergent decision-taking structures: administrative decision-taking* of flexibility, will increase the chance that line—staff frictions will be reduced, and that the professions will play a bigger part in the development of appropriate administrative rules. The concept and approach advanced by Algie is similar to this,[23] but what must be built into the arrangement is flexibility. The creation of a 'permanent' line-and-staff arrangement of the kind depicted there would seem to be self-defeating since it would re-introduce the rigidity which most authors seek to eliminate.

In addition, it is only realistic to recognise that in our developing culture other mechanisms will be required to carry forward the normal negotiating processes between management and workers. Much of this takes the form of joint regulation of what are essentially administrative matters (looked at, that is, from the point of view of the enterprise).[24] Whether this process is termed 'negotiation' or 'consultation', it is orientated towards the determination of levels of contribution and of wages and other conditions of those who, from an organisational standpoint, are the means by which enterprise purpose is achieved.

Despite the predisposition of these types of public service to regard such conditions as being settled at 'a national level', there is every reason to respond to the need for machinery of this sort at the local level. If, on the face of it, it appears that the 'pooling' and 'rotation' of worker talents renders the need for representational systems of this sort unnecessary, it may still be argued that – in line with the matrix approach to organisation – there is a need for a sharing in technical (task or organisational) decisions in separation from any sharing in personnel (career and personal welfare) decisions.

Developing Compliance

These suggestions may deal with two problems:

(*a*) the problem of providing opportunity for professional or worker influence upon the corporate planning process on a representative basis; and

(*b*) the problem of encouraging professional or worker participation in the establishment of the administrative rule-making process on a rotational basis supplemented by representative monitoring.

If, however, this is not to operate to make the front-line workers mere instruments of enterprise purpose from whom little more than compliance is required, then some attention is required to the manner in which the work roles are carried out.

There does not seem to be *any* system within which the worker can do as he or she likes; some degree of compliance must therefore be exacted. The provision of some opportunity to influence corporate plans and administrative rules may facilitate a process of mutual influence by which adjustments and accommodations become more possible, with consequences for motivation; but these leave largely untouched the individual's basic (generic or specialist) work role. If these roles must be constrained by the pursuit of an enterprise purpose, whilst at the same time the individual must remain possessed of a discretion to decide, when confronted with the client, the area of potentially greatest promise for improvement would seem to lie in the organisation of work roles themselves as opportunities for learning (and therefore for personal if not indeed career development).

In this area, there are perhaps two main problems: first, the problem of making provision for continuing learning by the individual role incumbent; second, the problem of diminishing the artificial barriers to development which spring from the operation of a contractual division of labour at this executive level, whereby individuals must be, say, either social workers, or domestics, or van drivers.

The first of these seems to call for two things:

(*a*) a conscious development of a work (or case) rota which will provide the individual with opportunity for developing skills – a requirement which is often asserted to be within the 'purview of the supervisor' but which may be more honoured in the breach than the observance in departments over-burdened with work; *and*

(*b*) a more deliberate utilisation of the case-conference method, as a means of effecting learning opportunity for *all* of those involved.

The second seems to call for a progressive diminution of the barriers between occupations grouped within teams, and this is much more likely to prove intractable because of the threat which such action would be perceived to produce to basic securities (such as salary and status differentials). This is, however, the area of organisation which, generally speaking, is being subjected to a good deal of attack in modern society, partly through the exercise of organisational power by trade unions and other occupational associations, and partly through legislative provision. In effect, this may force enterprises to develop new policies, not only in the narrow job-enrichment sense, but also in the way of providing new career and developmental opportunities.

This is not wildly inconsistent with what authors like Rowbottom and Kogan and Terry seem to be seeking; they seek a reduction of rigidity and an increase in flexibility within a framework of organisation which – in Rowbottom's approach – has something of a membrane quality in place of the formally defined hierarchy associated with the classical bureaucracy. But to characterise the need as one for a new 'style' may not be particularly helpful unless one can indicate its character and component structure.

The need for this style may be said to arise from the nature of the work to be done (that is the requirement of high discretion) and the predispositions of people towards rules governing co-ordination of that work within a team or organisational structure. As I have tried to suggest, there is a problem associated with the allocation of discretion in professional and administrator roles, but there are also other sources of potential conflict between individual worker and the enterprise, for example at the level of political decision about purposes and objectives. There is, however, a too-ready assumption that workers must *either* be committed to aims and methods *or* be alienated from them. However, it might prove to be more realistic to make the assumption that people are ambivalent to them and that, consequently, there is potential for both co-operation and conflict within modern enterprise systems. The style which would follow from this assumption would therefore be one which provides for criticism, conflict and co-operation, albeit within a framework of mutual influence or mutual change. It would then follow that criticism or dissatisfaction could be recognised as normal and natural, and that the enterprise itself should provide opportunity for this to be given due consideration along with co-operative postures of individuals.

The Development of 'Style'

Such a participatory style would therefore seek to provide avenues for criticism and commitment to be expressed, and it would then follow from this that the aim would be to prevent rigidity and ossification of the institutional arrangements. In particular, the approach would seem to require of those responsible that the enterprise:

(*a*) provide opportunity for ideas and emotions to be expressed, whether these indicate satisfaction or dissatisfaction with existing arrangements, as a part of the normal order of proceeding, thus helping to reduce the significance of autocratic omniscience;

(*b*) provide mechanisms by which dissatisfaction can be translated through an identification of causes into new or modified objectives or methods when the dissatisfaction can be significantly legitimated in someone's values;

(*c*) deploy appropriate working groups (working parties) to examine the dissatisfaction and the variations in objectives which it might suggest, treating these groups essentially as vehicles for individual and organisational learning;

(*d*) equip such groups with the leadership and the specialist and the physical resources which they would need to carry out a systematic examination of the cognitive and affective components of the problem thus identified;

(*e*) require that such exercises will follow certain defined procedures to ensure that all appropriate aspects of the problem are examined systematically so that persons within the enterprise who are not directly involved could have confidence that any conclusions emerging were worthy of serious attention;

(*f*) so define authority, responsibility and accountability that such working groups could acquire legitimate authority without destroying the authority and accountability of other members or teams of members within the enterprise; and

(*g*) generate the expectation that a dynamic enterprise consciously seeks to encourage criticism and constructive suggestions for improvement as part of its contribution to the society which contains it.

These seven objectives would then carry certain predictable consequences for different component sub-systems and sub-cultures within the enterprise. It would be necessary to pursue the following, as enabling mechanisms for the development of such a style.

At the level of the enterprise as a whole

(1) Accept the *fact* that there are two categories of objective in the enterprise, although not necessarily their current form:
    (*a*) task achievement or output-related objectives; and
    (*b*) human consideration or input-related objectives.
(2) Derive criteria by which each of these might be evaluated, either by comparative measurement or assessment.
(3) Establish a broad structure within which both (*a*) the beneficiaries of the service, and (*b*) the providers of the service, have an opportunity to express their goals and aspirations in association with all other interest groups.
(4) Establish as a policy that the enterprise is concerned to provide opportunities for learning to those who are associated with it, whether as customer-clients, or as employees.

At the level of the management unit

(1) Prepare a 'constitution' of the unit which will cover statements of objectives and criteria as these are seen to apply at that level, and establish the basic constituent decision-taking mechanisms for that unit.
(2) Establish the ground rules, within that constitution, for effecting changes in objectives *and* methods of realising them, such that both the managers and the non-managers within the system may be aware of the way to set about making changes.
(3) Establish the appropriate structural mechanisms required for

decision-taking and for 'consultation' with interested parties within the unit, including structures for communications within work teams.

(4) Develop a policy by which normal communications within the unit will be approached and the opportunities for learning (both in-service and external) will be provided in supplementation of these normal processes.

At the level of the individual (manager or workers)

(1) Establish what are the objectives and what are the criteria which will be applied to his (or her) work, and what are the broad limits of discretion which will be expected to apply, together with an indication of where those limits abut those of others.

(1*a*) At the level of the individual manager who carries responsibility for the work of others in the enterprise, policies with respect to the development of style will need articulation, along with those criteria which apply specifically to the successful promulgation of that style.

(2) Establish the procedures which will be necessary both to the successful carrying out of the role and to the representation by the individual of changes which might be needed in that role in the light of his (or her) experience in it.

(3) Indicate the place of the individual in the scheme of things and the opportunities which exist for his self-development and advancement within the organisation or enterprise.

At the level of ad hoc working groups

(1) Review reasons for present practice and the reasons why a change is sought in order to determine what objectives ought to be pursued in the working group's investigations.

(2) Assess potential benefits or advantages of the work being undertaken, including those concerned with the training of the individuals concerned against the costs in effort, time and money involved in undertaking it.

(3) Prepare a budgeted plan of activity for the working group, presenting the result in a systematic form which can be used to evaluate progress.

(4) Prepare a separate budget for 'outside' help required to reach a conclusion, including help from 'experts' and from those who will ultimately have to accept responsibility for any conclusion or change.

(5) Maintain a check on progress towards the working group's objectives against the time budget and record the experience at the end where this offers constructive suggestions for future working groups.

(6) Undertake the 'selling' of any conclusions which might require changes in thinking, feeling or behaviour by others in the organisation.

The Participative Professional Organisation

What is thus suggested is that in professional organisations there is some need to explore means of increasing participation and role flexibility, consistent with the recognition of the need for high discretion in the worker roles, without on the one hand producing anarchical situations and on the other building rigid joint-consultative arrangements which meet few if any of the real needs of the situation. The avoidance of anarchic non-organisation seems to require that some element of coercion must be adopted, although this can be confined to a constitutional determination of the rules governing change; the avoidance of rigidity of organisation seems to require that emphasis be placed upon the generic and the contributive nature of the work role, so that specialisation does not become a permanent feature of the organisational landscape even though it must be present for most people at any one point in time.

The suggestion made is not, however, a proposal for something completely new. The various reports which have been published in the past five years on the management of the various reorganised public services all seem to lean in the directions which this chapter has sought to crystallise. If, as has happened in the personal social services, these proposals have tended to create doubt and confusion (for example, as people seek to accommodate consensus decision-taking within the textbook's emphasis upon individual authority and accountability), the reason may lie in the failure to articulate the real need of professional organisations for more organic structures in language which is not dependent upon the basic bureaucratic model. This is, perhaps, not surprising in view of the recency of 'management' in those professional service areas which are now to be managed under the various new dispensations; and of the confinement of management concepts to those situations in which simplification and standardisation of the front-line work roles has proceeded so far as to make the problem of allocation of discretion capable of solution by means which are beyond the bounds of possibility in the personal social services.

What has been proposed here may also be taken as 'a footnote to Weber', but it is one which applies to his concept of 'collegial administration' rather than to his more widely known concept of 'bureaucracy'. Curiously enough, what is proposed is also to be found in the literature of scientific management, but it lies in F. W. Taylor's treatment of 'functional management organisation' rather than in his more widely known pronouncements on work study and standardisation.[25] The argument that I have sought to advance is therefore one which suggests that consideration of the situational needs of the personal-service organisation throws up the requirement of organic organisation; if this appears to be new because it is only now that society demands that these services be managed, it has nevertheless been well-recognised for a long time that the monocratic bureaucracy resting on increasingly specialised work roles was only one of at least two models of rational organisation discernible in modern society. Perhaps now is the time to bring the other out of its apparent hibernation.

12 Comparative Studies in Social Policy and Administration

Barbara Rodgers

Introduction

In the final chapter of a book dealing with so many fundamental aspects of social administration, there is no need for me to define or defend it as a subject of academic study, or to be over-worried about its boundaries. While we would all agree that 'The quality of our understanding of current problems depends largely on the broadness of our frame of reference', we have also had demonstrated to us that understanding of the many different ways in which social policies are being, or could be, implemented depends on our willingness and ability to subject these ways to much more detailed analysis. But whether we are principally concerned with the frame of reference or the practical possibilities of different forms of administration, we are now confident enough in the core, the main focus, of our studies in social policy and administration to welcome the important contribution to be made to almost any aspect of them, by political scientists, economists, sociologists, lawyers and others.

There are few other countries in which the subject has achieved this definition and status. At a UNESCO Conference held at Sigriswil in 1973 to consider research and teaching of social policy (*la politique sociale*) in Universities, the fragmented nature of social-policy studies in most European countries was evident.[1] Generalised courses in the development of social policy, or special studies in health economics, social-security systems, industrial relations, and so on, were to be found in different university faculties, or in para-governmental research institutes. Research on some horizontal themes, such as social indicators, was developing, and the French delegate, while still expressing some doubts about the 'coherence' of social policy — as a co-ordinated collection of objectives and of alternative means of achieving them which could be subjected to systematic analysis — admitted that the move towards the teaching of a more general 'overview' of social policy came from their contacts with administrators and the expressed need to give them a wider perspective.

In discussing the possibilities and limitations, the use and abuse, of comparative studies, I am therefore assuming a measure of agreement about this area of academic study, its coherence and its context — the overview within which any closer study of its parts must be made. More British universities and polytechnics are teaching, and more writers in this and other countries are adopting, a comparative approach than was the case even a decade ago. This is evident from Michael Lund's useful study of the literature, *Comparing the Social Policies of Nations*, prepared for a Seminar on Cross-National Research in Social Policy, held at the Center for the Study of Welfare Policy, University of Chicago, in 1972.[2] Yet more studies have been published since.

I shall therefore start by emphasising, or reiterating, the difficulties and dangers inherent in all studies of social policy and administration, and their implications for comparative studies. As my main concern is with methodology, I shall then take a hard look at the status of any generalisations, or theories, we may hope to draw out of our comparative studies. What help can we get from the logicians in formulating definitions and classifications? How far can 'constructive description' or case studies, preceded by, and leading to, further analysis, help us to make the relevant social phenomena more intelligible?

I shall then go on to follow my own advice, and try to spell out some ways in which we can analyse this 'collective action for social welfare' (my chosen definition for the focus of our studies in social administration), and submit it to comparative study, despite the limitations set by the peculiar self-identity and different culture-complex of each country under consideration. My examples will be taken from the well-trodden field of social-security systems and from that of the personal social services which still await any serious comparative study, and present methodological problems of definition and analysis in a particularly acute form.

Students of social administration no longer need to be persuaded of the value of comparative studies,[3] but they do perhaps still need to be warned that they cannot be undertaken lightly, and that comparative studies involve more than the drawing of a few comparisons with other countries in the last few lectures of a course, or chapter of a book. It would hardly seem necessary to draw such an elementary distinction in an academic treatise on the 'foundations of social administration' were it not that teachers and students alike are exposed to a constant stream of such comparisons, more often than not made in support of such good causes that their validity is too rarely questioned. One might well ask what these off-the-cuff comparisons have to do with serious comparative studies? Nothing, except that they are made with such assurance by people who often have so much detailed knowledge of the British counterpart of the particular aspect of social administration under discussion — be it family allowances, pensions or day-care facilities — that they tend to be taken seriously, and only those who are disciplined in comparative studies are proof against them.

I use the term 'disciplined' advisedly. It is not only in the comparative approach that students of social administration too often show a lamentable lack of intellectual discipline. So many of them are drawn to study social administration because they care; and in the face of social deprivation of all kinds, the heart naturally tends to rule the head. That is understandable; but a more subtle danger is that from being on the side of the angels is but a short step to a self-righteousness rooted in a confusion of detachment with indifference. To tear a shred from T. S. Elliot:

> There are three conditions which often look alike
> Yet differ completely, flourish in the same hedgerow:
> Attachment . . . detachment
> . . . and growing between them, indifference
> Which resembles the others as death resembles life,
> Being between two lives — unflowering, between
> The live and the dead nettle (*Little Gidding*).

It is this confusion more than anything else which militates against any keen, objective definition and analysis of ends and means. And that is surely what studies of social policy and administration are all.about?

One would expect that many of those who write for pressure groups, or who are in some other way politically committed to some general or specific scheme for advancing the welfare of a particular citizen group in their country, might be something less than objective in their analysis of the political, economic and administrative implications of the measures they advocate. But when they look at apparently comparable measures and achievements of another country, the political, economic and administrative concomitants for that country and its almost certainly different economic, social, cultural, demographic and political history and geography are more often than not left right out of the account.

Nevertheless, some exceptionally useful and valid comparative studies have been made when researchers sufficiently steeped in the discipline of a comparative approach have undertaken to report on what is happening in other countries for a committee which is overtly concerned, but in a responsible way, to influence policies for a particular group. Appendix III in Volume 2 of the Finer Report on 'Income Maintenance for One-Parent Families in Other Countries: an Appraisal', by Christine Cockburn and Hugh Heclo, is a recent example.[4] (An excellent exercise for students might lie in a critical evaluation of such studies, recognising the auspices and purposes for which they were undertaken.)

If, on the one hand, we must be wary of the comparisons drawn, or the pseudo-comparative studies made, by those who are less concerned with the validity of the comparisons than their purpose, we should also, I think, be wary of the academics whose major preoccupation is theory-building, and who may be equally unconcerned with the validity of their deductive comparisons. Yet another pitfall is a failure to distinguish between ends and means, the goals and the instruments. A common example is the indiscriminate use of the ill-defined concepts of 'universalism' and 'selectivity' as applied to the social-security and other supportive services of different countries, leading to superficial evaluations of a country's objectives and/or ways of achieving them.

Some Logical Problems of Comparative Studies

It is important to be clear about the status of any generalisations made in comparative studies. In discussing the difficulties and dangers of applying the comparative method to the studies of social institutions, Ginsberg warns against attempts to use comparative studies to formulate theories regarding the nature of society as a whole, or any claims 'to formulate the general laws of its evolution or development'. He stresses the difficulties of 'comparing the institutions of a given area with the "similar" institutions of other areas, on the grounds that each area is a unity, having a peculiar self-identity, with the result that the nature of institutions is distorted when they are studied apart from the culture-complex to which they belong'. However, assuming that the comparative method as such is not committed to any particular theory of sociology — or social policy:

> It is in essence nothing but an application of a general principle of methodology to vary the conditions of a phenomenon under investigation with the object of eliminating irrelevancies and the discovery of essentials. When applied to the study of social facts this involves the use of data from various periods of time and from the

life of different peoples. The primary object is the attainment of a classification of cultural phenomena and the establishment of a social morphology which would facilitate the discovery of empirical generalisations and perhaps eventually of more ultimate laws.[5]

Indeed there seems no reason why we should not be able to formulate many interesting if tentative generalisations of this kind about the development of social policy and forms of social administration from wide inductive comparisons. But in view of the interrelatedness of all social phenomena, and of these 'social facts' in particular, we clearly need many more intensive case studies of different areas, as well as great caution and humility in the tracing of similarities and differences, remembering that our analyses (not theories) of social policies are only useful so long as they illuminate and in some measure help to 'explain' the facts better than any others. So, too, any generalisations we draw should be stated as hypotheses to be tested out in further studies.

In other words, what we need are more 'constructive descriptions' of the many aspects of social policy and administration in this and other countries. A constructive description is 'descriptive, for it is dependent upon and checked at every stage by exact observation, it is constructive since it renders these [phenomena] . . . intelligible'.[6] To make social phenomena intelligible in this way, we must proceed *pari passu* by definition and classification. By this process of analysis we are able to clarify our ideas about the facts, revealing the implications of the expressions we use, and seeing what follows from their analysis. As we start from the sensible facts, the realities, which remain unaffected by how we think about them, so any 'experimental generalisations' or hypotheses which we formulate in our studies must be tested against other observed similarities, with all the accuracy and objectivity – and modesty – which the scientific approach adds to any common-sense observation.

As John Ford pointed out in a paper prepared for the Joint University Council for Public and Social Administration (J.U.C.) Comparative Social Administration Group,[7] we are dependent for so many of our facts not only on secondary sources but on translations of them. An appreciation of what is meant by particular terms – even such common terms as 'social security' – is as important as it is difficult. It means that we have to be careful about our own definitions, and aware of other people's definitions, or lack of them, before we embark on any comparative analysis. Thus, before we consider the peculiar difficulties of arriving at any agreed definitions and useful classifications for our comparative studies in social administration, it would be as well to remind ourselves of the logician's usual criteria for a definition:

(1) a definition should state the essential attributes of the species[8] defined;

(2) a definition must not contain the name defined — or a synonym of the name defined;

(3) the definition must be exactly equivalent to the species defined — it must denote the species, the whole species and nothing but the species;

(4) a definition must not be expressed in obscure, figurative or ambiguous language — there is no worse logical fault than to define the unknown by the still more unknown; and

(5) a definition must not be negative where it can be affirmative — though this rule is often not applicable and therefore not always binding.

Where a definition complies with all these rules and contains an analysis of a common idea — for example 'danger' is 'exposure to harm' — it can express a notable advance in understanding to enable us to see what it was we were meaning when we used the expression. Where it breaks the rules — and how easy it is to think of flagrant examples — it may obscure more than it clarifies, and provides no logical basis for any subsequent argument. As Wright Mills has pointed out, we must agree on a definition before we can disagree about the facts, never mind compare them.

A definition of any kind is of course only a kind of classification, and when we come to distinguish the special characteristics of the genus and species, we are up against the same difficulties in discovering and describing uniformities in large numbers of phenomena. Moreover, the number of classifications which can be made out of almost any body of social phenomena is exceedingly large. The likenesses and differences may be in terms of place, time, circumstance, quality, magnitude, activity, behaviour or function, coexistence or sequence, and so on; but the characteristics we use as a basis of classification should always be determined by the end sought. So the difficulties are not insuperable, once we abandon the attempt to make classifications which will hold for all purposes, and recognise all classifications as valid only for specific purposes.

To stress the importance — and difficulties — of arriving at agreed definitions and developing useful classifications, particularly for the 'micro' aspects of social administration, is not to advocate a Platonic/Aristotelian approach, which could all too easily lead us into an arid scholasticism. Popper's methodological nominalism suits our case much better.[9] He suggests that while the essentialist interpretation (Plato) normally reads a definition from left to right, the nominalist reads from right to left. It starts from the defining formula and asks for a short label to it. To take his example: 'A puppy is a young dog' is for the nominalist an answer to the question: what shall we call a young dog? rather than to the question: what is a puppy? It is because I favour this approach that I stress the importance to comparative studies of constructive descriptions. To embark on these we do not have to wait until we have precise definitions, satisfying all the logician's criteria, for the social phenomena we are proposing to study. Indicative guidelines will suffice. It is only later, as we come to sort out the raw material of our observations, that we must try to formulate more refined definitions and relevant (for our purpose) classifications, if we wish to submit our data to comparative analysis.

As with our hypotheses there is nothing definitive about our definitions. They can be discarded as soon as someone comes up with a better one. But, meanwhile, having 'defined the meaning of our terms', we must be unambiguous in our use of them.

A Definition for Further Analysis

If we can then start from an agreement that 'collective action for social welfare' is a useful short-hand term for the focus of our studies in social policy and administration, we can go on to enlarge upon this short-hand term, using it as a basis for further analysis.

It is commonly agreed that this collective action involves the setting of goals, the choice of instruments and the operation of particular programmes. Our studies are therefore potentially concerned with all the social phenomena which influence decisions taken at the level of policy formation and legislation, at the middle level of administration, and at consumer level where services are 'delivered'. Finally, we must be concerned with some evaluation of what has been achieved — since we purport to be dealing with a real world.

A dynamic process

It is also commonly agreed that this whole process of collective action for social welfare is normally a dynamic one; even if in some countries at some times it comes near to grinding to a halt. There is something rather naive about the present-day obsession with policies or instruments of 'change'. (I am reminded of the contribution of a weighty German professor of social policy to a European seminar: 'That social conditions will change is a possibility verging on the probable.')

The need for constant change — for adjustment, innovation and, most difficult of all, for getting rid of outdated attitudes and practices — is patently obvious to the sensitive and intelligent, who operate at the consumer level of the welfare services. Constant changes in the economic and political climate, in the conditions of life of different sections of the population, in the perceptions of the providers, and in the expectations of the receivers, demand changes in our collective action for social welfare. But what is not so obvious is *what* changes? Often it is a matter of recognising the welter of changes which are anyway occurring or likely to occur, and deciding which to encourage, which to try and restrain, which to try to redirect, which to ignore — and how then to reconcile them so as to minimise disharmony in their combined effect.

There is always a time lag in collecting the relevant facts, never mind understanding the implications, of all these changes. We cannot keep up with them, and we find ourselves more often than not trying to solve the problems of the last decade, or acting on inadequate information. Yet the social-policy question is not the simple ideological one of 'Where do we go?' but 'Where do we go from here?'[10] Improved ways of collecting and interpreting data relevant to the current situation are vital if our collective action is to be more effective — as vital as the historical perspective which affects the judgement of those who have studied and analysed how collective action for social welfare has developed in the past.

Interactions and interrelationships

The interaction and interrelatedness of policies and programmes are equally obvious, but the precise nature of these interrelationships in given situations often defies analysis. Nevertheless, with more studies of this particular aspect of social administration, we can hope to arrive at more empirical generalisations, which will be of practical value to those who have to take these interactions into account in formulating and implementing social policies. To be of any immediate practical value, such studies will need to suggest, if they do not actually spell out, how

(1) cost—benefit analysis can be made, or opportunity costs assessed; and how

(2) more effective co-ordination between different administrations can be achieved.

At the highest policy level, cost—benefit analysis must be concerned with the interaction of the economic and the social — with the economic aspects of social policies and the social aspects of economic policies — and with the scarcity factor, which reduces so many social-policy decisions to decisions about priorities. The case to be established is not usually for doing something *per se* (except in emergencies and crises when the need for immediate action is obvious), but for doing one thing rather than another, or for doing one thing before another.[11]

Co-ordination, whether vertical or horizontal, takes so many different forms, and needs to take account of such different factors at each of the three levels of collective action, that it warrants much more study and analysis than it has received so far.[12]

Again it is at the consumer level, in assessing the benefits derived and the price paid (in terms of benefits lost or forgone), that the results of the failure to co-ordinate basic policies and programmes regarding housing, income maintenance, residential and community care, and so on, are most vividly seen and appreciated. At this level, we see it in terms of individuals, who obviously fail to derive full benefit from the wide range of social services available to them, or who pay too high a cost (in loss of familiar surroundings or community support, of freedom or dignity) for the new dwelling, or for the medical or social care. We see it in its starkest form in the 'poverty trap'.

This interrelatedness is probably most easily forgotten at the middle level of administration, where broad policies laid down in legislation have to be implemented. At this point I would risk one empirical generalisation, or hypothesis: that the larger the administration, the more functional and monopolistic the service (for example the National Health Service in the United Kingdom), the more introverted and concerned with its own internal problems of co-ordination it is likely to become.

Too broad or too narrow an interpretation? outputs and outcomes

While this analysis and discussion of what is involved in the study of social policy and administration has so far followed fairly well-worn tracks, it will have done little to dispel the anxiety felt by most students: how to avoid the Scylla and Charybdis of too broad or too narrow an interpretation of the subject. My initial definition — collective action for social welfare — helps here, if we do not lose sight of the conscious purpose expressed in the 'for'. At the level of policy-making this sometimes means a purposeful inaction. 'As used here, policy will designate a course of action or inaction pursued under the authority of government', writes Heclo.[13]

Policy may or may not be expressed through programmes. But if it is, it is useful to distinguish between the 'outputs' of a particular programme, in terms of the benefits directly provided by it, which may well admit of precise description and even qualitative and quantitative measurement, and the 'outcomes' of broader, less easily measured effects of policies, and/or the side-effects of particular programmes.[14]

A further analysis of these concepts of outputs and outcomes will help in the difficult task of evaluating the achievements of a country's collective action for social welfare. The output of a programme is to be evaluated in relation to its stated objectives, and to the input of resources allocated to it. The more specific these objectives are, the easier it will be to measure the output. The income-maintenance services, because they are concerned with quantifiable cash benefits, admit of more measurable outputs than the health or personal social services, where the quality of the service rendered is less easily measured – although indicators of standards of care, often in terms of staff ratios, are continually being sought.

Outputs in the personal social services are particularly difficult to assess, as the functions or objectives of these services are vaguer and less well understood than those of social security, health or education. In the personal social services, outputs could presumably be measured in terms of the benefits: for example residential or foster-home placements, home helps, social workers, protection or rehabilitation services, which the personal-social-service agencies, whether generic or specialised, provide to meet the 'need' for social care and protection of children or adults. But there can be no precise or absolute definition of this 'need', and in many cases it could be met by a number of alternatives, or a combination of different services. The short- or medium-term objectives in relation to which output of these services is measured will be more concerned with 'needs to be met', a concept which takes account of policy decisions about priorities of need and of resources available in a particular locality.

How far can outputs reflect attempts to meet the obvious need for co-ordination between services, particularly when most major services are organised, as in the United Kingdom, according to function rather than to target groups? The concept of primary and secondary functions helps here. Many of these functional services, or service organisations, are required, by legislation or administrative advice or regulation, to exercise secondary functions, for example the health visitor's secondary function to give social advice, or the local education authorities to provide ancillary services. Others are required to co-ordinate their services with those of others in certain formal ways – through joint-consultative committees, case conferences or the keeping of registers. Presumably the amount of staff time given to such secondary or co-ordinating functions, and the attendant adminstrative expenses, could be measured and expressed in terms of output as well as that given to the primary function of the organisation. But too often these outputs are ignored, and so never costed in terms of the input of resources needed to achieve these important objectives. Accepting that one of the primary functions of social workers is to co-ordinate services on behalf of their clients, any organisation employing social workers has presumably taken some steps to see that its service output, at the delivery level at least, is co-ordinated with that of others.

Management by objectives is an attempt to break down the over-all long-term aims of a large organisation into short-term objectives for particular departments or sections, while involving the staff of each section in the setting of its targets, and agreeing with them on the ways in which outputs will be measured. However, the difficulties of finding precise statements of objectives and of measuring the quality of service outputs remain, and must not be conveniently forgotten when we come to compare quantified outputs of similar (according to their objectives) programmes, whether in the same or different countries.

If outputs are related to programmes, outcomes are more appropriately related to policies. In assessing outcomes, account must be taken of the same wide range of economic, political and social factors as influence the policy-makers in setting their goals/objectives and in deciding on their strategy for implementation. The outputs of relevant programmes are of course an important part of any assessment of the outcomes of a particular policy; or, put in another way, estimates of outputs, of measurable direct benefits are seen in a wider context, which takes account of side-effects, of indirect and less tangible welfares and diswelfares. Outcomes are concerned with who has actually benefited, indirectly as well as directly, by the provision of particular services, and who has been affected to their detriment, by how much and in what way?

How far can one go in trying to trace the repercussions of the implementation of social policies? As suggested earlier, the problem of identifying and selecting the most relevant data is the same, whether you are studying how policies developed, or their outcomes. Either way, such academic study follows after the event — it is already history. The policy-makers themselves will be much more limited in the factors they can consciously take into account and use in actually making their decisions. It would therefore seem important that students of policy development should distinguish between policy decisions which were based on conscious attempts to collect and use data about the factors likely to influence outcomes, and those which were based, perhaps, on sound hunches or instincts but took no conscious account of factors which, with hindsight, are seen to have been highly relevant.

Heclo discusses how far the academic can go in his comparative studies of social policy in Britain and Sweden:

> There is not a single decision dealt with in this book that could not alone have occupied at least a year's study of just how and why it

occurred. Even if there were the resources to approach such finality, however, common sense would require that the investigation be limited to what seems sufficient to arrive at reasonably probable answers to the questions posed . . . [He goes on to suggest that] settling on the level of analysis requires choices about the scope of policies to be covered, the number of countries, and the period of study.[15]

Strategies and tactics

How far can policy-makers go in tracing the influences on, and repercussions of, their policy decisions? Much depends on the level at which policy decisions are being taken, and how far they are seen as strategic rather than tactical and therefore worked out on a broader canvas. But 'strategy' and 'tactics', like 'genus' and 'species', are basically relative concepts. What the man at the top of the hierarchy of policy-makers (those who make the primary political decisions) regards as a tactic to be left to the man below him, the man below may regard as a strategy in relation to the man below *him*. Even those at the bottom, in the sense that they are involved in the actual delivery of services — and this includes many professional people like doctors or social workers — may well distinguish between *their* strategies and tactics. However, the concept is a useful one in that it underlines the continuum of 'policy' decisions, which are not all made discretely by politicians and legislators. Policy and its implementation, policy-making and administration, are not in fact completely separate activities, although we often talk about them as though they were. There may be a certain ambiguity about how far social policies and their outcomes are intended or could be foreseen, but strategies are unequivocally a conscious attempt to relate ends and means.

Strategic thinking about collective action for social welfare is therefore basically concerned with 'determining the relative importance and urgency of different desirable objectives',[16] and at the same time choosing which instruments are most likely to achieve, directly or indirectly, the appropriate outcomes. There are two characteristic features of social-policy strategies.

(1) They almost always involve choices in timing — the time dimension is important in most policy decisions. (One is reminded of the conversation about Burke: 'Burke was right, you know.' 'Oh yes, Burke is always right, but he is right too soon.')

(2) The choices to be made about ends and means can rarely be made independently — in spite of the favourite rhetorical question: 'Can we afford not to do this?' If the choices are made independently,

you may end up by trying to get a quart out of a pint pot, or failing to recognise that certain objectives are incompatible. Any academic analysis of particular social-policy objectives and of the means of implementing them will be of little help to the strategist unless it takes account of these two characteristics.

An example from Rimlinger. A good example of hard-headed strategical thinking is given by Rimlinger in his 'constructive description' of the development of social-welfare policies in Germany.[17] As it is concerned with primary political decisions about objectives, and the interaction of economic and social policies in seeking to implement them, it illustrates my point well.

In the post war period, Professor Mackenroth was attacking the problem of (social security) protection, not from the viewpoint of individual need but from one of the aggregate amount of resources a society is willing and able to allocate to social security and social services. Having made the point that the amounts allocated to social security in the real sense must come out of current GNP, he argues that there are three ways in which the amounts allocated to social security can be increased:

(1) through the redistribution of the aggregate amounts available for consumption;
(2) through the reduction of aggregate investment; or
(3) through an increase in the national product.

He did not believe that much could be gained by a redistribution of income allocated to consumption, and considered a reduction in the rate of investment undesirable. The only remaining degree of freedom, therefore, was to increase the national product.

This line of argument tied the development of social rights directly to economic growth and had an important influence in shaping the structure and growth of social-security benefits in post-war Germany. On the other hand, when Mackenroth goes on to stress that 'There must be no provisions that conflict with the productivity of the economy or the growth of the national product', and criticises programmes for their tendency to 'sterilise' and misallocate labour, he is only giving negative advice and not providing the positive strategy within a strategy which is needed if social-security objectives, other than those of maintaining workers' productivity, are to be met.

An example from Beveridge. Beveridge's strategies, on the other hand, were directed towards planning on several levels. In his Report, warnings were given — but not taken — about the importance of timing rises in the rates of benefit to his 'national minimum', with due regard to the post-war economic situation and to the demands of other forms of social expenditure, particularly on a national health service, which he saw as an essential part of his broader social-security strategy. Equal emphasis was given to economic policies directed at maintaining full employment, and a warning about the dangers of inflation. However, the main focus of his Report, in accordance with his terms of reference, was on his proposals for a comprehensive national insurance scheme, which was to be the principal instrument by which, he argued, 'freedom from want' could be secured and a national minimum established (his stated objectives). With hindsight one could argue that the weakness of his strategy for a comprehensive social-security (income-maintenance) plan was that one of the six principles of his main instrument of social insurance, that is 'adequacy' of benefits, was more properly an objective of over-all social-security policy. Again with hindsight, one can see that his analysis of what could, and what could not, in the 1970s as much as in the 1950s, be achieved through a contributory 'insurance' scheme, however comprehensive and however financed, was inadequate. The residual and supplementary function of the national assistance scheme, which he saw as necessary in the early years, was to wither away, as practically all became entitled to a flat-rate insurance benefit which would provide an adequate national minimum for all except exceptional cases. In the event, this social-insurance scheme, and indeed no social-insurance scheme as comprehensive in coverage as the British was to become, has ever been able to guarantee an acceptable *national* minimum,[18] least of all one based on flat-rate contributions.

In the United Kingdom the national assistance/supplementary benefit scales, including the rent element, have always been higher than those of the basic national insurance scheme. In fact the relativities between the scale rates of the two schemes have scarcely changed over the twenty-seven years they have been in operation. Comparative studies in social-security policies have shown that most other Western countries, less obsessed than we are with *guaranteeing* a national minimum to *all* citizens, have also found it necessary to provide some special categorical assistance supplement to their minimum insurance benefit for pensioners, as well as maintaining a residual, needs-tested, assistance scheme for exceptional cases.

An analytical framework

The basis for sound strategies. These two illustrations demonstrate, I hope, how important it is to apply a most stringent analysis of objectives, of the resources allocated and of the instruments selected for achieving them at every level of collective action for social welfare. Sound strategies are dependent on such analyses. How often does one find academics (or academic politicians and journalists), as well as politicians, condemning particular proposals for being unlikely to achieve objectives at which they are not primarily directed? One recent example was the tax-credit scheme put forward in the United Kingdom by the Conservative Government of 1970—4. These particular proposals were designed, not to abolish poverty nor even to bring relief to the poorest section of the population, but to provide a more rational and co-ordinated system of tax allowances and social-security benefits. It was a strategy to benefit tax administration generally and also those who were caught in a poverty trap due to the failure to relate the tax threshold to basic social-security and other means-tested benefits. As far as 'abolishing poverty' was concerned, that tax-credit scheme ought to have been seen as a strategy within a strategy.

One could give endless illustrations of similar failures to deal with this basic (and one would have thought obvious) problem of social-policy analysis — to use the current American 'short label':[19] how to relate the different levels of policy-making, the strategies and the tactics, or the strategies within strategies, and to define the objectives and explore the most appropriate instruments, at each level of collective action for social welfare.

The basis for any comparative study. Those who would undertake comparative studies of social policy and administration must start from some such analysis (or conceptual framework, to use a more popular term) as this, and be prepared to follow it through with as much objectivity as they can muster. And that includes rejecting the analysis, and looking for a better one, if it, or the 'short-label' definitions, no longer fit the social phenomena being studied.

More Constructive Descriptions

With more recognition of the methodological problems of studies in social policy and administration, and more thought given to the kind of analysis our subject-matter demands, we can hope for many more constructive descriptions of different aspects of this collective action for social welfare, in our own and other countries. Only from such national studies can we safely proceed to comparative studies. Indeed we already have many writers in comparative administration who have themselves contributed some of the most valuable of these constructive descriptions.

Related to parallel political and social studies

He who would make a comparative analysis out of such national studies is not only dependent on his colleagues in social administration. If he is to write in any depth about the development of social policy or about present practices in social administration in other countries, he will be as dependent as he is in writing about his own country on the analytic or constructive descriptions of social and economic historians, political scientists and others. Since the focus of his studies on the development of social policy, or of particular social policies, is different from theirs, he needs considerable understanding and skill if he is to relate and use what is relevant from their political, economic or sociological analysis to his own.

Rimlinger's comparative study on *Welfare Policy and Industrialization in Europe, America and Russia*[20] is really composed of three such constructive descriptions (Germany, the United States and Russia), out of which he draws his tentative conclusions. What impresses is the way in which he uses the writings of a wide range of historians and social scientists from these different countries in order to develop his theme, the development of social-income protection: 'The main objective of this study is to explain the forces that have shaped modern social security systems; it is a comparative historical analysis of the responses to the challenge of insecurity in different environments.'[21] His national studies are constructive in their analysis of the historical, political, economic and social facts which he and others saw as relevant to his theme; and descriptive, in that they are checked at every stage, not by 'direct observation', but by a thorough research of mainly secondary sources.

Students of society, perhaps in self-defence against the overwhelming mass of facts and interpretations to which they are exposed, tend to compartmentalise their knowledge; it seems more manageable if kept strictly within the channels of different 'courses' — though hopefully something seeps through to irrigate and cross-fertilise the whole. While unwilling to recognise social administration as a subject in its own right, some social-science professors have nevertheless found that a problem-focused course in social administration provides a useful exercise in crossing boundaries. In analysing social problems and how they are being tackled, students learn to pay more than lip-service to the obvious relevance of political, economic and social studies to each other.

Students specialising in social administration who are continually encouraged 'to connect',[22] and succeed in some measure in doing this in their analysis of problems of social policy and administration in their own country, may still have difficulties when it comes to comparative studies. Even when, for example,[23] their first-year course in 'politics' was itself based on a comparative approach, they are not necessarily able to put to good use what one would presume they had learnt about political influences and structures of government in other countries. The trouble was that they had 'learnt' their constitutional models, but had not in fact read enough (or any?) good constructive descriptions of government and administration in particular countries. There was no flesh on the skeleton of the analysis which had been presented to them, and so, for many of them, no real understanding. They had been fed on too much pre-digested fare. Before they could be set to analyse the collective action for social welfare of France or the United States, they had to be sent back to read some of the more descriptive texts which they had avoided reading earlier.

A constructive description increases understanding because it has a focus which indicates (rather than determines) the range of other studies, or of primary sources for original studies, which can be analysed in the ways suggested in the previous section. In making the preliminary decisions about what the aim or focus of the study should be, in selecting relevant data, whether from primary or secondary sources, and in settling on the depth or level of analysis which is practicable, judgement is everything.[24] There can be no right or wrong decisions, only more or less good judgement brought to the making of them. How can we cultivate good judgement in these matters? There are no short cuts, no substitute for knowledge and experience – a wide, and in relevant areas a quite detailed, knowledge of the factors affecting collective action for social welfare in the countries to be compared, and experience of teaching and writing, if not comparative studies then something in a comparative vein.

It is particularly important that the first and most vital choice – of the focus or theme of the study on which one is embarking – be closely related to one's own knowledge and experience. Incompetence and superficiality in comparative studies almost always stem from the authors having over-reached themselves. Some have too superficial a knowledge, or perhaps little real understanding, of the framework of reference of collective action for social welfare in the countries chosen, and so cannot handle what they like to call the 'background facts'. Others choose to focus on a particular policy or service without adequate knowledge and understanding of how policy decisions are made and services actually operate at all three levels of collective action for social welfare. Thus we sometimes get social economists, well equipped to write about the wider, economic implications of social-security policies, but with too little knowledge of operational problems of administering and 'delivering' different kinds of insurance or assistance benefits, and therefore ill-equipped to assess outcomes – what the policies are able to achieve. At other times it is social workers writing about some aspect of the personal social services, for example social work or child care, whose understanding of the dynamics and inter-relatedness of all collective action for social welfare, as well as of economic and social policies, is so limited that anything they have to say about the service(s) under consideration in their own country, and even more so in others, is at best superficial and at worst positively misleading.

Asking the right questions

An inadequate approach of either kind is almost invariably signalled by a failure in asking the relevant questions and so in the initial analysis of the focus of the study. What are the policy or programme objectives (or, if it is a developmental study, how did they come to be formulated), what instruments are being used to implement them, and with what results? How carefully were these ends, means and outcomes defined, if only with 'short-label' definitions at the start of the project? What attempts were made to analyse by classification — by 'eliminating irrelevancies and the discovery of essentials'[25] — in order to make comparisons between the 'same' institutions from different culture-complexes possible? Examples of such a failure in policy analysis (an academic exercise), or in the strategies proposed (by policy-makers), in the field of social security have already been given. One could give many more — of success as well as failure — in all social fields. But I am not so much concerned with a critique of the comparative studies made to date, as with a consideration of methodological problems, which if they can be overcome can add a much needed discipline and stringency to all our studies in social administration.

Comparative studies of social work and the personal social services

For this reason, and because most major comparative studies have so far been focused on social-security or health services, or on assessments of the total input and output (not outcomes) of social policies in different countries,[26] I shall end by considering some of the methodological problems facing those who would undertake comparative studies focused on social work or the personal social services.

Either way, whether it is social work (an activity) or any or all of the personal social services (organisations, many of which employ social workers) to be studied, there is the initial problem of finding agreed, even 'short-label' definitions which can help us to identify similar institutions in different countries. This lack of agreed definitions, particularly of social work, has not encouraged further systematic analysis, which needs a framework for constructive descriptions of parts or the whole of this area of social-service provision seen within the context of a country's over-all collective action for social welfare. Such constructive descriptions would help us to refine and develop the rough definitions with which we start, particularly if they are to be used in a comparative study. In trying to compare like with like, one is forced into trying to eliminate irrelevancies and discover essentials.

Definitions. Having just participated in a cross-national study[27] of the way in which 'personal social services' (more commonly known as 'general social services' in the United States; the French had no name for them!) are delivered in seven countries, I am convinced of the wisdom of starting with a fairly broad definition, so that one does not miss out anything of relevance. From this one proceeds by further analysis of some of the concepts which are the common currency of this area of study: 'need', social work, community care, co-ordination, participation, and so on; thence to constructive descriptions of policies and programmes, national and local, in particular countries; and so back to a refined and more explicit definition of what it is one is comparing.

In comparative studies at least, we are likely to make most progress if we define social work and the personal social services by function, rather than by what 'social workers' (or the apparently nearest equivalent, for example *assistant social* in France) do; and by what kinds of services (residential care, home helps, social workers, and so on) the personal social services provide. What social workers actually do, and the many different kinds of personal social services provided, how and by whom, will of course be described as honestly and objectively as possible in the national studies. We may then find 'social workers' doing other things than social work (as defined), and other agencies, whose primary function is health or education, employing social workers or providing personal social services (as defined). But if we are agreed on the essentials, the core function of social work or of the personal social services, we can eliminate these facts as irrelevant to our definitions; but not of course irrelevent to our study of how the personal social services, including social-work services, are administered and delivered. We end up by reinforcing our original definition by function, by asking ourselves what is the peculiar contribution which the personal social services make to the over-all objectives of collective action for social welfare in each country.

The leading article in *The Times* of 26 May 1975, under the heading of 'A Special Kind of Help', discussed the present predicament of social workers who are going through a crisis of identity – 'a period of self-examination and even of doubt'. After discussing the alternative claims and aspirations of caseworkers and community action workers as to what social work is (or should be) all about, it concludes: 'Both these criticisms of social work exaggerate the power of the social worker [to change persons or systems] and ignore the special contribution that he can make.' After analysing what the leader writer thinks that special contribution to be, the article ends: 'It is in providing that kind of specialised assistance that the social worker has a distinctive contribution to make. It is on that, and on monitoring somewhat more rigorously its success in doing so, that the profession now should concentrate.' A strategy for making the best use of social workers? But the writer has proceeded, as I am advocating the academic should, by defining by function.

At this point I should perhaps give the refined definitions of social work and the personal social services at which I arrived after spending the best part of two years working with colleagues on Professor A. J. Kahn's Cross-National Study. They are not very different from those drawn out of the constructive description of social work (in this country) given in the conclusions of *Portrait of Social Work*,[28] and of the personal social services in *A New Portrait of Social Work*.[29] But they have been reformulated to take account of the findings of the national case studies made by my American, Canadian, French, West German, Polish, Israeli and Yugoslav colleagues. Not that they or Professor Kahn are to be held in any way responsible for or committed to them. I put them forward as an academic exercise in definition in a difficult area: something people can get their intellectual teeth into, agree or disagree with, and hopefully come up with something better.

I suggested that the three basic functions of social *work* (the generalist basis?), wherever it is found, are the following:

(1) encouraging access, helping people to avail themselves of community resources of all kinds (client advocacy);

(2) recognising the need for case integration (an American 'short label') in the many cases where more than one service is involved in helping an individual, group or community, and being able to play one's part in case — and service — co-ordination (co-ordinating function); and

(3) responding sensitively to the 'needs' of the individual(s), which means leaving as much choice and encouraging as much participation as possible, while ensuring such care and protection for the individual(s) and society as each situation demands (the art of helping).

As for the personal social *services* — or, as I prefer to call them, the social-care services — they are primarily concerned, in the interests of individuals *and* society, with the following:

(1) providing the practical supports needed by those who for any reason have become dependent on others in their day-to-day living;

(2) creating substitute 'homes' for those who are temporarily or permanently homeless;

(3) providing parent or friend substitutes, again when the real thing is not available; and

(4) providing the social element in the treatment of deviants.

Although many of these services may be, or are, provided by medical or education staff or administrators, social workers, because of their primary functions as defined above, have a peculiarly important and relevant contribution to make to their planning, administration and delivery.

This last tentative generalisation could be set up as a hypothesis — to be tested out in a future comparative study?

Having dealt, *pro tem*, with the problem of definition, we are then faced with the daunting problem of selecting what are the significant factors (in relation to policies and programmes for the personal social services) about the 'culture-complex',[30] living conditions, political/ economic policies, forms of government and administration, and the other organised social services available in each country. If one is to refer to all these factors in a necessarily brief but meaningful way, one must assume that the reader has some knowledge and understanding of all these aspects of the country(ies) compared, or can be advised as to what to read to get it. Otherwise the brief references may do more harm than good, particularly if the relevance of these factors to the focus of the study, for example to a comparative study of 'child care', is not spelt out later — sometimes because the writer has not really seen the relevance himself.

Comparisons with developing countries. For these reasons it would be unwise, at first at least, to attempt to compare the personal social services of countries whose culture-complex and living conditions are too different from our own, as in developing or recently industrialised countries. Comparative studies have already shown the importance of the time scale — the sheer length of time particular institutions have been in existence. Heclo refers to 'the historical tenacity of welfare bureaucracies[31] and to 'the emulative effects of politics on social policy and substantive feed backs from inherited policy itself'.[32] In his study, Lund quotes a similar finding from the comparative studies of three economists (Aaron, Gordon and Pryor):

> Other more frequently considered differences, such as in political ideologies and types of political and economic systems, appear to be less important than has been assumed. The earlier a program was

started — whatever the circumstances surrounding its initiation and whatever subsequent changes may have occurred in value climate or regime — the greater is the degree of investment in welfare programs.

And he goes on to draw on a fourth study of nineteen Western nations by Kilby and Taira which comes to the same conclusion about 'program age' while isolating yet another determining variable in this group — geography:

> The highest social welfare expenditures were found among those countries on or closest to the European continent. This suggests the possible early influence of a factor we might label the 'diffusion of innovation' or a Western 'climate of opinion', reflecting perhaps the power of emulation on the international influence of critical national elites.[33]

Although these were all primarily economic studies concerned with comparing the social-security expenditures of different nations, their conclusions were substantially the same as those of Heclo, who was more concerned with forms of government intervention than total expenditure. They could probably be shown to hold good for the personal social services too. Another hypothesis to be tested out?

The 'diffusion of innovation' or the 'emulative effects of politics on social policy', fostered by bodies like the International Social Security Association (I.S.S.A.) and the International Labour Office (I.L.O.), by international gatherings and by the one-way traffic (with the developing countries) of 'welfare consultants', ensures that the aims/objectives of social policies, the techniques for their implementation, and the expectations aroused in recipients and providers by each, become common currency in the countries of the Far East, and in India and Africa too. What are not so easily passed on are models of strategies which help to decide: Where do we go from *here*? and to plan: *How* do we get from here to there? The development of similar institutions in the West was on such a different time scale that, for this if for no other reason, little guidance can be given to developing countries on strategies beyond emphasising the crucial importance of finding one which takes account of the time factor and, equally important for the personal social services particularly, the culture-complex of the particular country.

Once again, the academic needs many more longitudinal studies, constructive descriptions, of the ways in which organisation for social welfare has developed to date in non-Western countries before he can begin to identify and analyse likenesses and differences in the aims, strategies and tactics of their personal social services today.

Japan. Japan suggests itself as a particularly interesting country for such a study. Now one of the richest industrialised countries, but with a much shorter industrial history, it has been characterised by a very rapid experience and adoption of many Western ideas, aspirations and techniques, especially since the Second World War. How far has it been formulating its own strategies for developing its personal social services? Such a study would also highlight, for subsequent use in comparative studies, the relative importance of the culture-complex, and of other background factors. For instance, Dr McGranahan at the Chicago Seminar on Cross-National Research, pointed out:

> The family system in Japan has been less disrupted by urbanisation than family systems in other countries. People went to the city but it wasn't that far. In emphasising values and culture, we should not forget the role of elementary factors such as space and size.[34]

The culture-complex and the personal social services

Dr McGranahan's example aptly illustrates the danger of quoting for comparison facts and figures about a country's demography and occupational patterns (age groupings, family size, numbers of married women working, and so on), its urban and rural populations, as well as such social indicators as we now have (of housing conditions, health, income distributions, incomplete families, and so on) without having understood that country's unique culture-complex. Only so can one *judge* how significant, insignificant, or positively misleading, tables comparing these demographic and cultural facts are likely to be, bearing in mind what area or aspect of the country's collective action for social welfare is under consideration.

The culture-complex, rather than the cultural factors, as it affects families and communities, is obviously vital to any but the most superficial analysis of a country's social problems which the personal social services are designed to meet. By (our) definition, the personal social services are concerned to help those who through personal inadequacy or the lack of family care or community support, and too often through lack of effective provision of the basic social services of health or housing, etc., need social care or protection of some kind or another. It is not facts and figures about the average citizen, family or community which bring understanding of the problems with which the personal social services have to cope. Their concern is primarily with broken families, or with those who have outlived their families, or with non-communities with socially unacceptable sub-cultures; and their clients' problems are frequently aggravated by the failure of other services. At the same time, it is the peculiar contribution of the personal social services to the whole gamut of collective action for social welfare to endeavour to bring people back to, or to provide some acceptable substitute for, these natural resources of family and community – just as its peculiar preventive work lies in strengthening them. (All of which, like our definition, cannot be assumed to hold good for countries other than the Western democracies.)

Local government and the personal social services

The constitutional factors, which are of special signficance in any study focused on the personal social services, are those concerned with forms of decentralisation and local government: with the extent to which policy decisions about which particular personal social services should be developed – and how – are made close to local communities and with their participation. Here again any general statements, often with unspoken assumptions, about which services are administered by central or local government are of limited value. They must spell out, or assume a knowledge and understanding of, the kinds of local government, the kinds of autonomous local areas and the kinds of relationship between statutory and non-statutory social-service organisations in each country being compared. In analysing this area of social-welfare action, the strategies within strategies for the interpretation and implementation of national policies are of the greatest significance – far more so than in the implementation of social-security policies – though the different forms of decentralisation or local government used in the administration of discretionary, emergency and 'last-resort' financial assistance are, in comparative studies, often insufficiently studied.

Output and outcome

As suggested earlier, any attempt to estimate output, leaving aside any assessment of outcomes, cannot ignore the quality of the service actually delivered and the individual consumer's reaction to it. While consumers' reactions to any government intervention for personal welfare can never be assumed, reactions to the more obvious and tangible benefits of income maintenance, housing or health schemes are more easily anticipated than those of the less tangible, less certain remedies of the personal social services. Moreover, the personal social services, as defined, are usually and rightly regarded by the recipient as basically substitute or second-best forms of caring or protection; most people prefer to manage their own lives, or to be supported and helped by a 'real' mother or friend.

Conclusions

I have spent longer than I intended, when I set out to write this chapter on the methodology of comparative studies on the personal social services; but it has served to highlight some of the most intractable problems of analysing social policies, whether in our own country or in others. I have argued that these problems are best tackled if we proceed by a methodological nominalism which seeks definitions and classifications which will 'hold' for the purposes of the particular study, but which we will always be ready to discard if and when a better analysis, leading to a further elimination of irrelevancies and discovery of essentials, presents itself. Any social-policy analysis must take account of the dynamics and interactions which run through all collective action for social welfare, whichever part of it we happen to be studying. But the process of identifying the major factors/influences which determine long- and short-term objectives, and the choice of instruments for achieving them, in any particular country at any particular time, is much the same. One can then go on to distinguish the particular strategies and tactics/techniques adopted, and to quantify the outputs and assess the outcomes which result from these policies.

To do all this, particularly in the personal social services, I have constantly emphasised the need for many more national studies in depth – or constructive descriptions, to continue with Susan Stebbing's term to the end. For instance, in the Cross-National Study, in searching for a working definition and classification of the personal social services, we found a hard core of similar functions to be discharged in all the societies studied, and were thus able to distinguish the different institutional ways in which the actual services were planned and delivered.

With more of these studies, and with the intellectual honesty to accept the inevitable constraints of the comparative approach, we may well be led to sharpen our powers of social-policy analysis. We may not arrive at many 'empirical generalisations' from such studies of the social policies and welfare institutions of different countries, each with its 'peculiar self-identify',[35] but by persistently clarifying our statements we can look forward to drawing many more valid and interesting comparisons.

List of Contributors

JOHN CARRIER, a Lecturer in Social Administration at the London School of Economics and Political Science, is the author of articles on minority groups and co-author of 'Social Policy and Social Change — Explorations of the Development of Social Policy' in the *Journal of Social Policy* (1973). He is an elected member of a local authority and of its Social Services Committee.

BLEDDYN DAVIES is Director of the Personal Social Services Research Unit at the University of Kent at Canterbury. He is the author of a trilogy of books developing what he calls 'the theory of territorial justice' and books on such subjects as gambling, university costs and outputs, and the principles of universality and selectivity in social policy. Bleddyn Davies is editor of *Policy and Politics*.

NEIL FRAZER is a Lecturer in the Department of Social Administration, University of Edinburgh, and the co-author of *Investment Decisions in the Nationalised Fuel Industries* (1974).

HELMUTH HEISLER is Dean of the Faculty of Social Science, Lanchester Polytechnic, Coventry. He is author of articles on African affairs and welfare and *Urbanisation and the Government of Migration* (1974).

HOWARD JONES is Professor and Head of the Department of Social Administration, University College, Cardiff. He is the author of *Reluctant Rebels* (1961), *Crime and the Penal System* (1965), *Alcoholic Addiction* (1963), *Crime in a Changing Society* (1971), joint editor of *Criminology in Transition* (1965) and editor of *Towards a New Social Work* (1975). His various researches have been assisted by substantial research grants and the Ministry of Overseas Development financed his major investigation into crime in Guyana.

PETER KAIM-CAUDLE is Professor of Social Administration, University of Durham, having worked previously as an economist, barrister and statistician. He has published studies of social administration in Ireland as well as *Comparative Social Policy and Society* (1973) and *Team Care in General Practice* (1976). Professor Kaim-Caudle is Chairman of the Durham C.A.B. and a co-opted member of the Durham County Council Social Services Committee.

IAN KENDALL is a Lecturer in Social Administration at Portsmouth Polytechnic and is co-author of 'Social Policy and Social Change — Explorations of the Development of Social Policy' in the *Journal of Social Policy* (1973). He is a member of the Executive Committee of the Social Administration Association and Secretary of the Joint University Council Social Administration Committee's Comparative Social Administration Group.

THOMAS McPHERSON is Professor of Philosophy and Dean of Students, University College, Cardiff. His publications include *The Philosophy of Religion* (1965), *Political Obligation* (1967), *Social Philosophy* (1970), *The Argument from Design* (1972) and *Philosophy and Religious Belief* (1974).

DELLA ADAM NEVITT is Professor of Social Administration at the London School of Economics and Political Science. As well as being the author of numerous articles on housing policy and related issues, Professor Nevitt is a member of the Housing Finance Review Panel and of the Construction and Housing Research Advisory Council.

MURIEL NISSEL, who was until recently a Chief Statistician in charge of one of the social statistics branches in the Central Statistical Office, originated and edited the first five issues of the Government annual publication *Social Trends*. Mrs Nissel is at present advising a foreign government on the reorganisation of their statistical service and the O.E.C.D. on social indicators. Married to Siegmund Nissel of the Amadeus Quartet, she is keenly interested in the arts and is currently a member of the inquiry, instituted by the Gulbenkian Foundation, into the training of musicians.

BARBARA RODGERS, O.B.E., retired from the Readership in Social Administration at the University of Manchester and is now Honorary Senior Fellow at the Centre for Studies in Social Policy, London. She is the senior author of *A Portrait of Social Work* (1960), *A New Portrait of Social Work* (1973) and *Comparative Social Administration* (1968). Mrs Rodgers has been an independent member of several Wages Councils and the Supplementary Benefits Commission and is on the panel of the Manchester Industrial Tribunal.

J. D. STEWART is Deputy Director of the Institute of Local Government Studies, University of Birmingham. Featuring among his publications are *Management in Local Government — A Viewpoint* (1971), *The Responsive Local Authority* (1974) and *Corporate Planning in English Local Government* (1974). Professor Stewart was a member of the Layfield Committee of Inquiry into Local Government Finance, which reported in 1976.

GEORGE F. THOMASON is Montague Burton Professor of Industrial Relations and Head of the Department of Industrial Relations and Management Studies, University College, Cardiff. He has published contributions to community development and industrial affairs. His most recent work is *A Textbook on Personnel Management* (1976). Professor Thomason is a member of the Advisory, Conciliation and Arbitration Service's Panel of 'Single Arbitrators' and Vice-President of the Council for Social Service in Wales.

Notes and References

Chapter 1

1. Cf. M. Gluckman (ed.), *Closed Systems and Open Minds* (Edinburgh: Oliver & Boyd, 1964).

2. A. Gerschenkron, *Economic Backwardness in Historical Perspective* (New York: Praeger, 1965) p. 6.

3. R. Law, 'The Individual and the Community', in *The Character of England*, ed. E. Barker (Oxford University Press, 1950) p. 29.

4. Speech to the Electors of Bristol (3 November 1774), quoted by B. Newman, *Edmund Burke* (London: G. Bell, 1927) p. 106.

5. L. S. Amery, *Thoughts on the Constitution* (Oxford University Press, 1947) p. 10.

6. Ibid. p. 2.

7. L. Curtis, *Civitas Dei* (London: Allen & Unwin, 1950) p. 39.

8. *The Times Higher Education Supplement* (20 June 1975).

9. Quoted in H. L. Beales, *The Making of Social Policy*, L. T. Hobhouse Memorial Trust Lecture No. 15 (Oxford University Press, 1946) p. 6.

10. Quoted in K. Hutchison, *The Decline and Fall of British Capitalism* (London: Cape, 1951) pp. 323, 326.

11. *Macaulay: Prose and Poetry*, selected by G. M. Young (London: Rupert Hart-Davis, 1952) pp. 766–7.

12. T. Paine, *The Rights of Man* (London: Dent, 1915) p. 158.

13. G. W. Keeton, *The Passing of Parliament* (London: Ernest Benn, 1952) p. 116.

14. H. Heisler, 'Economic Competition and the Political Stability of Plural Societies', *Sociological Review Monograph No. 14*, ed. P. Halmos (Keele University, 1969) pp. 140–3.

15. Ibid.

16. *The Times* (3 July 1975).

17. *The Times* (8 July 1975).

18. Curtis, *Civitas Dei*, p. 204.

19. D. Landes, 'Technological Change and Development in Western Europe 1750–1914', in *The Cambridge Economic History of Europe*, ed. H. J. Habakkuk and M. Postan (Cambridge University Press, 1965) vol. VI, pp. 274–603, esp. 354, 561.

20. D. E. Apter, 'System, Process, and Politics of Economic Development',

226   *Foundations of Social Administration*

in *Industrialisation and Society*, ed. B. F. Hoselitz and W. E. Moore (UNESCO–Mouton, 1963) pp. 135–58; A. Etzioni, *The Active Society* (London: Collier-Macmillan, 1968) pp. 503–48; E. Pusic, 'The Interdependence between Social and Economic Planning with Special Reference to Yugoslavia', in *Social Welfare Policy*, First Collection, ed. J. A. Ponsioen ('s Gravenhage: Mouton, 1962) p. 286.

21. Gerschenkron, *Economic Backwardness*, p. 8.

22. Lord Beveridge, *Power and Influence* (London: Hodder & Stoughton, 1953) p. 175.

23. Quoted in T. Parsons, *The Structure of Social Action*, vol. I (New York: The Free Press, 1968) p. 10.

24. Quoted in T. S. Simey, 'The Contribution of Sidney and Beatrice Webb to Sociology', *British Journal of Sociology*, 12 (1961) pp. 106–23.

25. G. Myrdal, *An American Dilemma*, vol. II (New York: McGraw-Hill, 1964) pp. 1041–51.

26. J. R. Hicks, *The Social Framework* (Oxford: Clarendon Press, 1960) pp. 3, 8.

27. R. K. Merton, *Social Theory and Social Structure* (New York: The Free Press, 1957) p. 10.

28. T. Parsons, 'General Theory in Sociology', in *Sociology Today*, ed. R. K. Merton *et al.* (New York: Basic Books, 1959) pp. 3–38.

29. W. J. H. Sprott, *Sociology* (London: Hutchinson, n.d.) p. 40.

30. A. Seldon, 'Commitment to Welfare', *Social and Economic Administration*, 2 (1968) p. 198.

31. G. Myrdal, *Beyond the Welfare State* (London: Duckworth, 1960).

32. R. H. Tawney, *The Acquisitive Society* (London: Fontana, 1961).

33. R. M. Titmuss, *The Gift Relationship* (London: Allen & Unwin, 1970).

34. R. Pinker, *Social Theory and Social Policy* (London: Heinemann, 1971) pp. 135–75.

35. Landes, 'Technological Change and Development', p. 587.

36. H. Gaitskill, 'An Appreciation', in *The Radical Tradition*, R. H. Tawney (Harmondsworth: Penguin, 1966) p. 221.

37. T. S. Simey, *Welfare and Planning in the West Indies* (Oxford: Clarendon Press, 1946).

38. R. M. Titmuss *et al.*, *Social Policies and Population Growth in Mauritius* (London: Methuen, 1961).

39. Gerschenkron, *Economic Backwardness*, p. 7.

40. R. K. Merton, 'Social Problems and Sociological Theory', in *Contemporary Social Problems*, ed. R. K. Merton and R. Nisbet (New York: Harcourt Brace Jovanovich, 1971) pp. 818–23.

41. J. P. Roos, *Welfare Theory and Social Policy* (Helsinki: Societas Scientiarum Fennica, 1973) pp. 29–59.

42. J. S. Furnivall, *Colonial Policy and Practice* (New York University Press, 1956) p. 442.

43. R. M. Titmuss, *Commitment to Welfare* (London: Allen & Unwin, 1968) p. 22.

44. V. George and P. Wilding, 'Values, Class and Social Policy', *Social and Economic Administration*, 6 (1972) pp. 243–7; cf. D. Birrell and A. Murie, 'Ideology, Conflict and Social Policy', *Journal of Social Policy*, 4 (1975) pp. 243, 258.

45. A. L. Rowse, *The England of Elizabeth* (London: Macmillan, 1951) p. 354.

46. *Macaulay: Prose and Poetry*, pp. 780–1.

47. P. Thane, 'The History of Social Welfare', *New Society* (29 August 1974) pp. 540–2.

48. M. Cole, *Beatrice Webb* (London: Longmans, Green, 1945) pp. 150–1.
49. R. Hinden, 'Editor's Preface', in *Radical Tradition*, p. 8.
50. T. H. Marshall, *Citizenship and Social Class* (Cambridge University Press, 1950) pp. 1–85.
51. R. M. Titmuss, *Essays on the Welfare State* (London: Allen & Unwin, 1958).
52. George and Wilding, 'Values, Class and Social Policy', pp. 236–48; A. W. Gouldner, *The Coming Crisis of Western Sociology* (London: Heinemann, 1971) pp. 342–51.
53. F. Lafitte, 'Social Policy in a Free Society', Inaugural Lecture (University of Birmingham, 1962).
54. Titmuss, *Essays on the Welfare State*, pp. 34–55.
55. T. Parsons, 'An Outline of the Social System', in *Theories of Society I*, ed. T. Parsons *et al.* (New York: The Free Press, 1961) p. 41.
56. D. Lockwood, 'Social Integration and System Integration', in *Explorations in Social Change*, ed. G. K. Zollschan and W. Hirsch (London: Routledge & Kegan Paul, 1964) pp. 244–56; N. Mouzelis, 'Social and System Integration: Some Reflections on a Fundamental Distinction', *British Journal of Sociology*, 25 (1974) pp. 395–409.
57. H. Heisler, 'The Civic Culture of Africa: Planning Solidarity and Development', *Civilisations*, 17 (1967) pp. 224–39; A. C. Pigou, *The Economics of Welfare* (London: Macmillan, 1950) pp. 12–21.
58. P. Ford, *Social Theory and Social Practice* (Irish University Press, 1968) p. 2.
59. Heisler, 'Economic Competition and the Political Stability of Plural Societies', pp. 121–46.
60. Merton, 'Social Problems and Sociological Theory', pp. 795–7.
61. A. S. Milward, *The Economic Effects of the World Wars on Britain* (London: Macmillan, 1970) pp. 16–24; A. T. Peacock and J. Wiseman, *The Growth of Public Expenditure in the United Kingdom* (London: Allen & Unwin, 1967) pp. xiii–xv, 24–30.
62. See, for example, W. Bell, 'Social Change and Elites in an Emergent Nation', in *Social Change in Developing Areas*, ed. H. R. Barringer *et al.* (Cambridge, Mass.: Schenkman, 1965) pp. 155–204, esp. 165–8; H. Heisler, 'Approaches to the Study of Social Change and Zambia', *Sociologus*, 21 (1971) pp. 118–38.
63. J. A. Ponsioen, 'Social Planning as an Instrument of Social Policy', in *Social Welfare Policy*, pp. 72–82.
64. H. Heisler, 'A Reconsideration of the Theory of Community Development', *International Social Work*, 14 (1971) pp. 26–33; H. Heisler, 'Social Service in Africa: Western Approaches', *Social and Economic Administration*, 1 (1967) pp. 56–69.
65. M. Oakeshott, *Political Education* (Cambridge: Bowes & Bowes, 1951) p. 22.
66. K. R. Popper, *The Poverty of Historicism* (London: Routledge & Kegan Paul, 1961) pp. 67, 69.
67. J. Hart, 'Nineteenth Century Social Reform: A Tory Interpretation of History', in *Essays in Social History*, ed. M. W. Flinn and T. C. Smout (Oxford: Clarendon Press, 1974) pp. 197–217.
68. J. H. Goldthorpe, 'The Development of Social Policy in England 1900–1914', *Transactions of the Fifth World Congress of Sociology*, IV (Louvain: International Sociological Association, 1964) pp. 50–1.
69. Ford, *Social Theory and Social Practice*.

70. H. Heisler, 'Class and Class Competition in a Plural Society', Doctoral Thesis (University College, Cardiff, 1971) pp. 151–8.

71. R. K. Merton, 'The Unanticipated Consequences of Purposive Social Action', *American Sociological Review*, 1 (1936) pp. 894–904.

72. W. E. Moore and M. M. Tumin, 'Some Social Functions of Ignorance', *American Sociological Review*, 14 (1949) pp. 787–95.

73. W. F. Maunder (ed.), 'Introduction', *Reviews of United Kingdom Statistical Sources*, vol. I. (London: Heinemann, 1974) p. ix.

74. W. Baldamus, 'Sociological Trends', *British Journal of Sociology*, 25 (1974) pp. 378–83.

75. P. M. Hauser, 'Social Accounting', in *The Uses of Sociology*, ed. P. F. Lazarsfeld *et al.* (London: Weidenfeld & Nicolson, 1968) pp. 839–75.

76. B. Wootton, *Social Science and Social Pathology* (London: Allen & Unwin, 1959) p. 326.

77. Ibid. p. 324.

78. Cf. I. D. J. Bross, 'Statistical Criticism', in *The Quantitative Analysis of Social Problems*, ed. E. R. Tufte (Reading, Mass.: Addison-Wesley, 1970) pp. 97–108.

79. F. X. Sutton, 'The Uses of Social Research in the Developing Countries', in *Industrialisation and Society*, ed. B. F. Hoselitz and W. E. Moore, p. 394.

80. Ford, *Social Theory and Social Practice.*

81. E. Shils, 'The Calling of Sociology', in *Theories of Society*, ed. T. Parsons *et al.*, p. 1441.

82. G. Schubert, *The Public Interest* (New York: The Free Press, 1960) pp. 220, 223.

83. Shils, 'The Calling of Sociology', p. 1422.

84. Sutton, 'The Uses of Social Research in the Developing Countries', p. 409.

85. P. Halmos, *The Personal Service Society* (London: Constable, 1970) pp. 63–144.

86. Pigou, *The Economics of Welfare*, pp. 8–10.

87. Wootton, *Social Science and Pathology*, pp. 308 ff.

88. J. Galtung, *Theory and Methods of Social Research* (London: Allen & Unwin, 1967) p. 1.

89. Pigou, *The Economics of Welfare*, p. 10.

90. Furnivall, *Colonial Policy and Practice*, p. 438.

91. Pigou, *The Economics of Welfare*, p. 21.

92. See, for example, D. Wedderburn (ed.), *Poverty, Inequality and Class Structure* (Cambridge University Press, 1974).

93. A. W. Gouldner, 'Explorations in Applied Social Science', *Social Problems*, III (1956) pp. 169–81.

94. Edward, Earl of Clarendon, *A Collection of Tracts* (London: T. Woodward, 1727) p. 200.

Chapter 2

1. R. M. Titmuss, *Commitment to Welfare* (London: Allen & Unwin, 1968) p. 22.

2. See, for example, M. Brown, *Introduction to Social Administration in Britain* (London: Hutchinson, 1971) p. 11; T. H. Marshall, *Social Policy* (London: Hutchinson, 1972) p. 9; A. Forder, *Concepts in Social Administration* (London: Routledge & Kegan Paul, 1974) p. 1; K. M. Slack, *Social Administration and the Citizen* (London: Michael Joseph, 1965) chs 1 and 2.

3. See, for example, D. V. Donnison *et al., Social Policy and Administration Revisited* (London: Allen & Unwin, 1975) p. 13; Forder, *Concepts in Social Administration*, p. xi; Kathleen Slack says:

it is as well to state explicitly what has been implicit throughout; that social administration is not one more social science with its own theory and body of knowledge. It makes use of the findings of any of the social sciences which are relevant to its sphere, which includes . . . . The solving of social problems, the implementation of social policy, and the promotion of social welfare. It may focus attention on one area or synthesise various areas of knowledge of social institutions and human behaviour and thereby increase understanding. But its distinctive character is that it combines and benefits from any of the conclusions of the social sciences which assist it and uses them as tools in the performance of the functions which are its particular concern. In other words the student must see social administration as benefiting from the social sciences, not as one more. He must not contrast it with them as if it were itself a discipline but recognise its purposes and appreciate that the knowledge which enables it to pursue those purposes comes to a considerable extent from the subjects he sometimes queries as necessary to his field of work or interest (see *Social Administration and the Citizen*, p. 39).

4. R. Pinker notes that it is possible to construe the relationship between sociological theory and social administration in these terms – that is to say, that the latter is 'largely parasitic' upon the former – see R. Pinker, *Social Theory and Social Policy* (London: Heinemann, 1971) p. 5.
5. See, for example, Brown, *Introduction to Social Administration,* p. 11; Marshall, *Social Policy*, p. 9; and D. V. Donnison, 'The Teaching of Social Administration', *British Journal of Sociology*, XII, no. 3 (September 1961). Donnison states that 'narrowly defined, social administration is the study of the development, structure and practices of the social services; broadly defined, it is an attempt to apply the social sciences, including philosophy, to the analysis and solution of a changing range of social problems' (p. 221).
6. See, for example, Brown, *Introduction to Social Administration*, p. 11; P. Hall, *The Social Services of Modern England* (London: Routledge & Kegan Paul, 1962) p. 5; and Forder, *Concepts in Social Administration*, who says: 'Social administration is concerned with the study of the welfare system, and particularly the government-sponsored social services. It is therefore concerned with the problems of relating needs and resources in contrast to the capitalist market economy which relates supply with demand, that is backed by monetary resources' (p. 1).
7. D. G. MacRae, 'The Crisis of Sociology', in *Crisis in the Humanities*, ed. J. H. Plumb (Harmondsworth: Penguin, 1964) pp. 133–4; see also D. G. MacRae's observation in the Foreword to *Social Theory and Social Policy*, where he says:

'It is increasingly and almost universally the case that students of social administration are turning to a knowledge of some of the methods and ideas of sociology even more than of economics or even psychology' (p. vi); and K. Slack's opinion that sociology 'is no more than an initial assistance to students of social administration who find themselves required for the first time to appreciate the meaning and scope of sociology, and its relationship to the other subjects of their study' (see *Social Administration and the Citizen*, p. 34).

8. See, for example, G. Myrdal's statement that 'in the advanced welfare state the internal political debate is becoming increasingly technical in character, ever more concerned with detailed arrangements, and less involved with broad issues since those are slowly disappearing', in *Beyond the Welfare State* (London: Methuen, 1965) p. 56. A similar point is made in A. W. Gouldner, *The Coming Crisis of Western Sociology* (London: Heinemann, 1971) ch. 9, pp. 344–5:

'Above all, what one sees is a vast growth in the demand for *applied* social science: the *policy* orientated use of social sciences by government both for welfare and warfare purposes.'

9. C. Wright-Mills, *The Sociological Imagination* (Harmondsworth: Penguin, 1970) ch. 1; P. Berger and T. Luckmann, *The Social Construction of Reality* (New York: Doubleday Anchor, 1967) pt III; W. Pelz, *The Scope of Understanding in Sociology: Towards a More Radical Reorientation in the Social and Humanistic Sciences* (London: Routledge & Kegan Paul, 1974) esp. ch. 3, 'Diverse Approaches to the Problem of Understanding'; J. Rex, *Discovering Sociology* (London: Routledge & Kegan Paul, 1973) esp. ch. 3, 'The Need for Theory'. The above-mentioned writers are foremost amongst those who argue for a historically based *and* interpretative sociology in order that sociology remains a distinct area of study.

10. Pinker, *Social Theory and Social Policy*, p. 5.

11. Those of A. Briggs, T. H. Marshall, D. Wedderburn and R. M. Titmuss in the following texts: M. Zald (ed.), *Social Welfare Institutions* (New York: Wiley, 1965) p. 43; T. H. Marshall, *Sociology at the Crossroads* (London: Heinemann, 1963) p. 294; R. Miliband and J. Saville (eds), *The Socialist Register* (London: Merlin Press, 1965) p. 128; Titmuss, *Commitment to Welfare*, p. 20.

12. See R. M. Titmuss, *Essays on the Welfare State* (London: Allen & Unwin, 1963) pp. 34–55.

13. Pinker, *Social Theory and Social Policy*, p. 148.

14. Ibid. p. 148; see also Myrdal, *Beyond the Welfare State*, pp. 68–9.

15. Martin Rein uses the term 'externality' to refer to the fact that the failure to meet the needs of certain individuals might have significant consequences for the wider community – see P. Townsend (ed.), *The Concept of Poverty* (London: Heinemann, 1971) p. 46. It is interesting to note that, as T. H. Marshall points out, the leading article in *The Times* (1 Aug 1884) utterly failed to grasp this point:

> celebrating the downfall of these two men and the suppression of the Board of Health . . . . If there is such a thing as a political certainty among us, it is that nothing autocratic can exist in this country. The British nature abhors absolute power . . . . The Board of Health has fallen. We all of us claim the privilege of changing our doctors, throwing away their medicine when we are sick of it, or doing without them altogether whenever we feel tolerably well. . . . Esculpapius and Chiron, in the form of Mr. Chadwick and Dr. Southwood Smith, have been deposed, and we prefer to take our chance of cholera and the rest than be bullied into health (quoted in Marshall, *Social Policy* (London: Hutchinson, 1975) p. 28).

16. See Titmuss, *Essays on the Welfare State*, p. 41.

17. Pinker, *Social Theory and Social Policy*, p. 150.

18. Food and legal services are two examples of the growth of concern with areas that might have been thought tangential to welfare activities. See J. Harris, 'Food and Fairness: the History of Food Subsidies', *New Society* (2 August 1973) pp. 273–5; I. Paulus, *The Search for Pure Food* (London: Martin Robertson, 1974); H. Street, *Justice in the Welfare State* (London: Stevens & Sons, 1968); and P. Morris *et al.*, *Social Needs and Legal Action* (London: Martin Robertson, 1973).

19. MacRae, 'The Crisis of Sociology', p. 133.

20. P. Berger, *Invitation to Sociology* (Harmondsworth: Penguin, 1963) p. 39.

21. T. Bottomore, *Sociology: A Guide to Problems and Literature* (London: Allen & Unwin, 1962) p. 20.

22. Pinker, *Social Theory and Social Policy*, p. 44.

23. See, for example, Bottomore, *Sociology*; S. Cotgrove, *Science of Society* (London: Allen & Unwin, 1967); P. Worsley *et al.*, *Introducing Sociology* (Harmondsworth: Penguin, 1970).

24. A notable exception is in Joyce Warham, *An Introduction to Administration for Social Workers* (London: Routledge & Kegan Paul, 1975).

25. J. Carrier and I. Kendall, 'Social Policy and Social Change – Explanations of the Development of Social Policy', *Journal of Social Policy*, vol. 2, no. 3 (July 1973) p. 209.

26. Pinker, *Social Theory and Social Policy*, p. 45, suggests that the atheoretical nature of social administration may have deterred sociologists. Students of social administration may not have utilised sociology because of the absence of a well-developed sociology of welfare from which to draw.

27. See, for some examples, ibid. p. 5.

28. Ibid. p. 5.

29. See Carrier and Kendall, 'Social Policy and Social Change', pp. 209–24.

30. Pinker, *Social Theory and Social Policy*, p. 5.

31. See, for example, P. Filmer *et al.*, *New Directions in Sociological Theory* (London: Collier-Macmillan, 1972) where much traditional sociological theorising is accused of leading its practitioners up a 'blind alley' (p. 15).

32. Comment by Donnison in D. V. Donnison *et al.*, *Social Policy and Administration* (London: Allen & Unwin, 1965) p. 26.

33. J. Warham, 'Social Administration and Sociology', *Journal of Social Policy*, vol. 2, no. 3 (July 1973) p. 205.

34. R. Tawney, *Equality* (London: Allen & Unwin, 1964) Preface to 1938 Edition, p. 32 (with an Introdution by Richard Titmuss).

35. Reflecting an implicit commitment to 'rational determinism'; see Carrier and Kendall, 'Social Policy and Social Change', pp. 209–24.

36. See R. G. Lipsey, *Introduction to Positive Economics*, 2nd edn (London: Weidenfeld & Nicholson, 1963) p. 4:

It is possible to classify statements into positive and normative statements. Positive statements concern what *is, was or will be*, and normative statements concern what *ought to be*. Positive statements, assertions, or theories may be simple or they may be very complex but they are basically about what *is* the case. *Thus disagreements over positive statements are appropriately settled by an appeal to the facts.* Normative statements concern what ought to be. They are thus inextricably bound up with our whole philosophical, cultural and religious position. They depend upon our judgements about what is good and what is bad. We say that normative statements depend upon our value judgements .... Disagreements may arise over normative statements because different individuals have different ideas about what is good and bad and thus of what constitutes the good life. *Disagreements over normative statements cannot be settled merely by an appeal to facts.*

Gunnar Myrdal discusses the conflict between positive and normative statements by looking at what he calls 'the mechanism of rationalisation'. See G. Myrdal, *An American Dilemma* (New York: McGraw-Hill, 1964) vol. 2, appendix 1, 'A Methodological Note on Valuations and Beliefs':

People have ideas about how reality actually is or was, and they have ideas about how it ought to be, or ought to have been. The former we call 'beliefs'. The latter we call 'valuations'. A person's beliefs, that is, his knowledge, can be objectively judged to be true or false and more or less complete. His valuations – that a social situation or relation is, or was, 'just', 'right', 'fair', 'desirable', or the opposite, in some degree of intensity or other – cannot be judged by such objective standards as science provides. In their 'opinions' people express both their beliefs and their valuations. Usually people do not distinguish between what they think they know and what they like or dislike [and] The temptation will be strong to deny the very existence of a valuation conflict. This will sometimes bring in its wake grossly distorted notions about social reality. There is a sort of social ignorance which is most adequately explained as an attempt to avoid the twinges of conscience. It is, for instance, an experience of every social-scientist who has been working on problems of social policy and has taken some interest in people's reactions, that the strongest psychic resistance is aroused when an attempt is made to teach the better situated classes in a society about actual lower class standards of living and what causes them (pp. 1027, 1029–30).

37. Economics is possibly the main exception to this statement.
38. Warham, 'Social Administration and Sociology', p. 206.

Chapter 3

1. J. S. Mill, *Utilitarianism* (London: Dent, 1910) p. 33.
2. W. B. Gallie, 'Liberal Morality and Socialist Morality', in *Philosophy, Politics and Society*, ed. Peter Laslett, first series (Oxford: Blackwell, 1963) p. 123.
3. Ibid. pp. 125–6.
4. Other writers may detect other strands. See, for example, W. H. Walsh, 'Open and Closed Morality', in *The Morality of Politics*, ed. Bhikhu Parekh and R. N. Berki (London: Allen & Unwin, 1972). For further discussion, largely historical, of the connection between people's political views and their views of justice, see David Miller, 'The Ideological Backgrounds to Conceptions of Social Justice', *Political Studies*, XXII (1974) pp. 387–99.
5. W. G. Runciman, *Relative Deprivation and Social Justice* (London: Routledge & Kegan Paul, 1966).
6. Mill, *Utilitarianism*, pp. 59–60.
7. John Rawls, *A Theory of Justice* (Oxford University Press, 1972) p. 316.
8. Ibid. p. 27.

Chapter 4

1. Bertrand Russell, *Human Knowledge: its Scope and Limits* (London: Allen & Unwin, 1948) pp. 38–9, 439 ff.
2. M. Jahoda, M. Deutsch and S. W. Cook, *Research Methods in Social Relations* (New York: Drydan Press, 1958) p. 60.
3. H. Mannheim and L. T. Wilkins, *Prediction Studies in Relation to Borstal Training* (London: H.M.S.O., 1965).
4. Lionel Robbins, *An Essay on the Nature and Significance of Economic Science* (London: Macmillan, 1952) p. 147.
5. I. M. D. Little, *A Critique of Welfare Economics* (Oxford University Press, 1963) esp. chs IV, V.
6. Margaret Mead, *Sex and Temperament in Three Primitive Societies* (New York: Mentor, 1958); A. Kardiner, *Psychological Frontiers of Society* (New York: Columbia, 1963) esp. ch. VIII.

7. Josephine Klein, *Sample from English Cultures* (London: Routledge & Kegan Paul, 1965).
8. See, for example, D. K. Henderson and R. D. Gillespie, *A Textbook of Psychiatry* (Oxford University Press, 1962) p. 326.
9. Max Weber, *Methodology of the Social Sciences* (New York: The Free Press, 1949).
10. E. Durkheim, *Rules of Sociological Method* (New York: The Free Press, 1962).
11. I. Taylor, P. Walton and J. Young (eds), *Critical Criminology* (London: Routledge & Kegan Paul, 1975).
12. Sir Keith Joseph, 'Equality', *Journal of Social Policy*, an address to the Social Administration Association (Edinburgh, 1975).
13. W. G. Runciman, *Relative Deprivation and Social Justice* (London: Routledge & Kegan Paul, 1966).
14. K. Coates and R. Silburn, *Poverty: the Forgotten Englishmen* (Harmondsworth: Penguin, 1970) pp. 185–6.
15. R. K. Merton, *Social Theory and Social Structure* (New York: The Free Press, 1961) p. 51.
16. Karl Mannheim, *Ideology and Utopia* (London: Routledge & Kegan Paul, 1972).
17. This is the general purport of Max Weber's writings, but particular reference might be made to *The Protestant Ethic and the Spirit of Capitalism* (London: Allen & Unwin, 1962) p. 54; and to 'Social Psychology of World Religions', in *From Max Weber*, ed. H. H. Gerth and C. Wright Mills (London: Routledge & Kegan Paul, 1961) ch. XI. Note also the significance attached to the development of a money economy in *The Theory of Social and Economic Organisation* (New York: The Free Press, 1964).
18. G. Rusche and O. Kirchheimer, *Punishment and Social Structure* (New York: Columbia, 1939).
19. Immanuel Kant, *Metaphysic of Morals* (University of Pennsylvania Press, 1971).
20. Jeremy Bentham, *Introduction to the Principles of Morals and Legislation* (London: Athlone Press, 1970); for a modern exposition, see Anthony Quinton, *Utilitarian Ethics* (London: Macmillan, 1973).
21. Klein, *Samples from English Cultures* (London: Routledge & Kegan Paul, 1965).

Chapter 5

1. M. Shepherd, B. Cooper, A. C. Brown and G. Kalton, *Psychiatric Illness in General Practice* (Oxford University Press, 1966).

The publications listed below cover the main sources of the statistics quoted in this chapter. A comprehensive list of references may be found in the Central Statistical Office publication, *Social Trends*.

Central Statistical Office, *Social Trends* (London: H.M.S.O., Nov–Dec annually).
Central Statistical Office, *Annual Abstract of Statistics* (London: H.M.S.O., Nov annually).
Department of Employment, *Family Expenditure Survey Reports* (London: H.M.S.O., July annually).
Department of Employment, *New Earnings Survey Reports* (London: H.M.S.O., annually as a complete report – also in six separate parts, as each part is completed).

Department of Employment, *British Labour Statistics* (London: H.M.S.O., summer annually); historical abstract also available (from 1886–1969).
Department of Education and Science, *Statistics of Education*, several vols (London: H.M.S.O., annually).
Department of Health and Social Security, *Social Security Statistics* (London: H.M.S.O., annually).
Office of Population Censuses and Surveys (previously the General Register Office) and the General Register Offices of Scotland and Northern Ireland, *Census of Population* (1951, 1961, 1966, 1971 – various vols).
Office of Population Censuses and Surveys, *General Household Survey Reports 1971 and 1972* (London: H.M.S.O., annually).
Royal Commission on the Distribution of Income and Wealth, *Initial Report on the Standing Reference*, Report No. 1 (London: H.M.S.O., July 1975).

Chapter 6

1. R. H. Tawney, *Equality* (London: Allen & Unwin, 1964).
2. In ibid.
3. R. J. Lampman, 'Transfer and Redistribution as Social Process', in *Social Security in International Perspective*, ed. Shirley Jenkins (Columbia University Press, 1969).
4. Royal Commission, *Report No. 1 Royal Commission on the Distribution of Income and Wealth* (London: H.M.S.O., 1975).
5. See R. M. Titmuss, *Income Distribution and Social Change* (London: Allen & Unwin, 1962); A. B. Atkinson, *The Economics of Inequality* (Oxford: Clarendon Press, 1975); 'The Distribution of Income and Wealth: An Agenda', *New Society* (22 May 1975); 'Income Distribution and Social Change Revisited', *Journal of Social Policy*, vol. 4, pt I (1975); H. Lydall, *The Structure of Earnings* (Oxford University Press, 1968); 'The Economics of Inequality', *Lloyds Bank Review* (July 1975); and G. Polanyi and J. B. Wood, *How Much Inequality?* Research Monograph (London: Institute of Economic Affairs, 1974).
6. A. R. Thatcher, 'Year to Year Variations in the Earnings of Individuals', *Journal of the Royal Statistical Society*, series A, vol. 134 (1971); and 'Low Pay and Changes in Earnings', *Department of Employment Gazette*, vol. 81, no. 4 (London: H.M.S.O., 1973).
7. The following paragraphs draw heavily on the Royal Commission on the Distribution of Income and Wealth, *Report No. 1*.
8. See ibid. para. 140.
9. Ibid. table 20.
10. Ibid. tables G5 and G7.
11. M. H. Cooper, *Rationing Health Care* (London: Croom Helm, 1974) p. 37.
12. Office of Population Censuses and Surveys, *General Household Survey 1972* (London: H.M.S.O., 1975).
13. F. Field, *Unequal Britain* (London: Arrow Books, 1974).
14. *General Household Survey 1972*.
15. Lydall, *Structure of Earnings*.
16. Christopher Jenks, *Inequality* (New York: Harper & Row, 1973).
17. J. Coleman, *Equality of Educational Opportunity* (Washington D.C.: U.S. Office of Education, 1966); P. Blau and O. D. Duncan, *The American Occupational Structure* (New York: Wiley, 1967).
18. Review Symposium 1973, 'Inequality by Christopher Jenks *et al.*', *American Journal of Sociology*, vol. 78, no. 6 (1974).

Chapter 7

1. R. Titmuss, *Social Policy* (London: Allen & Unwin, 1974) ch. 2.

2. Arguments and evidence about the importance of labour supply to economic growth are contained in C. P. Kindleberger, *Europe's Postwar Growth: The Role of Labour Supply* (Oxford University Press, 1967).

3. I. Gough, 'State Expenditure in Advanced Capitalism', *New Left Review* (June/July 1975) p. 75.

4. For use of the social-wage argument, see ibid. and J. O'Connor, *Fiscal Crisis of the State* (New York: St Martin's Press, 1973). I would like to acknowledge my indebtedness to these stimulating sources.

5. H. L. Wilensky and C. N. Lebeaux, *Industrial Society and Social Welfare* (New York: The Free Press, 1958) is much more about industrialisation's effect on the demand for welfare than on its social-capital demand.

6. See L. Hunter and D. Robertson, *Economics of Wages and Labour* (London: Macmillan, 1969) ch. 11.

7. P. B. Doeringer and M. J. Piore, *Internal Labour Markets and Manpower Analysis* (Lexington, Mass.: D. C. Heath, 1971).

8. See G. McCrone, *Regional Policy in Britain* (London: Allen & Unwin, 1969) especially chs I and VIII.

9. H. J. Habakkuk, *American and British Technology in the Nineteenth Century* (Cambridge University Press, 1967).

10. 'Capital deepening' is the substitution of capital for labour, and 'capital widening' involves capital and employment growing at the same rate.

11. D. S. Landes, *The Unbound Prometheus* (Cambridge University Press, 1969) chs 3—5, quotation p. 340.

12. G. V. Rimlinger, *Welfare Policy and Industrialisation in Europe, America, and Russia* (New York: Wiley, 1971) ch. 6.

13. R. Matthews, 'Why has Britain had Full Employment since the War?', *Economic Journal* (1968).

14. Rimlinger, *Welfare Policy and Industrialisation*, ch. 7.

15. For an attempt at a structure for the analysis of this, see Commission of the E.E.C., *The Economic Impact of Social Security*, Social Policy Series No. 21 (Brussels, 1970).

16. Rimlinger, *Welfare Policy and Industrialisation*, p. 159.

17. Kindleberger, *Europe's Postwar Growth*, ch. 11.

18. H. Heclo, *Modern Social Politics in Britain and Sweden* (Yale University Press, 1974).

19. For an analysis of such a manpower policy, see E. W. Bakke, 'An Integrated Positive Manpower Policy', in *Employment Policy and the Labour Market*, ed. A. Ross (University of California Press, 1965). Sweden's approach to labour supply is compared with other European countries in Kindleberger, *Europe's Postwar Growth*.

20. O'Connor, *Fiscal Crisis of the State*, ch. 4.

21. Organisation for Economic Co-operation and Development, *Manpower Policy in the United Kingdom* (Paris, 1970).

22. E. Robinson, *The New Polytechnics* (Harmondsworth: Penguin, 1968).

23. E. Boyle and A. Crosland, *The Politics of Education* (Harmondsworth: Penguin, 1971) p. 103.

24. Central Statistical Office, *Social Trends* (London: H.M.S.O., 1974) table 124.

25. Ibid.

26. R. Layard, J. Sargan, M. Ager and D. Jones, *Qualified Manpower and Economic Performance* (London: Allen Lane, 1971).

27. The economic arguments against long-range manpower planning and specialisation are developed in M. Blaug, *An Introduction to the Economics of Education* (Harmondsworth: Penguin, 1972).

28. See M. Wynn, *Family Policy* (Harmondsworth: Penguin, 1972).

29. See *Social Trends* (1974) pp. 15—16 for figures.

30. R. Klein (ed.), *Inflation and Priorities* (London: Centre for Studies in Social Policy, 1975) ch. 6, 'Schools' by J. Barnes.

31. But this recent extension in day release should be seen against the fact that a commitment was made in the *Education Act* of 1944 (section 44) for day release for all young persons in employment. (My thanks to Michael Adler for this point.)

32. S. Mukherjee, *Changing Manpower Needs*, Political and Economic Planning Broadsheet 523 (1970).

33. Heclo, *Modern Social Politics in Britain and Sweden*, ch. 3.

34. F. F. Piven and R. Cloward, *Regulating the Poor* (London: Tavistock, 1972).

35. O.E.C.D., *Manpower Policy in the United Kingdom*, pp. 61, 176.

36. For example, in R. Bacon and W. Eltis, 'How We Went Wrong', *Sunday Times* (2 November 1975) and following issues.

37. Figures in this paragraph are on the same basis as those in Table 7.1, column 3, and from the same source.

38. H.M. Treasury, *Public Expenditure to 1979—80*, Cmnd. 6393 (London: H.M.S.O., 1976) p. 1.

39. D. Jackson, H. Turner, F. Wilkinson, *Do Trade Unions Cause Inflation?* (Cambridge University Press, 1972) ch. 3. The figures in the following sentence are from Klein (ed.), *Inflation and Priorities*, table 1.4 (relating to 1963 to 1968) and H. Turner and F. Wilkinson, 'The Seventh Pay Policy', *New Society* (17 July 1975) relating to 1964 to 1969.

40. Central Statistical Office, *Social Trends* (London: H.M.S.O., 1972) p. 58.

41. *Department of Employment Gazette* (London: H.M.S.O., October 1975).

42. O'Connor, *Fiscal Crisis of the State*, discusses the chances of a movement to bring the expertise of the big corporations into social services in the United States to increase their productivity ('a social-industrial complex'). He thinks it would be unlikely to get the political backing required.

43. See the analysis in Gough, 'State Expenditure in Advanced Capitalism'.

Chapter 8

1. William Stanley Jevons, *Political Economy* (London: Macmillan, 1878).

2. J. G. K. Wicksell, *Lectures in Political Economy* English trans. with introduction by L. C. Robbins (London: Routledge, 1934).

3. Alfred Marshall, *Principles of Economics*, 1st edn (London: Macmillan, 1890).

4. Philip H. Wicksteed, *The Common Sense of Political Economy* (London: Macmillan, 1910).

5. For elegant statements of the revealed-preference approach to demand theory, see Geoffrey P. E. Clarkson, *The Theory of Consumer Demand: A Critical Appraisal* (London: Gower Press, 1963); or Robert Dorfman, *The Price System* (Englewood Cliffs, N.J.: Prentice-Hall, 1964) chs 1 and 3; see also P. A. Samuelson, *Foundations of Economic Analysis* (Harvard University Press, 1947) ch. 5; and Sir John R. Hicks, *Revision of Demand Theory* (Oxford: Clarendon Press, 1956). For correct usage of the term 'demand' see Leslie L. Roos Jr,

'Quasi-Experiments and Environmental Policy', *Policy Sciences*, vol. 6. no. 3 (September 1975) where studies of the *demand* for various underpriced goods and of programmes for changing usage of a collective good are suggested; see also James M. Buchanan, 'Public Finance and Public Choice', *National Tax Journal*, vol. XXVIII, no. 4 (Dec 1975).

6. Alan Williams and Robert Anderson, *Efficiency in the Social Services* (Oxford: Blackwell, 1975); see especially chs 4, 5 and 6.

7. J. Bradshaw, 'A Taxonomy of Social Need', in *Problems and Progress in Medical Care*, ed. Gordon McLachlan, 7th series (Oxford University Press, 1972).

8. Alan Williams, ' "Need" as a Demand Concept', in *Economic Policies and Social Goals*, ed. A. J. Culyer (London: Martin Robertson, 1974).

9. P. Townsend *et al.*, *The Fifth Social Service* (London: Fabian Society, 1970) p. 9.

10. D. F. J. Piachaud, *Do the Poor Pay More?* Poverty Research Series no. 3 (London: Child Poverty Action Group, 1974).

11. John L. Nicholson, 'The Distribution and Redistribution of Income in the United Kingdom', in *Poverty, Inequality and Class Structure*, ed. Dorothy Wedderburn (Cambridge University Press, 1974).

12. *Report of Committee of Inquiry into the Pay of Non-University Teachers* (London: H.M.S.O., 1975).

13. Lionel C. Robbins, *An Essay on the Nature and Significance of Economic Science* (London: Macmillan, 1932); see also Fritz Machlup, 'Essay on the Universal Bogey', in *Essays in Honour of Lord Robbins*, ed. M. Peston and B. Corry (London: Weidenfeld & Nicolson, 1972).

14. Dorfman, *The Price System*.

Chapter 9

1. C. Carter, B. Reddaway and R. Stone, *The Measurement of Production Movements* (Cambridge University Press, 1956); and K. Lancaster, 'A New Approach to Consumer Theory', *Journal of Political Economy* (April 1966).

2. See V. Fuchs, *Production and Productivity in the Service Industries* (Columbia University Press, 1969).

3. Martin S. Feldstein, *The Contribution of Economic Analysis to Health Service Efficiency* (Amsterdam: North-Holland, 1965).

4. Ibid.

5. G. Bowles, 'Towards an Educational Production Function', in *Education, Income and Human Capital*, ed. W. L. Hansen (New York: National Bureau of Economic Research, 1970).

6. E. Hanushek, 'Teacher Characteristics and Gains in Student Achievement', *American Economic Review*, vol. 61, no. 2 (1971) pp. 280–8.

7. H. M. Levin, 'A New Model of School Effectiveness', in *Do Teachers Make a Difference?* (Washington, D.C.: Department of Health, Education and Welfare, 1970).

8. S. Michelson, 'The Association of Teacher Resourceness with Children's Characteristics', in *Do Teachers Make a Difference?*

9. R. E. Attiyeh *et al.*, 'The Efficiency of Programmed Learning in Teaching Economics', *American Economic Review*, vol. 59, no. 2 (1969) pp. 217–23.

10. S. Mushkin, *The Economics of Health and Medical Care* (University of Michigan Press, 1964).

11. J. Garrad and A. E. Bennett, 'A Validated Interview Schedule for use in Population Surveys of Chronic Disease and Disability', *British Journal of Preventive and Social Medicine*, vol. 25, no. 2 (1971).

12. Donald Verry and Bleddyn Davies, *University Costs and Outputs* (Amsterdam: Elsevier, 1976).

13. R. A. Parker, *Decision in Child Care* (London: Allen & Unwin, 1966); and V. George, *Foster Care: Theory and Practice* (London: Routledge & Kegan Paul, 1970).

14. I. Sinclair, *Hostels for Probationers* (London: H.M.S.O., 1971).

15. Burton Weisbrod, *Economics of Public Health: Measuring the Economic Impact of Diseases* (Pennsylvania University Press, 1963).

16. Verry and Davies, *University Costs and Outputs.*

17. A. Ziderman and V. Morris, 'The Economic Returns on Higher Education in England and Wales', *Economic Trends*, no. 211 (May 1971).

18. Terry N. Clark, 'Can You Cut a Budget Pie?' *Policy and Politics*, vol. 3, no. 2 (December 1974) pp. 3–31; and T. N. Clark (ed.), 'Citizen Preferences and Urban Public Policy', *Policy and Politics*, vol. 4, no. 4 (June 1976) pp. 1–130.

19. Elinor Ostrom *et al., Community Organisation and the Provision of Police Services* (Beverley Hills: Sage, 1973).

20. F. S. Chapin and S. F. Weiss, *Urban Growth Dynamics in a Cluster of Cities* (New York: Wiley, 1962).

21. C. Hoinville, 'Evaluating Community Preferences', *Environment and Planning*, vol. 3 (1970) pp. 33–50.

22. Richard Berthoud and Roger Jowell, *Creating a Community* (London: Social and Community Planning Research, 1973).

23. On this whole area, see Clark, 'Citizen Preferences and Urban Public Policy'.

24. See, for instance, M. Clawson, *Methods of Measuring the Demand for and Value of Outdoor Recreation* (Washington, D.C.: Resources for the Future, 1959); and N. W. Mansfield, 'The Estimation of Benefits from Recreation Sites and the Provision of a New Recreation Facility', *Regional Studies*, vol. 5 (1971) pp. 56–9.

25. A. K. Sen, 'Behaviour and the Concept of Preference', *Economica*, n.s., vol. 40, no. 159 (August 1971) pp. 241–59.

26. Martin S. Feldstein, 'Economic Analysis, Operational Research, and National Health Service Efficiency', *Oxford Economic Papers* (1963).

27. A. J. Culyer, R. Lavers and A. Williams, 'Social Indicator: Health', *Social Trends* (London: H.M.S.O., 1971).

28. A. Etzioni, *Modern Organisations* (Englewood Cliffs, N.J.: Prentice-Hall, 1964).

29. G. Majone, 'The Feasibility of Social Policies', *Policy Sciences*, vol. 6, no. 1 (March 1975) pp. 49–70.

30. Bleddyn Davies and Michael Reddin, *University, Selectivity and Effectiveness* (London: Heinemann, 1976).

31. Bleddyn Davies, *Social Needs and Resources in Local Services* (London: Michael Joseph, 1968); Bleddyn Davies *et al., Variations in Services for the Aged* (London: Bell, 1971); and Bleddyn Davies *et al., Variations in Children's Services amongst British Urban Authorities* (London: Bell, 1972).

32. P. Flynn *et al., Social Malaise in Liverpool* (Liverpool City Planning Department, 1970).

33. B. T. Robson, *Urban Analysis* (Cambridge University Press, 1969).

34. John Edwards, 'Social Indicators, Urban Deprivation and Positive Discrimination', *Journal of Social Policy*, vol. 4, no. 3 (July 1975) pp. 275–88.

35. Davies, *Social Needs and Resources in Local Services.*

36. One interesting review is contained in Richard Thayer, 'Measuring Need in

the Social Services', *Social and Economic Administration*, vol. 7, no. 2 (May 1973) pp. 91–104.

37. Stephen Hatch and Roger Sherrott, 'Positive Discrimination and the Distribution of Deprivations', *Policy and Politics*, vol. 1, no. 3 (March 1973) pp. 223–40.

38. Edwards, 'Social Indicators, Urban Deprivation and Positive Discrimination'.

39. Jonathan Bradshaw, 'The Concept of Social Need', *New Society* (30 March 1972) pp. 640–2.

40. B. L. Neugarten, R. J. Havighurst and S. S. Tobin, 'The Measurement of Life Satisfaction', *Journal of Gerontology*, vol. 16 (1971) pp. 134–43.

41. D. L. Adams, 'Analysis of a Life Satisfaction Index', *Journal of Gerontology*, vol. 29, no. 1 (1969) pp. 73–8.

42. A. Bigot, 'Relevance of American Life Satisfaction Indices for Research on British Subjects Before and After Retirement', *Age and Ageing*, vol. 3 (1974) pp. 113–21.

43. For a review of the literature handling this problem, see J. Hull *et al.*, 'Utility and its Measurement', *Journal of the Royal Statistical Society*, series A, vol. 136, no. 2 (1975) pp. 226–46.

44. H. Glennerster, *Social Service Budgets and Social Policy* (London: Allen & Unwin, 1975) pp. 161–2.

45. C. F. Lindblom, *The Intelligence of Democracy* (New York: The Free Press, 1965).

46. C. Jencks *et al.*, *Inequality* (London: Allen Lane, 1972).

47. Ibid. p. 109.

48. Ibid. p. 96.

49. Davies and Reddin, *Universality, Selectivity and Effectiveness*.

50. J. Townsend and A. Kimbell, 'Caring Regimes in Old People's Homes', *Health and Social Service Journal* (11 October 1975) p. 2286.

51. See, for example, Verry and Davies, *University Costs and Outputs*.

52. Hospital Advisory Service, *Annual Report for 1974* (London: H.M.S.O., 1975) paras 27, 20, 22 respectively.

53. D. Easton, *A Systems Analysis of Political Life* (New York: Wiley, 1965).

54. D. Silverman, *The Theory of Organisation* (London: Heinemann, 1970).

55. Royston Greenwood and C. R. Hining, 'The Comparative Study of Local Government Organisation', *Policy and Politics*, vol. 1, no. 3 (1972) pp. 213–22.

56. D. S. Pugh *et al.*, 'A Conceptual Scheme for Organisational Analysis', *Administrative Science Quarterly*, vol. 8 (December 1963); 'Dimensions of Organisation Structure', *Administrative Science Quarterly*, vol. 13 (June 1968); and 'The Context of Organisation Structures', *Administrative Science Quarterly*, vol. 14 (March 1969).

57. J. Hage and M. Aiken, 'Relationship of Centralisation to other Structural Properties', *Administrative Science Quarterly*, vol. 12 (June 1967).

58. Joan Woodward, *Industrial Organisation* (Oxford University Press, 1965); and J. M. Stalker and T. Burns, *The Management of Innovation* (London: Tavistock, 1961).

59. David Braybrooke and Charles E. Lindblom, *A Strategy for Decision* (New York: The Free Press, 1963); and Lindblom, *Intelligence of Democracy*.

60. P. Self, 'Is Comprehensive Planning Possible and Rational?', *Policy and Politics*, vol. 2, no. 3 (March 1974) pp. 193–203.

61. Y. Dror, 'Muddling Through – "Science" or Inertia', *Public Administration Review*, vol. 24, no. 3 (September 1964).

62. Self, 'Is Comprehensive Planning Possible and Rational?'
63. Majone, 'The Feasibility of Social Policies'.
64. See, for example, G. Tullock, *The Politics of Bureaucracy* (Washington, D.C.: Public Affairs Press, 1965); and A. Downs, *An Economic Theory of Democracy* (New York: Harper & Row, 1967).
65. J. E. Davies, *The Evangelistic Bureaucrat* (London: Tavistock, 1972); Norman Dennis, *People and Planning* (London: Faber & Faber, 1970); and R. Batley, 'An Explanation of Non-Participation in Planning', *Policy and Politics*, vol. 1, no. 2 (December 1972) pp. 95–113.
66. Bryan Glastonbury *et al.*, 'Community Perceptions and the Personal Social Services', *Policy and Politics*, vol. 1, no. 3 (March 1972) pp. 191–211.
67. A. Sinfield, *Which Way for Social Work?* (London: Fabian Society, 1969).
68. Bleddyn Davies, 'Social and Economic Indicators: The Academic's Contribution', in K. Kirkland (ed.), *Proceedings of the Statistics Users Conference 1975 on Statistics for Local Government* (London: Standing Committee of Statistics Users, 1976) pp. 40–52.
69. P. Gregory, 'Waiting Lists and the Demand for Public Housing', *Policy and Politics*, vol. 3, no. 4 (1975) pp. 71–87.
70. See, for example, Davies and Reddin, *Universality, Selectivity and Effectiveness*; and Gareth L. Williams and A. Gordon, *Attitudes of Young People to School Work and Higher Education* (Lancaster University: Institute for Research and Development in Post Compulsory Education, 1976).
71. L. J. Sharpe, 'Instrumental Participation and Urban Government', in *From Policy to Administration*, ed. J. A. G. Griffith (London: Allen & Unwin, 1976).
72. Braybrooke and Lindblom, *A Strategy for Decision.*
73. Easton, *A Systems Analysis of Political Life.*
74. In Phoebe Hall *et al.*, *Choice, Change and Conflict in Social Policy* (London: Heinemann, 1975).

Chapter 10

This chapter draws upon a wide range of material in which this debate is pursued. Special reference should be made to the following:

D. Braybrooke and C. Lindblom, *A Strategy of Decision* (New York: The Free Press, 1963).
Y. Dror, *Public Policy Re-examined* (Scranton, Penn.: Chandler, 1968).
A. Etzioni, *The Active Society* (New York: The Free Press, 1968).
A. Faludi, *Planning Theory* (Oxford: Pergamon, 1973).
J. Friend and W. Jessup, *Local Government and Strategic Choice* (London: Tavistock, 1971).
R. Greenwood and J. D. Stewart (eds), *Corporate Planning in Local Government* (London: Charles Knight, 1974).
H. A. Simon, *Administrative Behaviour* (New York: The Free Press (paperback edition), 1965).
J. D. Stewart, *The Responsive Local Authority* (London: Charles Knight, 1974).
G. Vickers, *The Art of Judgment* (London: Methuen, 1965).

Chapter 11

1. R. Rowbottom, 'Organising Social Services: Hierarchy or ...?', *Public Administration*, vol. 51 (Autumn 1973) pp. 291–305.
2. M. Kogan and J. Terry, *The Organisation of a Social Services Department: A Blue-Print* (London: Bookstall Publications, 1971).

3. Committee on Local Authority and Allied Personal Social Services (Chairman: B. Seebohm), *Report*, Cmnd. 3703 (London: H.M.S.O., 1968); and *Local Authorities Social Services Act* (1970).

4. C. I. Barnard, *The Functions of the Executive* (Harvard University Press, 1968); H. A. Simon, *Administrative Behaviour* (New York: The Free Press (paperback edn), 1965); and A. Cochrane, *Effectiveness and Efficiency* (Nuffield Provincial Hospitals Trust, 1972).

5. E. L. Trist *et al.*, *Organisation Choice* (London: Tavistock, 1963).

6. Kogan and Terry, *Organisation of a Social Services Department*, p. 17.

7. Rowbottom, 'Organising Social Services', p. 293.

8. T. Caplow, *The Sociology of Work* (University of Minnesota Press, 1954); E. C. Hughes, *Men and Their Work* (New York: The Free Press, 1959); and H. L. Wilensky, 'The Professionalisation of Everyone?', *American Journal of Sociology*, vol. LXX (2) (September 1904) pp. 137–58.

9. A. Etzioni, *Complex Organisations* (New York: The Free Press, 1961) p. 12.

10. Royal Commission on Local Government (Chairman: Lord Redcliffe-Maud), *Report*, Cmnd. 4040 (London: H.M.S.O., 1969); *Local Government in England: Government Proposals for Reorganisation*, Cmnd. 4584 (London: H.M.S.O., February 1971) and *Local Government Act* (1972).

11. Ministry of Housing and Local Government, *Report of a Committee on the Management of Local Government*, Chairman: Sir John Maud (London: H.M.S.O., May 1967); Department of the Environment, *The New Local Authorities: Management and Structure*, Chairman: M. A. Bains (London: H.M.S.O., 1972).

12. F. X. Steggert, 'Organisation Theory: Bureaucratic Influences and the Social Welfare Task', in *Common Elements in Administration*, ed. E. W. Reed (National Conference on Social Welfare, Columbus, Ohio, 1965) quoted in H. A. Schatz (ed.), *Social Work Administration* (New York: Council on Social Work Education, 1970).

13. Ibid.

14. Rowbottom, 'Organising Social Services'.

15. F. Katz, 'The School as a Complex Social Organisation', *Harvard Educational Review*, vol. 34 (Autumn 1964) p. 431.

16. See G. F. Thomason, *Improving the Quality of Organisation* (London: Institute of Personnel Management, 1973).

17. Brunel University, *Working Papers on the Reorganisation of the National Health Service* (Brunel University: Health Services Organisation Research Unit, October 1973).

18. See Thomason, *Improving the Quality of Organisation.*

19. Ibid.

20. J. Algie, 'Management and Organisation in the Social Services', *British Hospital Journal* (26 June 1970) pp. 1245–8.

21. Brunel University, *Working Papers.*

22. M. Dalton, *Men Who Manage* (New York: Wiley, 1959).

23. Algie, 'Management and Organisation in the Social Services'.

24. N. W. Chamberlain, *The Union Challenge to Management Control* (New York: Harper, 1948).

25. F. W. Taylor, *Scientific Management* (New York: Harper, 1947).

Chapter 12

1. A Report containing (in French and English) some of the papers presented to this *Colloque sur la politique sociale* can be obtained from Patrick de Laubier, Département de Sociologie, Université de Genève.

2. Michael Lund's study, *Comparing the Social Policies of Nations: A Report on Issues, Methods and Resources* (Chicago University Press, forthcoming), along with the Report on the Seminar, can be obtained from the Center for the Study of Welfare Policy, University of Chicago.

3. As I felt it necessary to discuss them in the Introduction and Conclusions of Barbara N. Rodgers, with John Greve and John S. Morgan, *Comparative Social Administration* (London: Allen & Unwin, 1968).

4. This 'Report of a Research Project undertaken by the General Secretariat of ISSA for the British Committee on One-Parent Families' is reproduced in *International Social Security Review*, XXVIII, no. 1 (1975) pp. 3–60.

5. Morris Ginsberg, *Studies in Sociology* (London: Methuen, 1932) pp. 12–13.

6. L. S. Stebbing, *A Modern Introduction to Logic*, 3rd edn (London: Methuen, 1942) p. 395.

7. Presented at the J.U.C. and S.A.A. Conference in Edinburgh (July 1975).

8. 'Species' = 'A Class composed of individuals having some common qualities or characteristics, frequently as a sub-division of a larger class or genus', *Shorter Oxford English Dictionary*.

9. K. R. Popper, *The Open Society and Its Enemies*, vol. 2, 5th edn (London: Routledge & Kegan Paul, 1966) p. 13.

10. Hugh Heclo, *Modern Social Politics in Britain and Sweden* (Yale University Press, 1974) p. 16.

11. A further discussion of these points is to be found in Rodgers *et al.*, *Comparative Social Administration*, pt II, 'The Comparative Analysis', ch. 1, 'Social Policy and Planning'; also see the Introduction in Peter Kaim-Caudle, *Comparative Social Policy and Social Security* (London: Martin Robertson, 1973).

12. See Rodgers, *Comparative Social Administration*, pt II, 'The Comparative Analysis', ch. 3, 'Co-ordination'.

13. Heclo, *Modern Social Politics in Britain and Sweden*, p. 4.

14. There is a useful, well-illustrated discussion of the side-effects of social policies in the Introduction to Kaim-Caudle, *Comparative Social Policy and Social Security*.

15. Heclo, *Modern Social Politics in Britain and Sweden*, p. 12.

16. Kaim-Caudle, *Comparative Social Policy and Social Security*, p. 5.

17. Gaston V. Rimlinger, *Welfare Policy and Industrialization in Europe, America and Russia* (New York: Wiley, 1971) pp. 155–6.

18. A conclusion reached by Rimlinger too; ibid.; it is one of the 'experimental generalisations' of his conclusions, p. 320.

19. Ibid. p. 8.

20. Ibid.

21. Ibid. p. 7.

22. A favourite phrase of E. M. Forster and much used in *Howard's End* (1910).

23. The example is taken from my own teaching experience.

24. Kaim-Caudle, *Comparative Social Policy and Social Security*, p. 5: 'At the point of decision the *sine qua non* is judgement.'

25. My quotation from Ginsberg, p. 199 of this chapter.

26. Harold L. Wilensky, *The Welfare State and Equality* (University of California Press, 1975); Michael Lund's bibliographical study, *Comparing the Social Policies of Nations*, provides ample evidence of this bias.

27. *Cross-National Studies of Social Service Systems* (New York: Columbia University School of Social Work): Project Director, Alfred J. Kahn, Associate

Director, Sheila B. Kammerman. A series of national reports prepared at the initiative of the U.S. investigators can be obtained from A. J. Kahn (at cost price).

28. B. N. Rodgers and J. Dixon, *Portrait of Social Work* (Oxford University Press, 1960).

29. B. N. Rodgers and M. J. Stevenson, *A New Portrait of Social Work* (London: Heinemann, 1973).

30. As used by Ginsberg in quotation, p. 199 of this chapter.

31. Heclo, *Modern Social Politics in Britain and Sweden*, p. 15.

32. Ibid. p. 14.

33. Michael Lund, *Comparing the Social Policies of Nations*. The studies referred to are Henry Aaron, 'Social Security: International Comparisons', in *Studies in the Economics of Income Maintenance*, ed. Otto Eckstein (Washington D.C.: Brookings Institution, 1967); Margaret Gordon, *The Economics of Welfare Politicians* (Columbia University Press, 1963); Frederick L. Pryor, *Public Expenditures in Communist and Capitalist Nations* (London: Allen & Unwin, 1968); and Peter Kilby and Koji Taira, 'Differences in Social Security Development in Selected Countries', *International Social Security Review*, vol. 22, no. 2 (1969).

34. *Cross-National Research in Social Policy, Report on a Seminar* (April 1972) p. 21. (A copy of the Report can be obtained from The Center for the Study of Welfare Policy, University of Chicago.)

35. Ginsberg, *Studies in Sociology*, p. 5.

Index